Conspiracy of Catiline and The Jurgurthine War

Sallust

Contents

CONSPIRACY OF CATILINE. 7
   THE ARGUMENT. 7

THE JUGURTHINE WAR 116
   THE ARGUMENT. 116

CONSPIRACY OF CATILINE AND THE JURGURTHINE WAR

BY
Sallust

CONSPIRACY OF CATILINE.

THE ARGUMENT.

The Introduction, I.-IV. The character of Catiline, V. Virtues of the ancient Romans, VI.-IX. Degeneracy of their posterity, X.-XIII. Catiline's associates and supporters, and the arts by which he collected them, XIV. His crimes and wretchedness, XV. His tuition of his accomplices, and resolution to subvert the government, XVI. His convocation of the conspirators, and their names, XVII. His concern in a former conspiracy, XVIII., XIX. Speech to the conspirators, XX. His promises to them, XXI. His supposed ceremony to unite them, XXII. His designs discovered by Fulvia, XXIII. His alarm on the election of Cicero to the consulship, and his design in engaging women in his cause, XXIV. His accomplice, Sempronia, characterized, XXV. His ambition of the consulship, his plot to assassinate Cicero, and his disappointment in both, XXVI. His mission of Manlius into Etruria, and his second convention of the conspirators, XXVII. His second attempt to kill Cicero; his directions to Manlius well observed, XXVIII. His machinations induce the Senate to confer extraordinary power on the consuls, XXIX. His proceedings are opposed by various precautions, XXX. His effrontery in the Senate, XXXI. He sets out for Etruria, XXXII. His accomplice, Manlius, sends a deputation to Marcius, XXXIII. His representations to various respectable characters, XXXIV. His letter to Catulus, XXXV. His arrival at Manlius's camp; he is declared an enemy by the Senate; his adherents continue faithful and resolute, XXXVI. The discontent and disaffection of the populace in Rome, XXXVII. The old contentions between the patricians and plebeians, XXXVIII. The effect which a victory of Catiline would have produced, XXXIX. The

Allobroges are solicited to engage in the conspiracy, XL. They discover it to Cicero, XLI. The incaution of Catiline's accomplices in Gaul and Italy, XLII. The plans of his adherents at Rome, XLIII. The Allobroges succeed in obtaining proofs of the conspirators' guilt, XLIV. The Allobroges and Volturcius are arrested by the contrivance of Cicero, XLV. The principal conspirators at Rome are brought before the Senate, XLVI. The evidence against them, and their consignment to custody, XLVII. The alteration in the minds of the populace, and the suspicions entertained against Crassus, XLVIII. The attempts of Catulus and Piso to criminate Caesar, XLIX. The plans of Lentulus and Cethegus for their rescue, and the deliberations of the Senate, L. The speech of Caesar on the mode of punishing the conspirators, LI. The speech of Cato on the same subject, LII. The condemnation of the prisoners; the causes of Roman greatness, LIII. Parallel between Caesar and Cato, LIV. The execution of the criminals, LV. Catiline's warlike preparations in Etruria, LVI. He is compelled by Metullus and Antonius to hazard an action, LVII. His exhortation to his men, LVIII. His arrangements, and those of his opponents, for the battle, LIX. His bravery, defeat, and death, LX., LXI.

* * * * *

I. It becomes all men, who desire to excel other animals,[1] to strive, to the utmost of their power,[2] not to pass through life in obscurity, [3] like the beasts of the field,[4] which nature has formed groveling[5] and subservient to appetite.

All our power is situate in the mind and in the body.[6] Of the mind we rather employ the government;[7] of the body the service.[8] The one is common to us with the gods; the other with the brutes. It appears to me, therefore, more reasonable[9] to pursue glory by means of the intellect than of bodily strength, and, since the life which we enjoy is short, to make the remembrance of us as lasting as possible. For the glory of wealth and beauty is fleeting and perishable; that of intellectual power is illustrious and immortal.[10]

Yet it was long a subject of dispute among mankind, whether military efforts were more advanced by strength of body, or by force of intellect. For, in affairs of war, it is necessary to plan before beginning to act,[11] and, after planning, to act with promptitude and vigor.[12] Thus, each[13] being insufficient of itself, the one requires the assistance of the other.[14]

II. In early times, accordingly, kings (for that was the first title of sovereignty in the world) applied themselves in different ways;[15] some exercised the mind, others the body. At that period, however,[16] the life of man was passed without covetousness;[17] every one was satisfied with his own. But after Cyrus in Asia[18] and the Lacedaemonians and Athenians in Greece, began to subjugate cities and nations, to deem the lust of dominion a reason for war, and to imagine the greatest glory to be in the most extensive empire, it was then at length discovered, by proof and experience,[19] that mental power has the greatest effect in military operations. And, indeed,[20] if the intellectual ability[21] of kings and magistrates[22] were exerted to the same degree in peace as in war, human affairs would be more orderly and settled, and you would not see governments shifted from hand to hand,[23] and things universally changed and confused. For dominion is easily secured by those qualities by which it was at first obtained. But when sloth has introduced itself in the place of industry, and covetousness and pride in that of moderation and equity, the fortune of a state is altered together with its morals; and thus authority is always transferred from the less to the more deserving.[24]

Even in agriculture,[25] in navigation, and in architecture, whatever man performs owns the dominion of intellect. Yet many human beings, resigned to sensuality and indolence, un-instructed and unimproved, have passed through life like travellers in a strange country[26]; to whom, certainly, contrary to the intention of nature, the body was a gratification, and the mind a burden. Of these I hold the life and death in equal estimation[27]; for silence is maintained concerning both. But he only, indeed, seems to me to live, and to enjoy life, who, intent upon some employment, seeks reputation from some ennobling enterprise, or honorable pursuit.

But in the great abundance of occupations, nature points out different paths to different individuals. III. To act well for the Commonwealth is noble, and even to speak well for it is not without merit[28]. Both in peace and in war it is possible to obtain celebrity; many who have acted, and many who have recorded the actions of others, receive their tribute of praise. And to me, assuredly, though by no means equal glory attends the narrator and the performer of illustrious deeds, it yet seems in the highest degree difficult to write the history of great transactions; first, because deeds must be adequately represented[29] by words; and next, because most readers consider that whatever errors you mention with censure, are mentioned through malevolence and envy; while, when you speak of the great virtue and glory of eminent men, every one hears with acquiescence[30] only that which he himself thinks easy to be performed; all beyond his own conception he regards as fictitious and incredible[31].

I myself, however, when a young man[32], was at first led by inclination, like most others, to engage in political affairs[33]; but in that pursuit many circumstances were unfavorable to me; for, instead of modesty, temperance, and integrity[34], there prevailed shamelessness, corruption, and rapacity. And although my mind, inexperienced in dishonest practices, detested these vices, yet, in the midst of so great corruption, my tender age was insnared and infected[35] by ambition; and, though I shrunk from the vicious principles of those around me, yet the same eagerness for honors, the same obloquy and jealousy[36], which disquieted others, disquieted myself.

IV. When, therefore, my mind had rest from its numerous troubles and trials, and I had determined to pass the remainder of my days unconnected with public life, it was not my intention to waste my valuable leisure in indolence and inactivity, or, engaging in servile occupations, to spend my time in agriculture or hunting[37]; but, returning to those studies[38] from which, at their commencement, a corrupt ambition had allured me, I determined to write, in detached portions[39], the transactions of the Roman people, as any occurrence should seem worthy of mention; an undertaking to which I was the rather inclined, as my mind was uninfluenced by hope, fear, or political partisanship. I shall accordingly give a brief account, with as much truth as I can, of the Conspiracy of Catiline; for I think it an enterprise eminently deserving of record, from the unusual nature both of its guilt and of its perils. But before I enter upon my narrative, I must give a short description of the character of the man.

V. Lucius Catiline was a man of noble birth[40], and of eminent mental and personal endowments; but of a vicious and depraved disposition. His delight, from his youth, had been civil commotions, bloodshed, robbery, and sedition[41]; and in such scenes he had spent his early years.[42] His constitution could endure hunger, want of sleep, and cold, to a degree surpassing belief. His mind was daring, subtle, and versatile, capable of pretending or dissembling whatever he wished.[43] He was covetous of other men's property, and prodigal of his own. He had abundance of eloquence,[44] though but little wisdom. His insatiable ambition was always pursuing objects extravagant, romantic, and unattainable.

Since the time of Sylla's dictatorship,[45] a strong desire of seizing the government possessed him, nor did he at all care, provided that he secured power[46] for himself, by what means he might arrive at it. His violent spirit was daily more and more hurried on by the diminution of his patrimony, and by his consciousness of guilt; both which evils he had increased by those practices which I have mentioned above. The corrupt morals of the state, too, which extravagance and selfishness, pernicious and contending vices, rendered thoroughly depraved,[47] furnished him with additional incentives to action.

Since the occasion has thus brought public morals under my notice, the subject itself seems to call upon me to look back, and briefly to describe the conduct of our ancestors[48] in peace and war; how they managed the state, and how powerful they left it; and how, by gradual alteration, it became, from being the most virtuous, the most vicious and depraved.

VI. Of the city of Rome, as I understand,[49] the founders and earliest inhabitants were the Trojans, who, under the conduct of Aeneas, were wandering about as exiles from their country, without any settled abode; and with these were joined the Aborigines,[50] a savage race of men, without laws or government, free, and owning no control. How easily these two tribes, though of different origin, dissimilar language, and opposite habits of life, formed a union when they met within the same walls, is almost incredible.[51] But when their state, from an accession of population and territory, and an improved condition of morals, showed itself tolerably flourishing and powerful, envy, as is generally the case in human affairs, was the consequence of its prosperity. The neighboring kings and people, accordingly, began to assail them in war, while a few only of their friends came to their support; for the rest, struck with alarm, shrunk from sharing their dangers. But the Romans, active at home and in the field, prepared with alacrity for their defense.[52] They encouraged one another, and hurried to meet the enemy. They protected, with their arms, their liberty, their country, and their homes. And when they had at length repelled danger by valor, they lent assistance to their allies and supporters, and procured friendships rather by bestowing[53] favors than by receiving them.

They had a government regulated by laws. The denomination of their government was monarchy. Chosen men, whose bodies might be enfeebled by years, but whose minds were vigorous in understanding, formed the council of the state; and these, whether from their age, or from the similarity of their duty, were called FATHERS.[54] But afterward, when the monarchical power, which had been originally established for the protection of liberty, and for the promotion of the public interest, had degenerated into tyranny and oppression, they changed their plan, and appointed two magistrates,[55] with power only annual; for they conceived that, by this method, the human mind would be least likely to grow overbearing for want of control.

VII. At this period every citizen began to seek distinction, and to display his talents with greater freedom; for, with princes, the meritorious are greater objects of suspicion than the undeserving, and to them the worth of others is a source of alarm. But when liberty was secured, it is almost incredible[56] how much the state strengthened itself in a short space of time, so strong a passion for distinction had pervaded it. Now, for the first time, the youth, as soon as they were able to bear the toil of war,[57] acquired military skill by actual service in the camp, and took pleasure rather in splendid arms and military steeds than in the society of mistresses and convivial indulgence. To such men no toil was unusual, no place was difficult or inaccessible, no armed enemy was formidable; their valor had overcome every thing. But among themselves the grand rivalry was for glory; each sought to be first to wound an enemy, to scale a wall, and to be noticed while performing such an exploit. Distinction such as this they regarded as wealth, honor, and true nobility.[58] They were covetous of praise, but liberal of money; they desired competent riches but boundless glory. I could mention, but that the account would draw me too far from my subject, places in which the Roman people, with a small body of men, routed vast armies of the enemy; and cities, which, though fortified by nature, they carried by assault.

VIII. But, assuredly, Fortune rules in all things. She makes every thing famous or obscure rather from caprice than in conformity with truth. The exploits of the Athenians, as far as I can judge, were very great and glorious,[59] something inferior to what fame has represented them. But because writers of great talent flourished there, the actions of the Athenians are celebrated over the world as the most splendid achievements. Thus, the merit of those who have acted is estimated at the highest point to which illustrious intellects could exalt it in their writings.

But among the Romans there was never any such abundance of writers;[60] for, with them, the most able men were the most actively employed. No one exercised the mind independently of the body: every man of ability chose to act rather than narrate,[61] and was more desirous that his own merits should be celebrated by others, than that he himself should record theirs.

IX. Good morals, accordingly, were cultivated in the city and in the camp. There was the greatest possible concord, and the least possible avarice. Justice and probity prevailed among the citizens, not more from the influence of the laws than from natural inclination. They displayed animosity, enmity, and resentment only against the enemy. Citizens contended with citizens in nothing but honor. They were magnificent in their religious services, frugal in their families, and steady in their friendships.

By these two virtues, intrepidity in war, and equity in peace, they maintained themselves and their state. Of their exercise of which virtues, I consider these as the greatest proofs; that, in war, punishment was oftener inflicted on those who attacked an enemy contrary to orders, and who, when commanded to retreat, retired too slowly from the contest, than on those who had dared to desert their standards, or, when pressed by the enemy,[62] to abandon their posts; and that, in peace, they governed more by conferring benefits than by exciting terror, and, when they received an injury, chose rather to pardon than to revenge it.

X. But when, by perseverance and integrity, the republic had increased its power; when mighty princes had been vanquished in war;[63] when barbarous tribes and populous states had been reduced to subjection; when Carthage, the rival of Rome's dominion, had been utterly destroyed, and sea and land lay every where open to her sway, Fortune then began to exercise her tyranny, and to introduce universal innovation. To those who had easily endured toils, dangers, and doubtful and difficult circumstances, ease and wealth, the objects of desire to others, became a burden and a trouble. At first the love of money, and then that of power, began to prevail, and these became, as it were, the sources of every evil. For avarice subverted honesty, integrity, and other honorable principles, and, in their stead, inculcated pride, inhumanity, contempt of religion, and general venality. Ambition prompted many to become deceitful; to keep one thing concealed in the breast, and another ready on the tongue;[64] to estimate friendships and enmities, not by their worth, but according to interest; and to carry rather a specious countenance than an honest heart. These vices at first advanced but slowly, and were sometimes restrained by correction; but afterward, when their infection had spread like a pestilence, the state was entirely changed, and the government, from being the most equitable and praiseworthy, became rapacious and insupportable.

XI. At first, however, it was ambition, rather than avarice,[65] that influenced the minds of men; a vice which approaches nearer to virtue than the other. For of glory, honor, and power, the worthy is as desirous as the worthless; but the one pursues them by just methods; the other, being destitute of honorable qualities, works with fraud and deceit. But avarice has merely money for its object, which no wise man has ever immoderately desired. It is a vice which, as if imbued with deadly poison, enervates whatever is manly in body or mind.[66] It is always unbounded and insatiable, and is abated neither by abundance nor by want.

But after Lucius Sylla, having recovered the government[67] by force of arms, proceeded, after a fair commencement, to a pernicious termination, all became robbers and plunderers;[68] some set their affections on houses, others on lands; his victorious troops knew neither restraint nor moderation, but inflicted on the citizens disgraceful and inhuman outrages. Their rapacity was increased by the circumstance that Sylla, in order to secure the attachment of the forces which he had commanded in Asia,[69] had treated them, contrary to the practice of our ancestors, with extraordinary indulgence, and exemption from discipline; and pleasant and luxurious quarters had easily, during seasons of idleness, enervated the minds of the soldiery. Then the armies of the Roman people first became habituated to licentiousness and intemperance, and began to admire statues, pictures, and sculptured vases; to seize such objects alike in public edifices and private dwellings;[70] to spoil temples; and to cast off respect for every thing, sacred and profane. Such troops, accordingly, when once they obtained the mastery, left nothing to be vanquished. Success unsettles the principles even of the wise, and scarcely would those of debauched habits use victory with moderation.

XII. When wealth was once considered an honor, and glory, authority, and power attended on it, virtue lost her influence, poverty was thought a disgrace, and a life of innocence was regarded as a life of ill-nature.[71] From the influence of riches, accordingly, luxury, avarice, and pride prevailed among the youth; they grew at once rapacious and prodigal; they undervalued what was their own, and coveted what was another's; they set at naught modesty and continence; they lost all distinction between sacred and profane, and threw off all consideration and self-restraint.

It furnishes much matter for reflection,[72] after viewing our modern mansions and villas extended to the size of cities, to contemplate the temples which our ancestors, a most devout race of men, erected to the gods. But our forefathers adorned the fanes of the deities with devotion, and their homes with their own glory, and took nothing from those whom they conquered but the power of doing harm; their descendants, on the contrary, the basest of mankind,[73] have even wrested from their allies, with the most flagrant injustice, whatever their brave and victorious ancestors had left to their vanquished enemies; as if the only use of power were to inflict injury.

XIII. For why should I mention those displays of extravagance, which can be believed by none but those who have seen them; as that mountains have been leveled, and seas covered with edifices,[74] by many private citizens; men whom I consider to have made a sport of their wealth,[75] since they were impatient to squander disreputably what they might have enjoyed with honor.

But the love of irregular gratification, open debauchery, and all kinds of luxury,[76] had spread abroad with no less force. Men forgot their sex; women threw off all the restraints of modesty. To gratify appetite, they sought for every kind of production by land and by sea; they slept before there was any inclination for sleep; they no longer waited to feel hunger, thirst, cold,[77] or fatigue, but anticipated them all by luxurious indulgence. Such propensities drove the youth, when their patrimonies were exhausted, to criminal practices; for their minds, impregnated with evil habits, could not easily abstain from gratifying their passions, and were thus the more inordinately devoted in every way to rapacity and extravagance.

XIV. In so populous and so corrupt a city, Catiline, as it was very easy to do, kept about him, like a body-guard, crowds of the unprincipled and desperate. For all those shameless, libertine, and profligate characters, who had dissipated their patrimonies by gaming,[78] luxury, and sensuality; all who had contracted heavy debts, to purchase immunity for their crimes or offenses; all assassins[79] or sacrilegious persons from every quarter, convicted or dreading conviction for their evil deeds; all, besides, whom their tongue or their hand maintained by perjury or civil bloodshed; all, in fine, whom wickedness, poverty, or a guilty conscience disquieted, were the associates and intimate friends of Catiline. And if any one, as yet of unblemished character, fell into his society, he was presently rendered, by daily intercourse and temptation, similar and equal to the rest. But it was the young whose acquaintance he chiefly courted; as their minds, ductile and unsettled from their age, were easily insnared by his stratagems. For as the passions of each, according to his years, appeared excited, he furnished mistresses to some, bought horses and dogs for others, and spared, in a word, neither his purse nor his character, if he could but make them his devoted and trustworthy supporters. There were some, I know, who thought that the youth, who frequented the house of Catiline, were guilty of crimes against nature; but this report arose rather from other causes than from any evidence of the fact[80].

XV. Catiline, in his youth, had been guilty of many criminal connections, with a virgin of noble birth[81], with a priestess of Vesta[82], and of many other offenses of this nature, in defiance alike of law and religion. At last, when he was smitten with a passion for Aurelia Orestilla[83], in whom no good man, at any time of her life, commended any thing but her beauty, it is confidently believed that because she hesitated to marry him, from the dread of having a grown-up step-son[84], he cleared the house for their nuptials by putting his son to death. And this crime appears to me to have been the chief cause of hurrying forward the conspiracy. For his guilty mind, at peace with neither gods nor men, found no comfort either waking or sleeping; so effectually did conscience desolate his tortured spirit.[85] His complexion, in consequence, was pale, his eyes haggard, his walk sometimes quick and sometimes slow, and distraction was plainly apparent in every feature and look.

XVI. The young men, whom, as I said before, he had enticed to join him, he initiated, by various methods, in evil practices. From among them he furnished false witnesses,[86] and forgers of signatures; and he taught them all to regard, with equal unconcern, honor, property, and danger. At length, when he had stripped them of all character and shame, he led them to other and greater enormities. If a motive for crime did not readily occur, he incited them, nevertheless, to circumvent and murder inoffensive persons[87] just as if they had injured him; for, lest their hand or heart should grow torpid for want of employment, he chose to be gratuitously wicked and cruel.

Depending on such accomplices and adherents, and knowing that the load of debt was every where great, and that the veterans of Sylla,[88] having spent their money too liberally, and remembering their spoils and former victory, were longing for a civil war, Catiline formed the design of overthrowing the government. There was no army in Italy; Pompey was fighting in a distant part of the world;[89] he himself had great hopes of obtaining the consulship; the senate was wholly off its guard;[90] every thing was quiet and tranquil; and all those circumstances were exceedingly favorable for Catiline.

XVII. Accordingly, about the beginning of June, in the consulship of Lucius Caesar[91] and Caius Figulus, he at first addressed each of his accomplices separately, encouraged some, and sounded others, and informed them, of his own resources, of the unprepared condition of the state, and of the great prizes to be expected from the conspiracy. When he had ascertained, to his satisfaction, all that he required, he summoned all whose necessities were the most urgent, and whose spirits were the most daring, to a general conference.

At that meeting there were present, of senatorial rank, Publius Lentulus Sura,[92] Publius Autronius,[93] Lucius Cassius Longinus,[94] Caius Cethegus,[95] Publius and Servius Sylla[96] the sons of Servius Sylla, Lucius Vargunteius,[97] Quintus Annius,[98] Marcus Porcius Laeca,[99] Lucius Bestia,[100] Quintus Curius;[101] and, of the equestrian order, Marcus Fulvius Nobilior,[102] Lucius Statilius,[103] Publius Gabinius Capito,[104] Caius Cornelius;[105] with many from the colonies and municipal towns,[106] persons of consequence in their own localities. There were many others, too, among the nobility, concerned in the plot, but less openly: men whom the hope of power, rather than poverty or any other exigence, prompted to join in the affair. But most of the young men, and especially the sons of the nobility, favored the schemes of Catiline; they who had abundant means of living at ease, either splendidly or voluptuously, preferred uncertainties to certainties, war to peace. There were some, also, at that time, who believed that Marcus Licinius Crassus[107] was not unacquainted with the conspiracy; because Cneius Pompey, whom he hated, was at the head of a large army, and he was willing that the power of any one whomsoever should raise itself against Pompey's influence; trusting, at the same time, that if the plot should succeed, he would easily place himself at the head of the conspirators.

XVIII. But previously[108] to this period, a small number of persons, among whom was Catiline, had formed a design against the state: of which affair I shall here give as accurate account as I am able. Under the consulship of Lucius Tullus and Marcus Lepidus, Publius Autronius and Publius Sylla,[109] having been tried for bribery under the laws against it,[110] had paid the penalty of the offense. Shortly after Catiline, being brought to trial for extortion,[111] had been prevented from standing for the consulship, because he had been unable to declare himself a candidate within the legitimate number of days.[112] There was at that time, too, a young patrician of the most daring spirit, needy and discontented, named Cneius Piso,[113] whom poverty and vicious principles instigated to disturb the government. Catiline and Autronius,[114] having concerted measures with this Piso, prepared to assassinate the consuls, Lucius Cotta and Lucius Torquatus, in the Capitol, on the first of January,[115] when they, having seized on the fasces, were to send Piso with an army to take possession of the two Spains.[116] But their design being discovered, they postponed the assassination to the fifth of February; when they meditated the destruction, not of the consuls only, but of most of the senate. And had not Catiline, who was in front of the senate-house, been too hasty to give the signal to his associates, there would that day have been perpetrated the most atrocious outrage since the city of Rome was founded. But as the armed conspirators had not yet assembled in sufficient numbers, the want of force frustrated the design.

XIX. Some time afterward, Piso was sent as quaestor, with Praetorian authority, into Hither Spain; Crassus promoting the appointment, because he knew him to be a bitter enemy to Cneius Pompey. Nor were the senate, indeed, unwilling[117] to grant him the province; for they wished so infamous a character to be removed from the seat of government; and many worthy men, at the same time, thought that there was some security in him against the power of Pompey, which was then becoming formidable. But this Piso, on his march toward his province, was murdered by some Spanish cavalry whom he had in his army. These barbarians, as some say, had been unable to endure his unjust, haughty, and cruel orders; but others assert that this body of cavalry, being old and trusty adherents of Pompey, attacked Piso at his instigation; since the Spaniards, they observed, had never before committed such an outrage, but had patiently submitted to many severe commands. This question we shall leave undecided. Of the first conspiracy enough has been said.

XX. When Catiline saw those, whom I have just above mentioned,[118] assembled, though he had often discussed many points with them singly, yet thinking it would be to his purpose to address and exhort them in a body, retired with them into a private apartment of his house, where, when all witnesses were withdrawn, he harangued them to the following effect:

"If your courage and fidelity had not been sufficiently proved by me, this favorable opportunity[119] would have occurred to no purpose; mighty hopes, absolute power, would in vain be within our grasp; nor should I, depending on irresolution or ficklemindedness, pursue contingencies instead of certainties. But as I have, on many remarkable occasions, experienced your bravery and attachment to me, I have ventured to engage in a most important and glorious enterprise. I am aware, too, that whatever advantages or evils affect you, the same affect me; and to have the same desires and the same aversions, is assuredly a firm bond of friendship.

"What I have been meditating you have already heard separately. But my ardor for action is daily more and more excited, when I consider what our future condition of life must be, unless we ourselves assert our claims to liberty.[120] For since the government has fallen under the power and jurisdiction of a few, kings and princes[121] have constantly been their tributaries; nations and states have paid them taxes; but all the rest of us, however brave and worthy, whether noble or plebeian, have been regarded as a mere mob, without interest or authority, and subject to those, to whom, if the state were in a sound condition, we should be a terror. Hence, all influence, power, honor, and wealth, are in their hands, or where they dispose of them: to us they have left only insults,[122] dangers, persecutions, and poverty. To such indignities, O bravest of men, how long will you submit? Is it not better to die in a glorious attempt, than, after having been the sport of other men's insolence, to resign a wretched and degraded existence with ignominy?

"But success (I call gods and men to witness!) is in our own hands. Our years are fresh, our spirit is unbroken; among our oppressors, on the contrary, through age and wealth a general debility has been produced. We have therefore only to make a beginning; the course of events[123] will accomplish the rest.

"Who in the world, indeed, that has the feelings of a man, can endure that they should have a superfluity of riches, to squander in building over seas[124] and leveling mountains, and that means should be wanting to us even for the necessaries of life; that they should join together two houses or more, and that we should not have a hearth to call our own? They, though they purchase pictures, statues, and embossed plate; [125] though they pull down now buildings and erect others, and lavish and abuse their wealth in every possible method; yet can not, with the utmost efforts of caprice, exhaust it. But for us there is poverty at home, debts abroad; our present circumstances are bad, our prospects much worse; and what, in a word, have we left, but a miserable existence?

"Will you not, then, awake to action? Behold that liberty, that liberty for which you have so often wished, with wealth, honor, and glory, are set before your eyes. All these prizes fortune offers to the victorious. Let the enterprise itself, then, let the opportunity, let your poverty, your dangers, and the glorious spoils of war, animate you far more than my words. Use me either as your leader or your fellow-soldier; neither my heart nor my hand shall be wanting to you. These objects I hope to effect, in concert with you, in the character of consul; unless, indeed, my expectation deceives me, and you prefer to be slaves rather than masters."

XXI. When these men, surrounded with numberless evils, but without any resources or hopes of good, had heard this address, though they thought it much for their advantage to disturb the public tranquillity, yet most of them called on Catiline to state on what terms they were to engage in the contest; what benefits they were to expect from taking up arms; and what support and encouragement they had, and in what quarters. [126] Catiline then promised them the abolition of their debts;[127] a proscription of the wealthy citizens;[128] offices, sacerdotal dignities, plunder, and all other gratifications which war, and the license of conquerors, can afford. He added that Piso was in Hither Spain, and Publius Sittius Nucerinus with an army in Mauritania, both of whom were privy to his plans; that Caius Antonius, whom he hoped to have for a colleague, was canvassing for the consulship, a man with whom he was intimate, and who was involved in all manner of embarrassments; and that, in conjunction with him, he himself, when consul, would commence operations. He, moreover, assailed all the respectable citizens with reproaches, commended each of his associates by name, reminded one of his poverty, another of his ruling passion,[129] several others of their danger or disgrace, and many of the spoils which they had obtained by the victory of Sylla. When he saw their spirits sufficiently elevated, he charged them to attend to his interest at the election of consuls, and dismissed the assembly.

XXII. There were some, at the time, who said that Catiline, having ended his speech, and wishing to bind his accomplices in guilt by an oath, handed round among them, in goblets, the blood of a human body mixed with wine; and that when all, after an imprecation, had tasted of it, as is usual in sacred rites, he disclosed his design; and they asserted[130] that he did this, in order that they might be the more closely attached to one another, by being mutually conscious of such an atrocity. But some thought that this report, and many others, were invented by persons who supposed that the odium against Cicero, which afterward arose, might be lessened by imputing an enormity of guilt to the conspirators who had suffered death. The evidence which I have obtained, in support of this charge, is not at all in proportion to its magnitude.

XXIII. Among those present at this meeting was Quintus Curius,[131] a man of no mean family, but immersed in vices and crimes, and whom the censors had ignominiously expelled from the senate. In this person there was not less levity than impudence; he could neither keep secret what he heard, not conceal his own crimes; he was altogether heedless what he said or what he did. He had long had a criminal intercourse with Fulvia, a woman of high birth; but growing less acceptable to her, because, in his reduced circumstances, he had less means of being liberal, he began, on a sudden, to boast, and to promise her seas and mountains;[132] threatening her, at times, with the sword, if she were not submissive to his will; and acting, in his general conduct, with greater arrogance than ever.[133] Fulvia, having learned the cause of his extravagant behavior, did not keep such danger to the state a secret; but, without naming her informant, communicated to several persons what she had heard and under what circumstances, concerning Catiline's conspiracy. This intelligence it was that incited the feelings of the citizens to give the consulship to Marcus Tullius Cicero.[134] For before this period, most of the nobility were moved with jealousy, and thought the consulship in some degree sullied, if a man of no family,[135] however meritorious, obtained it. But when danger showed itself, envy and pride were laid aside. XXIV. Accordingly, when the comitia were held, Marcus Tullius and Caius Antonius were declared consuls; an event which gave the first shock to the conspirators. The ardor of Catiline, however, was not at all diminished; he formed every day new schemes; he deposited arms, in convenient places, throughout Italy; he sent sums of money borrowed on his own credit, or that of his friends, to a certain Manlius,[136] at Faesulae,[137] who was subsequently the first to engage in hostilities. At this period, too, he is said to have attached to his cause great numbers of men of all classes, and some women, who had, in their earlier days, supported an expensive life by the price of their beauty, but who, when age had lessened their gains but not their extravagance, had contracted heavy debts. By the influence of these females, Catiline hoped to gain over the slaves in Rome, to get the city set on fire, and either to secure the support of their husbands or take away their lives.

XXV. In the number of those ladies was Sempronia,[138] a woman who had committed many crimes with the spirit of a man. In birth and beauty, in her husband and her children, she was extremely fortunate; she was skilled in Greek and Roman literature; she could sing, play, and dance,[139] with greater elegance than became a woman of virtue, and possessed many other accomplishments that tend to excite the passions. But nothing was ever less valued by her than honor or chastity. Whether she was more prodigal of her money or her reputation, it would have been difficult to decide. Her desires were so ardent that she oftener made advances to the other sex than waited for solicitation. She had frequently, before this period, forfeited her word, forsworn debts, been privy to murder, and hurried into the utmost excesses by her extravagance and poverty. But her abilities were by no means despicable;[140] she could compose verses, jest, and join in conversation either modest, tender, or licentious. In a word, she was distinguished[141] by much refinement of wit, and much grace of expression.

XXVI. Catiline, having made these arrangements, still canvassed for the consulship for the following year; hoping that, if he should be elected, he would easily manage Antonius according to his pleasure. Nor did he, in the mean time remain inactive, but devised schemes, in every possible way, against Cicero, who, however, did not want skill or policy to guard, against them. For, at the very beginning of his consulship, he had, by making many promises through Fulvia, prevailed on

Quintus Curius, whom I have already mentioned, to give him secret information of Catiline's proceedings. He had also persuaded his colleague, Antonius, by an arrangement respecting their provinces,[142] to entertain no sentiment of disaffection toward the state; and he kept around him, though without ostentation, a guard of his friends and dependents.

When the day of the comitia came, and neither Catiline's efforts for the consulship, nor the plots which he had laid for the consuls in the Campus Martius,[143] were attended with success, he determined to proceed to war, and resort to the utmost extremities, since what he had attempted secretly had ended in confusion and disgrace.[144]

XXVII. He accordingly dispatched Caius Manlius to Faesulae, and the adjacent parts of Etruria; one Septimius, of Carinum,[145] into the Picenian territory; Caius Julius into Apulia; and others to various places, wherever he thought each would be most serviceable.[146] He himself, in the mean time, was making many simultaneous efforts at Rome; he laid plots for the consul; he arranged schemes for burning the city; he occupied suitable posts with armed men; he went constantly armed himself, and ordered his followers to do the same; he exhorted them to be always on their guard and prepared for action; he was active and vigilant by day and by night, and was exhausted neither by sleeplessness nor by toil. At last, however, when none of his numerous projects succeeded,[147] he again, with the aid of Marcus Porcius Laeca, convoked the leaders of the conspiracy in the dead of night, when, after many complaints of their apathy, he informed them that he had sent forward Manlius to that body of men whom he had prepared to take up arms; and others of the confederates into other eligible places, to make a commencement of hostilities; and that he himself was eager to set out to the army, if he could but first cut off Cicero, who was the chief obstruction to his measures.

XXVIII. While, therefore, the rest were in alarm and hesitation, Caius Cornelius, a Roman knight, who offered his services, and Lucius Vargunteius, a senator, in company with him, agreed to go with an armed force, on that very night, and with but little delay,[148] to the house of Cicero, under pretense of paying their respects to him, and to kill him unawares, and unprepared for defense, in his own residence. But Curius, when he heard of the imminent danger that threatened the consul, immediately gave him notice, by the agency of Fulvia, of the treachery which was contemplated. The assassins, in consequence, were refused admission, and found that they had undertaken such an attempt only to be disappointed.

In the mean time, Manlius was in Etruria, stirring up the populace, who, both from poverty, and from resentment for their injuries (for, under the tyranny of Sylla, they had lost their lands and other property) were eager for a revolution. He also attached to himself all sorts of marauders, who were numerous in those parts, and some of Sylla's colonists, whose dissipation and extravagance had exhausted their enormous plunder.

XXIX. When these proceedings were reported to Cicero, he, being alarmed at the twofold danger, since he could no longer secure the city against treachery by his private efforts, nor could gain satisfactory intelligence of the magnitude or intentions of the army of Manlius, laid the matter, which was already a subject of discussion among the people, before the senate. The senate, accordingly, as is usual in any perilous emergency, decreed that THE CONSULS SHOULD MAKE IT THEIR CARE THAT THE COMMONWEALTH SHOULD RECEIVE NO INJURY. This is the greatest power which, according to the practice at Rome, is granted[149] by the senate to the magistrate, and which authorizes him to raise troops; to make war; to assume unlimited control over the allies and the citizens; to take the chief command and jurisdiction at home and in the field; rights which, without an order of the people, the consul is not permitted to exercise.

XXX. A few days afterward, Lucius Saenius, a senator, read to the senate a letter, which, he said, he had received from Faesulae, and in which, it was stated that Caius Manlius, with a large force, had taken the field by the 27th of October. [150] Others at the same time, as is not uncommon in such a crisis, spread reports of omens and prodigies; others of meetings being held, of arms being transported, and of insurrections of the slaves at Capua and in Apulia. In consequence of these rumors, Quintus Marcius Rex[151] was dispatched, by a decree of the senate, to Faesulae, and Quintus Metellus Creticus[152] into Apulia and the parts adjacent; both which officers, with the title of commanders,[153] were waiting near the city, having been prevented from entering in triumph, by the malice of a cabal, whose custom it was to ask a price for every thing, whether honorable or infamous. The praetors, too, Quintus Pompeius Rufus, and Quintus Metellus Celer, were sent off, the one to Capua, the other to Picenum, and power was given them to levy a force proportioned to the exigency and the danger. The senate also decreed, that if any one should give information of the conspiracy which had been formed against the state, his reward should be, if a slave, his freedom and a hundred sestertia; if a freeman, a complete pardon and two hundred sestertia[154]. They further appointed that the schools of gladiators[155] should be distributed in Capua and other municipal towns, according to the capacity of each; and that, at Rome, watches should be posted throughout the city, of which the inferior magistrates[156] should have the charge.

XXXI. By such proceedings as these the citizens were struck with alarm, and the appearance of the city was changed. In place of that extreme gayety and dissipation,[157] to which long tranquillity[158] had given rise, a sudden gloom spread over all classes; they became anxious and agitated; they felt secure neither in any place, nor with any person; they were not at war, yet enjoyed no peace; each measured the public danger by his own fear. The women, also, to whom, from the extent of the empire, the dread of war was new, gave way to lamentation, raised supplicating hands to heaven, mourned over their infants, made constant inquiries, trembled at every thing, and, forgetting their pride and their pleasures, felt nothing but alarm for themselves and their country.

Yet the unrelenting spirit of Catiline persisted in the same purposes, notwithstanding the precautions that were adopted against him, and though he himself was accused by Lucius Paullus under the Plautian law.[159] At last, with a view to dissemble, and under pretense of clearing his character, as if he had been provoked by some attack, he went into the senate-house. It was then that Marcus Tullius, the consul, whether alarmed at his presence, or fired with indignation against him, delivered that splendid speech, so beneficial to the republic, which he afterward wrote and published.[160]

When Cicero sat down, Catiline, being prepared to pretend ignorance of the whole matter, entreated, with downcast looks and suppliant voice, that "the Conscript Fathers would not too hastily believe any thing against him;" saying "that he was sprung from such a family, and had so ordered his life from his youth, as to have every happiness in prospect; and that they were not to suppose that he, a patrician, whose services to the Roman people, as well as those of his ancestors, had been so numerous, should want to ruin the state, when Marcus Tullius, a mere adopted citizen of Rome,[161] was eager to preserve it." When he was proceeding to add other invectives, they all raised an outcry against him, and called him an enemy and a traitor.[162] Being thus exasperated, "Since I am encompassed by enemies," he exclaimed,[163] "and driven to desperation, I will extinguish the flame kindled around me in a general ruin."

XXXII He then hurried from the senate to his own house; and then, after much reflection with himself, thinking that, as his plots against the consul had been unsuccessful, and as he knew the city to be secured from fire by the watch, his best course would be to augment his army, and make provision for the war before the legions could be raised, he set out in the dead of night, and with a few attendants, to the camp of Manlius. But he left in charge to Lentulus and Cethegus, and others of whose prompt determination he was assured, to strengthen the interests of their party in every possible way, to forward the plots against the consul, and to make arrangements for a massacre, for firing the city, and for other destructive operations of war; promising that he himself would shortly advance on the city with a large army.

During the course of these proceedings at Rome, Caius Manlius dispatched some of his followers as deputies to Quintus Marcius Rex, with directions to address him[164] to the following effect:

XXXIII. "We call gods and men to witness, general, that we have taken up arms neither to injure our country, nor to occasion peril to any one, but to defend our own persons from harm; who, wretched and in want, have been deprived most of us, of our homes, and all of us of our character and property, by the oppression and cruelty of usurers; nor has any one of us been allowed, according to the usage of our ancestors, to have the benefit of the law,[165] or, when our property was lost to keep our persons free. Such has been the inhumanity of the usurers and of the praetor.[166]

Often have your forefathers, taking compassion on the commonalty at Rome, relieved their distress by decrees;[167] and very lately, within our own memory, silver, by reason of the pressure of debt, and with the consent of all respectable citizens, was paid with brass.[168]

Often too, we must own, have the commonalty themselves, driven by desire of power, or by the arrogance of their rulers, seceded[169] under arms from the patricians. But at power or wealth, for the sake of which wars, and all kinds of strife, arise among mankind, we do not aim; we desire only our liberty, which no honorable man relinquishes but with life. We therefore conjure you and the senate to befriend your unhappy fellow-citizens; to restore us the protection of the law, which the injustice of the praetor has taken from us; and not to lay on us the necessity of considering how we may perish, so as best to avenge our blood."

XXXIV. To this address Quintus Marcius replied, that, "if they wished to make any petition to the senate, they must lay down their arms, and proceed as suppliants to Rome;" adding, that "such had always been the kindness[170] and humanity of the Roman senate and people, that none had ever asked help of them in vain."

Catiline, on his march, sent letters to most men of consular dignity, and to all the most respectable citizens, stating that "as he was beset by false accusations, and unable to resist the combination of his enemies, he was submitting to the will of fortune, and going into exile at Marseilles; not that he was guilty of the great wickedness laid to his charge, but that the state might be undisturbed, and that no insurrection might arise from his defense of himself."

Quintus Catulus, however, read in the senate a letter of a very different character, which, he said, was delivered to him in the name of Catiline, and of which the following is a copy.

[171]XXXV. "Lucius Catiline to Quintus Catulus, wishing health. Your eminent integrity, known to me by experience,[172] gives a pleasing confidence, in the midst of great perils, to my present recommendation. [173] I have determined, therefore, to make no formal defense[174] with regard to my new course of conduct; yet I was resolved, though conscious of no guilt,[175] to offer you some explanation,[176] which, on my word of honor,[177] you may receive as true.[178] Provoked by injuries and indignities, since, being robbed of the fruit of my labor and exertion, [179] I did not obtain the post of honor due to me,[180] I have undertaken, according to my custom, the public cause of the distressed. Not but that I could have paid, out of my own property, the debts contracted on my own security;[181] while the generosity of Orestilla, out of her own fortune and her daughter's, would discharge those incurred on the security of others. But because I saw unworthy men ennobled with honors, and myself proscribed[182] on groundless suspicion, I have for this very reason, adopted a course,[183] amply justifiable in my present circumstances,

for preserving what honor is left to me. When I was proceeding to write more, intelligence was brought that violence is preparing against me. I now commend and intrust Orestilla to your protection;[184] intreating you, by your love for your own children, to defend her from injury.[185] Farewell."

XXXVI. Catiline himself, having stayed a few days with Caius Flaminius Flamma in the neighborhood of Arretium,[186] while he was supplying the adjacent parts, already excited to insurrection, with arms, marched with his fasces, and other ensigns of authority, to join Manlius in his camp.

When this was known at Rome, the senate declared Catiline and Manlius enemies to the state, and fixed a day as to the rest of their force, before which they might lay down their arms with impunity, except such as had been convicted of capital offenses. They also decreed that the consuls should hold a levy; that Antonius, with an army, should hasten in pursuit of Catiline; and that Cicero should protect the city.

At this period the empire of Rome appears to me to have been in an extremely deplorable condition;[187] for though every nation, from the rising to the setting of the sun, lay in subjection to her arms, and though peace and prosperity, which mankind think the greatest blessings, were hers in abundance, there yet were found, among her citizens, men who were bent with obstinate determination, to plunge themselves and their country into ruin; for, notwithstanding the two decrees of the senate,[188] not one individual, out of so vast a number, was induced by the offer of reward to give information of the conspiracy; nor was there a single deserter from the camp of Catiline. So strong a spirit of disaffection had, like a pestilence, pervaded the minds of most of the citizens.

XXXVII. Nor was this disaffected spirit confined to those who were actually concerned in the conspiracy; for the whole of the common people, from a desire of change, favored the projects of Catiline. This they seemed to do in accordance with their general character; for, in every state, they that are poor envy those of a better class, and endeavor to exalt the factious;[189] they dislike the established condition of things, and long for something new; they are discontented with their own circumstances, and desire a general alteration; they can support themselves amid tumult and sedition, without anxiety, since poverty does not easily suffer loss.[190]

As for the populace of the city, they had become disaffected[191] from various causes. In the first place,[192] such as every where took the lead in crime and profligacy, with others who had squandered their fortunes in dissipation, and, in a word, all whom vice and villainy had driven from their homes, had flocked to Rome as a general receptacle of impurity. In the next place, many, who thought of the success of Sylla, when they had seen some raised from common soldiers into senators, and others so enriched as to live in regal luxury and pomp, hoped, each for himself, similar results from victory, if they should once take up arms. In addition to this, the youth, who, in the country, had earned a scanty livelihood by manual labor, tempted by public and private largesses, had preferred idleness in the city to unwelcome toil in the field. To these, and all others of similar character, public disorders would furnish subsistence. It is not at all surprising, therefore, that men in distress, of dissolute principles and extravagant expectations, should have consulted the interest of the state no further than as it was subservient to their own. Besides, those whose parents, by the victory of Sylla, had been proscribed, whose property had been confiscated, and whose civil rights had been curtailed,[193] looked forward to the event of a war with precisely the same feelings.

All those, too, who were of any party opposed to that of the senate, were desirous rather that the state should be embroiled, than that they themselves should be out of power. This was an evil, which, after many years, had returned upon the community to the extent to which it now prevailed.[194]

XXXVIII. For after the powers of the tribunes, in the consulate of Cneius Pompey and Marcus Crassus, had been fully restored,[195] certain young men, of an ardent age and temper, having obtained that high office,[196] began to stir up the populace by inveighing against the senate, and proceeded, in course of time, by means of largesses and promises, to inflame them more and more; by which methods they became popular and powerful. On the other hand, the most of the nobility opposed their proceedings to the utmost; under pretense, indeed, of supporting the senate, but in reality for their own aggrandizement. For, to state the truth in few words, whatever parties, during that period, disturbed the republic under plausible pretexts, some, as if to defend the rights of the people, others, to make the authority of the senate as great as possible, all, though affecting concern for the public good, contended every one for his own interest. In such contests there was neither moderation nor limit; each party made a merciless use of its successes.

XXXIX. After Pompey, however, was sent to the maritime and Mithridatic wars, the power of the people was diminished, and the influence of the few increased. These few kept all public offices, the administration of the provinces, and every thing else, in their own hands; they themselves lived free from harm,[197] in flourishing circumstances, and without apprehension; overawing others, at the same time, with threats of impeachment,[198] so that when in office, they might be less inclined to inflame the people. But as soon as a prospect of change, in this dubious state of affairs, had presented itself, the old spirit of contention awakened their passions; and had Catiline, in his first battle, come off victorious, or left the struggle undecided, great distress and calamity must certainly have fallen upon the state, nor would those, who might at last have gained the ascendency, have been allowed to enjoy it long, for some superior power would have wrested dominion and liberty from them when weary and exhausted.

There were some, however, unconnected with the conspiracy, who set out to join Catiline at an early period of his proceedings. Among these was Aulus Fulvius, the son of a senator, whom, being arrested on his journey, his father ordered to be put to death.[199] In Rome, at the same time, Lentulus, in pursuance of Catiline's directions, was endeavoring to gain over, by his own agency or that of others, all whom he thought adapted, either by principles or circumstances, to promote an insurrection; and not citizens only, but every description of men who could be of any service in war.

XL. He accordingly commissioned one Publius Umbrenus to apply to certain deputies of the Allobroges,[200] and to lead them, if he could, to a participation in the war; supposing that as they were nationally and individually involved in debt, and as the Gauls were naturally warlike, they might easily be drawn into such an enterprise. Umbrenus, as he had traded in Gaul, was known to most of the chief men there, and personally acquainted with them; and consequently, without loss of time, as soon as he noticed the deputies in the Forum, he asked them, after making a few inquiries about the state of their country, and affecting to commiserate its fallen condition, "what termination they expected to such calamities?" When he found that they complained of the rapacity of the magistrates, inveighed against the senate for not affording them relief, and looked to death as the only remedy for their sufferings, "Yet I," said he, "if you will but act as men, will show you a method by which you may escape these pressing difficulties." When he had said this, the Allobroges, animated with the highest hopes, besought Umbrenus to take compassion on them; saying that there was nothing so disagreeable or difficult, which they would not most gladly perform, if it would but free their country from debt. He then conducted them to the house of Decimus Brutus, which was close to the Forum, and, on account of Sempronia, not unsuitable to his purpose, as Brutus was then absent from Rome.[201] In order, too, to give greater weight to his representations, he sent for Gabinius, and, in his presence, explained the objects of the conspiracy, and mentioned the names of the confederates, as well as those of many other persons, of every sort, who were guiltless of it, for the purpose of inspiring the embassadors with greater confidence. At length, when they had promised their assistance, he let them depart.

XLI. Yet the Allobroges were long in suspense what course they should adopt. On the one hand, there was debt, an inclination for war, and great advantages to be expected from victory;[202] on the other, superior resources, safe plans, and certain rewards[203] instead of uncertain expectations. As they were balancing these considerations, the good fortune of the state at length prevailed. They accordingly disclosed the whole affair, just as they had learned it, to Quintus Fabius Sanga,[204] to whose patronage their state was very greatly indebted. Cicero, being apprized of the matter by Sanga, directed the deputies to pretend a strong desire for the success of the plot, to seek interviews with the rest of the conspirators, to make them fair promises, and to endeavor to lay them open to conviction as much as possible.

XLII. Much about the same time there were commotions[205] in Hither and Further Gaul, in the Picenian and Bruttian territories, and in Apulia. For those, whom Catiline had previously sent to those parts, had begun, without consideration, and seemingly with madness, to attempt every thing at once; and, by nocturnal meetings, by removing armor and weapons from place to place, and by hurrying and confusing every thing, had created more alarm than danger. Of these, Quintus Metellus Celer, the praetor, having brought several to trial,[206] under the decree of the senate, had thrown them into prison, as had also Caius Muraena in Further Gaul,[207] who governed that province in quality of legate.

XLIII. But at Rome, in the mean time, Lentulus, with the other leaders of the conspiracy, having secured what they thought a large force, had arranged, that as soon as Catiline should reach the neighborhood of Faesulae, Lucius Bestia, a tribune of the people, having called an assembly, should complain of the proceedings of Cicero, and lay the odium of this most oppressive war on the excellent consul;[208] and that the rest of the conspirators, taking this as a signal, should, on the following night, proceed to execute their respective parts.

These parts are said to have been thus distributed. Statilius and Gabinius, with a large force, were to set on fire twelve places of the city, convenient for their purpose,[209] at the same time; in order that, during the consequent tumult,[210] an easier access might be obtained to the consul, and to the others whose destruction was intended; Cethegus was to beset the gate of Cicero, and attack him personally with violence; others were to single out other victims; while the sons of certain families, mostly of the nobility, were to kill their fathers; and, when all were in consternation at the massacre and conflagration, they were to sally forth to join Catiline.

While they were thus forming and settling their plans, Cethegus was incessantly complaining of the want of spirit in his associates; observing, that they wasted excellent opportunities through hesitation and delay;[211] that, in such an enterprise, there was need, not of deliberation, but of action; and that he himself, if a few would support him, would storm the senate-house while the others remained inactive. Being naturally bold, sanguine, and prompt to act, he thought that success depended on rapidity of execution.

XLIV. The Allobroges, according to the directions of Cicero, procured interviews, by means of Gabinius, with the other conspirators; and from Lentulus, Cethegus, Statilius, and Cassius, they demanded an oath, which they might carry under seal to their countrymen, who otherwise would hardly join in so important an affair. To this the others consented without suspicion; but Cassius promised them soon to visit their country,[212] and, indeed, left the city a little before the deputies.

In order that the Allobroges, before they reached home, might confirm their agreement with Catiline, by giving and receiving pledges of faith, Lentulus sent with them one Titus Volturcius, a native of Crotona, he himself giving Volturcius a letter for Catiline, of which the following is a copy:

"Who I am, you will learn from the person whom I have sent to you. Reflect seriously in how desperate a situation you are placed, and remember that you are a man.[213] Consider what your views demand, and seek aid from all, even the lowest." In addition, he gave him this verbal message: "Since he was declared an enemy by the senate, for what reason should he reject the assistance of slaves? That, in the city, every thing which he had directed was arranged; and that he should not delay to make nearer approaches to it."

XLV. Matters having proceeded thus far, and a night being appointed for the departure of the deputies, Cicero, being by them made acquainted with every thing, directed the praetors,[214] Lucius Valerius Flaccus, and Caius Pomtinus, to arrest the retinue of the Allobroges, by laying in wait for them on the Milvian Bridge;[215] he gave them a full explanation of the object with which they were sent,[216] and left them to manage the rest as occasion might require. Being military men, they placed a force, as had been directed, without disturbance, and secretly invested the bridge; when the deputies, with Volturcius, came to the place, and a shout was raised from each side of the bridge,[217] the Gauls, at once comprehending the matter, surrendered themselves immediately to the praetors. Volturcius, at first, encouraging his companions, defended himself against numbers with his sword; but afterward, being unsupported by the Allobroges, he began earnestly to beg Pomtinus, to whom he was known, to save his life, and at last, terrified and despairing of safety, he surrendered himself to the praetors as unconditionally as to foreign enemies.

XLVI. The affair being thus concluded, a full account of it was immediately transmitted to the consul by messengers. Great anxiety, and great joy, affected him at the same moment. He rejoiced that, by the discovery of the conspiracy, the state was freed from danger; but he was doubtful how he ought to act, when citizens of such eminence were detected in treason so atrocious. He saw that their punishment would be a weight upon himself, and their escape the destruction of the Commonwealth. Having, however, formed his resolution, he ordered Lentulus, Cethegus, Statilius, Gabinius, and one Quintus Coeparius of Terracina, who was preparing to go to Apulia to raise the slaves, to be summoned before him. The others came without delay; but Coeparius, having left his house a little before, and heard of the discovery of the conspiracy, had fled from the city. The consul himself conducted Lentulus, as he was praetor, holding him by the hand, and ordered the others to be brought into the Temple of Concord, under a guard. Here he assembled the senate, and in a very full attendance of that body, introduced Volturcius with the deputies. Hither also he ordered Valerius Flaccus, the praetor, to bring the box with the letters[218] which he had taken from the deputies.

XLVII. Volturcius, being questioned concerning his journey, concerning his letter,[219] and lastly, what object he had had in view,[220] and from what motives he had acted, at first began to prevaricate,[221] and to pretend ignorance of the conspiracy; but at length, when he was told to speak on the security of the public faith,[222] he disclosed every circumstance as it had really occurred, stating that he had been admitted as an associate, a few days before, by Gabinius and Coeparius; that he knew no more than the deputies, only that he used to hear from Gabinius, that Publius Autronius, Servius Sylla, Lucius Vargunteius, and many others, were engaged in the conspiracy. The Gauls made a similar confession, and charged Lentulus, who began to affect ignorance, not only with the letter to Catiline, but with remarks which he was in the habit of making, "that the sovereignty of Rome, by the Sibylline books, was predestined to three Cornelii; that Cinna and Sylla had ruled already;[223] and that he himself was the third, whose fate it would be to govern the city; and that this, too, was the twentieth year since the Capitol was burned; a year which the augurs, from certain omens, had often said would be stained with the blood of civil war."

The letter then being read, the senate, when all had previously acknowledged their seals,[224] decreed that Lentulus, being deprived of his office, should, as well as the rest, be placed in private custody.[225] Lentulus, accordingly, was given in charge to Publius Lentulus Spinther, who was then aedile; Cethegus, to Quintus Cornificius; Statilius, to Caius Caesar; Gabinius, to Marcus Crassus; and Coeparius, who had just before been arrested in his flight, to Cneius Terentius, a senator.

XLVIII. The common people, meanwhile, who had at first, from a desire of change in the government, been too much inclined to war, having, on the discovery of the plot, altered their sentiments, began to execrate the projects of Catiline, to extol Cicero to the skies; and, as if rescued from slavery, to give proofs of joy and exultation. Other effects of war they expected as a gain rather than a loss; but the burning of the city they thought inhuman, outrageous, and fatal, especially to themselves, whose whole property consisted in their daily necessaries and the clothes which they wore.

On the following day, a certain Lucius Tarquinius was brought before the senate, who was said to have been arrested as he was setting out to join Catiline. This person, having offered to give information of the conspiracy, if the public faith were pledged to him,[226] and being directed by the consul to state what he knew, gave the senate nearly the same account as Volturcius had given, concerning the intended conflagration, the massacre of respectable citizens, and the approach of the enemy, adding that "he was sent by Marcus Crassus to assure Catiline that the apprehension of Lentulus, Cethegus, and others of the conspirators, ought not to alarm him, but that he should hasten, with so much the more expedition to the city, in order to revive the courage of the rest, and to facilitate the escape of those in custody".[227] When Tarquinius named Crassus, a man of noble birth, of very great wealth, and of vast influence, some, thinking the statement incredible, others, though they supposed it true, yet, judging that at such a crisis a man of such power[228] was rather to be soothed than irritated (most of them, too, from personal reasons, being; under obligation to Crassus), exclaimed that he was "a false witness," and demanded that the matter should be put to the vote. Cicero, accordingly, taking their opinions, a full senate decreed "that the testimony of Tarquinius appeared false; that he himself should be kept in prison; and that no further liberty of speaking[229] should be granted him, unless he should name the person at whose instigation he had fabricated so shameful a calumny."

There were some, at that time, who thought that this affair was contrived by Publius Autronius, in order that the interest of Crassus, if he were accused, might, from participation in the danger, more readily screen the rest. Others said that Tarquinius was suborned by Cicero, that Crassus might not disturb the state, by taking upon him, as was his custom,[230] the defense of the criminals. That this attack on his character was made by Cicero, I afterward heard Crassus himself assert.

XLIX. Yet, at the same time, neither by interest, nor by solicitation, nor by bribes, could Quintus Catulus, and Caius Piso, prevail upon Cicero to have Caius Caesar falsely accused, either by means of the Allobroges, or any other evidence. Both of these men were at bitter enmity with Caesar; Piso, as having been attacked by him, when he was on[231] his trial for extortion, on a charge of having illegally put to death a Transpadane Gaul; Catulus, as having hated him ever since he stood for the pontificate, because, at an advanced age, and after filling the highest offices, he had been defeated by Caesar, who was then comparatively a youth.[232] The opportunity, too, seemed favorable for such an accusation; for Caesar, by extraordinary generosity in private, and by magnificent exhibitions in public,[233] had fallen greatly into debt. But when they failed to persuade the consul to such injustice, they themselves, by going from one person to another, and spreading fictions of their own, which they pretended to have heard from Volturcius or the Allobroges, excited such violent odium against him, that certain Roman knights, who were stationed as an armed guard round the Temple of Concord, being prompted, either by the greatness of the danger, or by the impulse of a high spirit, to testify more openly their zeal for the republic, threatened Caesar with their swords as he went out of the senate-house.

L. While these occurrences were passing in the senate, and while rewards were being voted, an approbation of their evidence, to the Allobrogian deputies and to Titus Volturcius, the freedmen, and some of the other dependents of Lentulus, were urging the artisans and slaves, in various directions throughout the city,[234] to attempt his rescue; some, too, applied to the ringleaders of the mob, who were always ready to disturb the state for pay. Cethegus, at the same time, was soliciting, through his agents, his slaves[235] and freedmen, men trained to deeds of audacity, to collect themselves into an armed body, and force a way into his place of confinement.

The consul, when he heard that these things were in agitation, having distributed armed bodies of men, as the circumstances and occasion demanded, called a meeting of the senate, and desired to know "what they wished to be done concerning those who had been committed to custody." A full senate, however, had but a short time before[236] declared them traitors to their country. On this occasion, Decimus Junius Silanus, who, as consul elect, was first asked his opinion, moved[237] that capital punishment should be inflicted, not only on those who were in confinement, but also on Lucius Cassius, Publius Furius, Publius Umbrenus, and Quintus Annius, if they should be apprehended; but afterward, being influenced by the speech of Caius Caesar, he said that he would go over to the opinion of Tiberius Nero,[238] who had proposed that the guards should be increased, and that the senate should deliberate further on the matter. Caesar, when it came to his turn, being asked his opinion by the consul, spoke to the following effect:

LI. "It becomes all men,[239] Conscript Fathers, who deliberate on dubious matters, to be influenced neither by hatred, affection, anger, nor pity. The mind, when such feelings obstruct its view, can not easily see what is right; nor has any human being consulted, at the same moment, his passion and his interest. When the mind is freely exerted, its reasoning is sound; but passion, if it gain possession of it, becomes its tyrant, and reason is powerless.

I could easily mention, Conscript Fathers, numerous examples of kings and nations, who, swayed by resentment or compassion, have adopted injudicious courses of conduct; but I had rather speak of these instances in which our ancestors, in opposition, to the impulse of passion, acted with wisdom and sound policy.

In the Macedonian war, which we carried on against king Perses, the great and powerful state of Rhodes, which had risen by the aid of the Roman people, was faithless and hostile to us; yet, when the war was ended, and the conduct of the Rhodians was taken into consideration, our forefathers left them unmolested lest any should say that war was made upon them for the sake of seizing their wealth, rather than of punishing their faithlessness. Throughout the Punic war, too, though the Carthaginians, both during peace and in suspension of arms, were guilty of many acts of injustice, yet our ancestors never took occasion to retaliate, but considered rather what was worthy of themselves, than what might be justly inflicted on their enemies.

Similar caution, Conscript Fathers, is to be observed by yourselves, that the guilt of Lentulus, and the other conspirators, may not have greater weight with you than your own dignity, and that you may not regard your indignation more than your character. If, indeed, a punishment adequate to their crimes be discovered, I consent to extraordinary measures;[240] but if the enormity of their crime exceeds whatever can be devised,[241] I think that we should inflict only such penalties as the laws have provided.

Most of those, who have given their opinions before me, have deplored, in studied and impressive language,[242] the sad fate that threatens the republic; they have recounted the barbarities of war, and the afflictions that would fall on the vanquished; they have told us that maidens would be dishonored, and youths abused; that children would be torn from the embraces of their parents; that matrons would be subjected to the pleasure of the conquerors; that temples and dwelling-houses would be plundered; that massacres and fires would follow; and that every place would be filled with arms, corpses, blood, and lamentation. But to what end, in the name of the eternal gods! was such eloquence directed? Was it intended to render you indignant at the conspiracy? A speech, no doubt, will inflame him whom so frightful and monstrous a reality has not provoked! Far from it: for to no man does evil, directed against himself, appear a light matter; many, on the contrary, have felt it more seriously than was right.

But to different persons, Conscript Fathers, different degrees of license are allowed. If those who pass a life sunk in obscurity, commit any error, through excessive anger, few become aware of it, for their fame is as limited as their fortune; but of those who live invested with extensive power, and in an exalted station, the whole world knows the proceedings. Thus in the highest position there is the least liberty of action; and it becomes us to indulge neither partiality nor aversion, but least of all animosity; for what in others is called resentment, is in the powerful termed violence and cruelty.

I am indeed of opinion, Conscript Fathers, that the utmost degree of torture is inadequate to punish their crime; but the generality of mankind dwell on that which happens last, and, in the case of malefactors, forget their guilt, and talk only of their punishment, should that punishment have been inordinately severe. I feel assured, too, that Decimus Silanus, a man of spirit and resolution, made the suggestions which he offered, from zeal for the state, and that he had no view, in so important a matter, to favor or to enmity; such I know to be his character, and such his discretion.[243] Yet his proposal appears to me, I will not say cruel (for what can be cruel that is directed against such characters?), but foreign to our policy. For assuredly, Silanus, either your fears, or their treason, must have induced you, a consul elect, to propose this new kind of punishment. Of fear it is unnecessary to speak, when by the prompt activity of that distinguished man our consul, such numerous forces are under arms; and as to the punishment, we may say, what is indeed the truth, that in trouble and distress, death is a relief from suffering, and not a torment;[244] that it puts an end to all human woes; and that, beyond it, there is no place either for sorrow or joy.

But why, in the name of the immortal gods, did you not add to your proposal, Silanus, that, before they were put to death, they should be punished with the scourge? Was it because the Porcian law[245] forbids it? But other laws[246] forbid condemned citizens to be deprived of life, and allow them to go into exile. Or was it because scourging is a severer penalty than death? Yet what can be too severe, or too harsh, toward men convicted of such an offense? But if scourging be a milder punishment than death, how is it consistent to observe the law as to the smaller point, when you disregard it as to the greater?

But who it may be asked, will blame any severity that shall be decreed against these parricides[247] of their country? I answer that time, the course of events,[248] and fortune, whose caprice governs nations, may blame it. Whatever shall fall on the traitors, will fall on them justly; but it is for you, Conscript Fathers, to consider well what you resolve to inflict on others. All precedents productive of evil effects,[249] have had their origin from what was good; but when a government passes into the hands of the ignorant or unprincipled, any new example of severity,[250] inflicted on deserving and suitable objects, is extended to those that are improper and undeserving of it. The Lacedaemonians, when they had conquered the Athenians,[251] appointed thirty men to govern their state. These thirty began their administration by putting to death, even without a trial, all who were notoriously wicked, or publicly detestable; acts at which the people rejoiced, and extolled their justice. But afterward, when their lawless power gradually increased, they proceeded, at their pleasure, to kill the good and the bad indiscriminately, and to strike terror into all; and thus the state, overpowered and enslaved, paid a heavy penalty for its imprudent exultation.

Within our own memory, too, when the victorious Sylla ordered Damasippus,[252] and others of similar character, who had risen by distressing their country, to be put to death, who did not commend the proceeding? All exclaimed that wicked and factious men, who had troubled the state with their seditious practices, had justly forfeited their lives. Yet this proceeding was the commencement of great bloodshed. For whenever anyone coveted the mansion or villa, or even the plate or apparel of another, he exerted his influence to have him numbered among the proscribed. Thus they, to whom the death of Damasippus had been a subject of joy, were soon after dragged to death themselves; nor was there any cessation of slaughter, until Sylla had glutted all his partisans with riches.

Such excesses, indeed, I do not fear from Marcus Tullius, or in these times. But in a large state there arise many men of various dispositions. At some other period, and under another consul, who, like the present, may have an army at his command, some false accusation may be credited as true; and when, with our example for a precedent, the consul shall have drawn the sword on the authority of the senate, who shall stay its progress, or moderate its fury?

Our ancestors, Conscript Fathers, were never deficient in conduct or courage; nor did pride prevent them from imitating the customs of other nations, if they appeared deserving of regard. Their armor, and weapons of war, they borrowed from the Samnites; their ensigns of authority,[253] for the most part, from the Etrurians; and, in short, whatever appeared eligible to them, whether among allies or among enemies, they adopted at home with the greatest readiness, being more inclined to emulate merit than to be jealous of it. But at the same time, adopting a practice from Greece, they punished their citizens with the scourge, and inflicted capital punishment on such as were condemned. When the republic, however, became powerful, and faction grew strong from the vast number of citizens, men began to involve the innocent in condemnation, and other like abuses were practiced; and it was then that the Porcian and other laws were provided, by which condemned citizens were allowed to go into exile. This lenity of our ancestors, Conscript Fathers, I regard as a very strong reason why we should not adopt any new measures of severity. For assuredly there was greater merit and wisdom in those, who raised so mighty an empire from humble means, than in us, who can scarcely preserve what they so honorably acquired. Am I of opinion, then, you will ask, that the conspirators should be set free, and that the army of Catiline should thus be increased? Far from it; my recommendation is, that their property be confiscated, and that they themselves be kept in custody in such of the municipal towns as are best able to bear the expense;[254] that no one hereafter bring their case before the senate, or speak on it to the people; and that the senate now give their opinion, that he who shall act contrary to this, will act against the republic and the general safety."

LII. When Caesar had ended his speech, the rest briefly expressed their assent,[255] some to one speaker, and some to another, in support of their different proposals; but Marcius Porcius Cato, being asked his opinion, made a speech to the following purport:

"My feelings, Conscript Fathers, are extremely different,[256] when I contemplate our circumstances and dangers, and when I revolve in my mind the sentiments of some who have spoken before me. Those speakers, as it seems to me, have considered only how to punish the traitors who have raised war against their country, their parents, their altars, and their homes;[257] but the state of affairs warns us rather to secure ourselves against them, than to take counsel as to what sentence we should pass upon them. Other crimes you may punish after they have been committed; but as to this, unless you prevent its commission, you will, when it has once taken effect, in vain appeal to justice.[258] When the city is taken, no power is left to the vanquished. But, in the name of the immortal gods, I call upon you, who have always valued your mansions and villas, your statues and pictures, at a higher price than the welfare of your country; if you wish to preserve those possessions, of whatever kind they are, to which you are attached; if you wish to secure quiet for the enjoyment of your pleasures, arouse yourselves, and act in defense of your country. We are not now debating on the revenues, or on injuries done to our allies, but our liberty and our life is at stake.

Often, Conscript Fathers, have I spoken at great length in this assembly; often have I complained of the luxury and avarice of our citizens, and, by that very means, have incurred the displeasure of many. I, who never excused to myself, or to my own conscience, the commission of any fault, could not easily pardon the misconduct,[259] or indulge the licentiousness, of others. But though you little regarded my remonstrances, yet the republic remained secure; its own strength[260] was proof against your remissness. The question, however, at present under discussion, is not whether we live in a good or a bad state of morals; nor how great, or how splendid, the empire of the Roman people is; but whether these things around us, of whatever value they are, are to continue our own, or to fall, with ourselves, into the hands of the enemy.

In such a case, does any one talk to me of gentleness and compassion? For some time past, it is true, we have lost the real name of things; [261] for to lavish the property of others is called generosity, and audacity in wickedness is called heroism; and hence the state is reduced to the brink of ruin. But let those, who thus misname things, be liberal, since such is the practice, out of the property of our allies; let them be merciful to the robbers of the treasury; but let them not lavish our blood, and, while they spare a few criminals, bring destruction on all the guiltless.

Caius Caesar, a short time ago, spoke in fair and elegant language, [262] before this assembly, on the subject of life and death; considering as false, I suppose, what is told of the dead; that the bad, going a different way from the good, inhabit places gloomy, desolate, dreary, and full of horror. He accordingly proposed ***that the property of the conspirators should be confiscated, and themselves kept in custody in the municipal towns***; fearing, it seems, that, if they remain at Rome, they may be rescued either by their accomplices in the conspiracy, or by a hired mob; as if, forsooth, the mischievous and profligate were to be found only in the city, and not through the whole of Italy, or as if desperate attempts would not be more likely to succeed where there is less power to resist them. His proposal, therefore, if he fears any danger from them, is absurd; but if, amid such universal terror, he alone is free from alarm, it the more concerns me to fear for you and myself.

Be assured, then, that when you decide on the fate of Lentulus and the other prisoners, you at the same time determine that of the army of Catiline, and of all the conspirators. The more spirit you display in your decision, the more will their confidence be diminished; but if they shall perceive you in the smallest degree irresolute, they will advance upon you with fury.

Do not suppose that our ancestors, from so small a commencement, raised the republic to greatness merely by force of arms. If such had been the case, we should enjoy it in a most excellent condition;[263] for of allies and citizens,[264] as well as arms and horses, we have a much greater abundance than they had. But there were other things which made them great, but which among us have no existence; such as industry at home, equitable government abroad, and minds impartial in council, uninfluenced by any immoral or improper feeling. Instead of such virtues, we have luxury and avarice; public distress, and private superfluity; we extol wealth, and yield to indolence; no distinction is made between good men and bad; and ambition usurps the honors due to virtue. Nor is this wonderful; since you study each his individual interest, and since at home you are slaves to pleasure, and here to money or favor; and hence it happens that an attack is made on the defenseless state.

But on these subjects I shall say no more. Certain citizens, of the highest rank, have conspired to ruin their country; they are engaging the Gauls, the bitterest foes of the Roman name, to join in a war against us; the leader of the enemy is ready to make a descent upon us; and do you hesitate; even in such circumstances, how to treat armed incendiaries arrested within your walls? I advise you to have mercy upon them;[265] they are young men who have been led astray by ambition; send them away, even with arms in their hands. But such mercy, and such clemency, if they turn those arms against you, will end in misery to yourselves. The case is, assuredly, dangerous, but you do not fear it; yes, you fear it greatly, but you hesitate how to act, through weakness and want of spirit, waiting one for another, and trusting to the immortal gods, who have so often preserved your country in the greatest dangers. But the protection of the gods is not obtained by vows and effeminate supplications; it is by vigilance, activity, and prudent measures, that general welfare is secured. When you are once resigned to sloth and indolence, it is in vain that you implore the gods; for they are then indignant and threaten vengeance.

In the days of our forefathers, Titus Manlius Torquatus, during a war with the Gauls, ordered his own son to be put to death, because he had fought with an enemy contrary to orders. That noble youth suffered for excess of bravery; and do you hesitate what sentence to pass on the most inhuman of traitors? Perhaps their former life is at variance with their present crime. Spare, then, the dignity of Lentulus, if he has ever spared his own honor or character, or had any regard for gods or for men. Pardon the youth of Cethegus, unless this be the second time that he has made war upon his country.[266] As to Gabinius, Slatilius, Coeparius, why should I make any remark upon them? Had they ever possessed the smallest share of discretion, they would never have engaged in such a plot against their country.

In conclusion, Conscript Fathers, if there were time to amend an error, I might easily suffer you, since you disregard words, to be corrected by experience of consequences. But we are beset by dangers on all sides; Catiline, with his army, is ready to devour us;[267] while there are other enemies within the walls, and in the heart of the city; nor can any measures be taken, or any plans arranged, without their knowledge. The more necessary is it, therefore, to act with promptitude. What I advise, then, is this: that since the state, by a treasonable combination of abandoned citizens, has been brought into the greatest peril; and since the conspirators have been convicted on the evidence of Titus Volturcius, and the deputies of the Allobroges, and on their own confession, of having concerted massacres, conflagrations, and other horrible and cruel outrages, against their fellow-citizens and their country, punishment be inflicted, according to the usage of our ancestors, on the prisoners who have confessed their guilt, as on men convicted of capital crimes."

LIII. When Cato had resumed his seat, all the senators of consular dignity, and a great part of the rest,[268] applauded his opinion, and extolled his firmness of mind to the skies. With mutual reproaches, they accused one another of timidity, while Cato was regarded as the greatest and noblest of men; and a decree of the senate was made as he had advised.

After reading and hearing of the many glorious achievements which the Roman people had performed at home and in the field, by sea as well as by land, I happened to be led to consider what had been the great foundation of such illustrious deeds. I knew that the Romans had frequently, with small bodies of men, encountered vast armies of the enemy; I was aware that they had carried on wars[269] with limited forces against powerful sovereigns; that they had often sustained, too, the violence of adverse fortune; yet that, while the Greeks excelled them in eloquence, the Gauls surpassed them in military glory. After much reflection, I felt convinced that the eminent virtue of a few citizens had been the cause of all these successes; and hence it had happened that poverty had triumphed over riches, and a few over a multitude. And even in later times, when the state had become corrupted by luxury and indolence, the republic still supported itself, by its own strength, under the misconduct of its generals and magistrates; when, as if the parent stock were exhausted,[270] there was certainly not produced at Rome, for many years, a single citizen of eminent ability. Within my recollection, however, there arose two men of remarkable powers, though of very different character, Marcus Cato and Caius Caesar, whom, since the subject has brought them before me, it is not my intention to pass in silence, but to describe, to the best of my ability, the disposition and manners of each.

LIV. Their birth, age, and eloquence, were nearly on an equality; their greatness of mind similar, as was also their reputation, though attained by different means. [271] Caesar grew eminent by generosity and munificence; Cato by the integrity of his life. Caesar was esteemed for his humanity and benevolence; austereness had given dignity to Cato. Caesar acquired renown by giving, relieving, and pardoning; Cato by bestowing nothing. In Caesar, there was a refuge for the unfortunate; in Cato, destruction for the bad. In Caesar, his easiness of temper was admired; in Cato, his firmness. Caesar, in fine, had applied himself to a life of energy and activity; intent upon the interest of his friends, he was neglectful of his own; he refused nothing to others that was worthy of acceptance, while for himself he desired great power, the command of an army, and a new war in which his talents might be displayed. But Cato's ambition was that of temperance, discretion, and, above all, of austerity; he did not contend in splendor with the rich, or in faction with the seditious, but with the brave in fortitude, with the modest in simplicity,[272] with the temperate[273] in abstinence; he was more desirous to be, than to appear, virtuous; and thus, the less he courted popularity, the more it pursued him.

LV. When the senate, as I have stated, had gone over to the opinion of Cato, the counsel, thinking it best not to wait till night, which was coming on, lest any new attempts should be made during the interval, ordered the triumvirs[274] to make such preparations as the execution of the conspirators required. He himself, having posted the necessary guards, conducted Lentulus to the prison; and the same office was performed for the rest by the praetors. There is a place in the prison, which is called the Tullian dungeon,[275] and which, after a slight ascent to the left, is sunk about twelve feet under ground. Walls secure it on every side, and over it is a vaulted roof connected with stone arches;[276] but its appearance is disgusting and horrible, by reason of the filth, darkness, and stench. When Lentulus had been let down into this place, certain men, to whom orders had been given,[277] strangled him with a cord. Thus this patrician, who was of the illustrious family of the Cornelii, and who filled the office of consul at Rome, met with an end suited to his character and conduct. On Cethegus, Statilius, Gabinius, and Coeparius, punishment was inflicted in a similar manner.

LVI. During these proceedings at Rome, Catiline, out of the entire force which he himself had brought with him, and that which Manlius had previously collected, formed two legions, filling up the cohorts as far as his number would allow;[278] and afterward, as any volunteers, or recruits from his confederates,[279] arrived in his camp, he distributed them equally throughout the cohorts, and thus filled up his legions, in a short time, with their regular number of men, though at first he had not more than two thousand. But, of his whole army, only about a fourth part had the proper weapons of soldiers; the rest, as chance had equipped them, carried darts, spears, or sharpened stakes.

As Antonius approached with his army, Catiline directed his march over the hills, encamping, at one time, in the direction of Rome, at another in that of Gaul.

He gave the enemy no opportunity of fighting, yet hoped himself shortly to find one,[280] if his accomplices at Rome should succeed in their objects. Slaves, meanwhile, of whom vast numbers [281] had at first flocked to him, he continued to reject, not only as depending on the strength of the conspiracy, but as thinking it impolitic [282] to appear to share the cause of citizens with runagates.

LVII. When it was reported in his camp, however, that the conspiracy had been discovered at Rome, and that Lentulus, Cethegus, and the rest whom I have named, had been put to death, most of those whom the hope of plunder, or the love of change, had led to join in the war, fell away. The remainder Catiline conducted, over rugged mountains, and by forced marches, into the neighborhood of Pistoria, with a view to escape covertly, by cross roads, into Gaul.

But Quintus Metellus Celer, with a force of three legions, had at that time, his station in Picenum, who suspected that Catiline, from the difficulties of his position, would adopt precisely the course which we have just described. When, therefore, he had learned his route from some deserters, he immediately broke up his camp, and took his post at the very foot of the hills, at the point where Catiline's descent would be, in his hurried march into Gaul[283]. Nor was Antonius far distant, as he was pursuing, though with, a large army, yet through plainer ground, and with fewer hinderances, the enemy in retreat.[284]

Catiline, when he saw that he was surrounded by mountains and by hostile forces, that his schemes in the city had been unsuccessful, and that there was no hope either of escape or of succor, thinking it best, in such circumstances, to try the fortune of a battle, resolved upon engaging, as speedily as possible, with Antonius. Having, therefore, assembled his troops, he addressed them in the following manner:

LVIII. "I am well aware, soldiers, that words can not inspire courage; and that a spiritless army can not be rendered active,[285] or a timid army valiant, by the speech of its commander. Whatever courage is in the heart of a man, whether from nature or from habit, so much will be shown by him in the field; and on him whom neither glory nor danger can move, exhortation is bestowed in vain; for the terror in his breast stops his ears.

I have called you together, however, to give you a few instructions, and to explain to you, at the same time, my reasons for the course which I have adopted. You all know, soldiers, how severe a penalty the inactivity and cowardice of Lentulus has brought upon himself and us; and how, while waiting for reinforcements from the city, I was unable to march into Gaul.

In what situation our affairs now are, you all understand as well as myself. Two armies of the enemy, one on the side of Rome, and the other on that of Gaul, oppose our progress; while the want of corn, and of other necessaries, prevents us from remaining, however strongly we may desire to remain, in our present position. Whithersoever we would go, we must open a passage with our swords. I conjure you, therefore, to maintain a brave and resolute spirit; and to remember, when you advance to battle, that on your own right hands depend[286] riches, honor, and glory, with the enjoyment of your liberty and of your country. If we conquer, all will be safe; we shall have provisions in abundance; and the colonies and corporate towns will open their gates to us. But if we lose the victory through want of courage, these same places[287] will turn against us; for neither place nor friend will protect him whom his arms have not protected. Besides, soldiers, the same exigency does not press upon our adversaries, as presses upon us; we fight for our country, for our liberty, for our life; they contend for what but little concerns them,[288] the power of a small party. Attack them, therefore, with so much the greater confidence, and call to mind your achievements of old.

We might,[289] with the utmost ignominy, have passed the rest of our days in exile. Some of you, after losing your property, might have waited at Rome for assistance from others. But because such a life, to men of spirit, was disgusting and unendurable, you resolved upon your present course. If you wish to quit it, you must exert all your resolution, for none but conquerors have exchanged war for peace. To hope for safety in flight, when you have turned away from the enemy the arms by which the body is defended, is indeed madness. In battle, those who are most afraid are always in most danger; but courage is equivalent to a rampart. When I contemplate you, soldiers, and when I consider your past exploits, a strong hope of victory animates me. Your spirit, your age, your valor, give me confidence; to say nothing of necessity, which makes even cowards brave. To prevent the numbers of the enemy from surrounding us, our confined situation is sufficient. But should Fortune be unjust to your valor, take care not to lose your lives unavenged; take care not to be taken and butchered like cattle, rather than fighting like men, to leave to your enemies a bloody and mournful victory."

LIX. When he had thus spoken, he ordered, after a short delay, the signal for battle to be sounded, and led down his troops, in regular order, to the level ground. Having then sent away the horses of all the cavalry, in order to increase the men's courage by making their danger equal, he himself, on foot, drew up his troops suitably to their numbers and the nature of the ground. As a plain stretched between the mountains on the left, with a rugged rock on the right, he placed eight cohorts in front, and stationed the rest of his force, in close order, in the rear.[290] From among these he removed all the ablest centurions,[291] the veterans,[293] and the stoutest of the common soldiers that were regularly armed, into the foremost ranks.[293] He ordered Caius Manlius to take the command on the right, and a certain officer of Faesulae[294] on the left; while he himself, with his freedmen[295] and the colonists,[296] took his station by the eagle,[297] which Caius Marius was said to have had in his army in the Cimbrian war.

On the other side, Caius Antonius, who, being lame,[298] was unable to be present in the engagement, gave the command of the army to Marcus Petreius, his lieutenant-general. Petreius, ranged the cohorts of veterans, which he had raised to meet the present insurrection,[299] in front, and behind them the rest of his force in lines. Then, riding round among his troops, and addressing his men by name, he encouraged them, and bade them remember that they were to fight against unarmed marauders, in defense of their country, their children, their temples, and their homes.[300] Being a military man, and having served with great reputation, for more than thirty years, as tribune, praefect, lieutenant, or praetor, he knew most of the soldiers and their honorable actions, and, by calling these to their remembrance, roused the spirits of the men.

LX. When he had made a complete survey, he gave the signal with the trumpet, and ordered the cohorts to advance slowly. The army of the enemy followed his example; and when they approached so near that the action could be commenced by the light-armed troops, both sides, with a loud shout, rushed together in a furious charge.[301] They threw aside their missiles, and fought only with their swords. The veterans, calling to mind their deeds of old, engaged fiercely in the closest combat. The enemy made an obstinate resistance; and both sides contended with the utmost fury. Catiline, during this time, was exerting himself with his light troops in the front, sustaining such as were pressed, substituting fresh men for the wounded, attending to every exigency, charging in person, wounding many an enemy, and performing at once the duties of a valiant soldier and a skillful general.

When Petreius, contrary to his expectation, found Catiline attacking him with such impetuosity, he led his praetorian cohort against the centre of the enemy, among whom, being thus thrown into confusion, and offering but partial resistance,[302] he made great slaughter, and ordered, at the same time, an assault on both flanks. Manlius and the Faesulan, sword in hand, were among the first[303] that fell; and Catiline, when he saw his army routed, and himself left with but few supporters, remembering his birth and former dignity, rushed into the thickest of the enemy, where he was slain, fighting to the last.

LXI. When the battle was over, it was plainly seen what boldness, and what energy of spirit, had prevailed throughout the army of Catiline; for, almost every where, every soldier, after yielding up his breath, covered with his corpse the spot which he had occupied when alive. A few, indeed, whom the praetorian cohort had dispersed, had fallen somewhat differently, but all with wounds in front. Catiline himself was found, far in advance of his men, among the dead bodies of the enemy; he was not quite breathless, and still expressed in his countenance the fierceness of spirit which he had shown during his life. Of his whole army, neither in the battle, nor in flight, was any free-born citizen made prisoner, for they had spared their own lives no more than those of the enemy.

Nor did the army of the Roman people obtain a joyful or bloodless victory; for all their bravest men were either killed in the battle, or left the field severely wounded.

Of many who went from the camp to view the ground, or plunder the slain, some, in turning over the bodies of the enemy, discovered a friend, others an acquaintance, others a relative; some, too, recognized their enemies. Thus, gladness and sorrow, grief and joy, were variously felt throughout the whole army.

NOTES.

[1] I. Desire to excel other animals--Sese student praestare
caeteris animalibus. The pronoun, which is usually omitted, is, says

Cortius, not without its force; for it is equivalent to *ut ipsi*: student *ut ipsi praestent*. In support of his opinion he quotes, with other passages, Plaut. Asinar. i. 3, 31: Vult placere sese amicae, i.e. vult *ut ipse amicae placeat*; and Coelius Antipater apud Festum in "Topper," Ita uti sese quisque vobis studeat aemulari, i.e. *studeat ut ipse aemuletur.* This explanation is approved by Bernouf. Cortius might have added Cat. 7: *sese* quisque hostem ferire --properabat. "Student," Cortius interprets by "cupiunt."

[2] To the utmost of their power--*Summa ope*, with their utmost ability. "A Sallustian mode of expression. Cicero would have said *summa opera, summo studio, summa contentione.* Ennius has 'Summa nituntur opum vi.'" Colerus.

[3] In obscurity--*Silentio.* So as to have nothing said of them, either during their lives or at their death. So in c. 2: Eorum ego vitam mortemque juxta aestumo, quoniam de utraque siletur. When Ovid says, **Bene qui latuit, bene vixit,** and Horace, Nec vixit male, qui vivens moriensque fefellit, they merely signify that he has some comfort in life, who, in ignoble obscurity, escapes trouble and censure. But men thus undistinguished are, in the estimation of Sallust, little superior to the brute creation. "Optimus quisque," says Muretus, quoting Cicero, "honoris et gloriae studio maxime ducitur;" the ablest men are most actuated by the desire of honor and glory, and are more solicitous about the character which they will bear among posterity. With reason, therefore, does Pallas, in the Odyssey, address the following exhortation to Telemachus:

"Hast thou not heard how young Orestes, fir'd
With great revenge, immortal praise acquir'd?

O greatly bless'd with ev'ry blooming grace,

With equal steps the paths of glory trace!
Join to that royal youth's your rival name,
And shine eternal in the sphere of fame."

[4] Like the beasts of the field--*Veluti pecora.* Many translators have rendered *pecora* "brutes" or "beasts;" *pecus*, however, does not mean brutes in general, but answers to our English word *cattle*.

[5] Groveling--*Prona.* I have adopted *groveling* from Mair's old translation. *Pronus*, stooping *to the earth*, is applied to *cattle*, in opposition to *erectus*, which is applied to *man*; as in the following lines of Ovid, Met. i.:

"*Prona* que cum spectent animalia caetera terram,
Os homini sublime dedit, coelumque tueri
Jussit, et *erectos* ad sidera tollere vultus."

"--while the mute creation downward bend
Their sight, and to their earthly mother tend,
Man looks aloft, and with erected eyes
Beholds his own hereditary skies."   *Dryden.*

Which Milton (Par. L. vii. 502) has paraphrased:

"There wanted yet the master-work, the end
Of all yet done; a creature, who not prone
And 'brute as other creatures, but endued
With sanctity of reason, might *erect*
His stature, and *upright with front serene*
Govern the rest, self-knowing, and from thence
Magnanimous to correspond with heaven."
"Nonne vides hominum ut celsos ad sidera vultus

> Sustulerit Deus, et sublimia fluxerit ora,
> Cum pecudes, voluerumque genus, formasque ferarum,
> Segnem atque obscoenam passim stravisset in alvum."

> "See'st thou not how the Deity has rais'd
> The countenance of man erect to heav'n,
> Gazing sublime, while prone to earth he bent
> Th' inferior tribes, reptiles, and pasturing herds,
> And beasts of prey, to appetite enslav'd"

"When Nature," says Cicero, de Legg. i. 9, "had made other animals abject, and consigned them to the pastures, she made man alone upright, and raised him to the contemplation of heaven, as of his birthplace and former abode;" a passage which Dryden seems to have had in his mind when he translated the lines of Ovid cited above. Let us add Juvenal, xv, 146.

> "Sensum a coelesti demissum traximus arce,
> Cujus egent prona et terram spectantia."

> "To us is reason giv'n, of heav'nly birth,
> Denied to beasts, that prone regard the earth."

[6] All our power is situate in the mind and in the body--Sed omnis nostra vis in animo et corpore sita. All our power is placed, or consists, in our mind and our body. The particle *sed,* which is merely a connective, answering to the Greek *de*, and which would be useless in an English translation, I have omitted.

[7] Of the mind we--employ the government--***Animi imperio--utimur***. "What the Deity is in the universe, the mind is in man; what matter is to the universe, the body is to us; let the worse, therefore, serve the better."--Sen. Epist. lxv. Dux et imperator vitae mortalium

animus est, the mind is the guide and ruler of the life of mortals. --Jug. c. 1. "An animal consists of mind and body, of which the one is formed by nature to rule, and the other to obey."--Aristot. Polit. i. 5. Muretus and Graswinckel will supply abundance of similar passages.

[8] Of the mind we rather employ the government; of the body, the service--***Animi imperio, corporis servitio, magis utimur***. The word ***magis*** is not to be regarded as useless. "It signifies," says Cortius, "that the mind rules, and the body obeys, ***in general***, and with greater reason.*" At certain times the body may* seem to have the mastery, as when we are under the irresistible influence of hunger or thirst.

[9] It appears to me, therefore, more reasonable, etc.--Quo mihi rectius videtur***, etc. I have rendered*** quo ***by*** therefore. "Quo," observes Cortius, "is ***propter quod***, with the proper force of the ablative case. So Jug. c. 84: ***Quo*** mihi acrius adnitendum est, etc; c. 2, ***Quo*** magis pravitas eorum admiranda est. Some expositors would force us to believe that these ablatives are inseparably connected with the comparative degree, as in ***quo minus, eo major***, and similar expressions; whereas common sense shows that they can not be so connected." Kritzius is one of those who interprets in the way to which Cortius alludes, as if the drift of the passage were, Quanto magis animus corpori praestat, tanto rectius ingenii opibus gloriam quaerere. But most of the commentators and translators rightly follow Cortius. "***Quo***," says Pappaur, "is for ***quocirca***."

[10] ***That of*** intellectual power is illustrious and immortal--Virtus clara aeternaque habetur. The only one of our English translators who has given the right sense of ***virtus*** In this passage, is Sir Henry Steuart, who was guided to it by the Abbe Thyvon and M. Beauzee. "It appears somewhat singular," says Sir Henry, "that none of the

numerous translators of Sallust, whether among ourselves or among foreign nations--the Abbe Thyvon and M. Beauzee excepted--have thought of giving to the word ***virtus***, in this place, what so obviously is the meaning intended by the historian; namely, 'genius, ability, distinguished talents.'" Indeed, the whole tenor of the passage, as well as the scope of the context, leaves no room to doubt the fact. The main objects of comparison, throughout the three first sections of this Proemium, or introductory discourse, are not vice and virtue, but body and mind; a listless indolence, and a vigorous, honorable activity. On this account it is pretty evident, that by ***virtus*** Sallust could never mean the [Greek ***aretae***], 'virtue or moral worth,' but that he had in his eye the well-known interpretation of Varro, who considers it ***ut viri vis*** (De Ling. Lat. iv.), as denoting the useful energy which ennobles a man, and should chiefly distinguish him among his fellow-creatures. In order to be convinced of the justice of this rendering, we need only turn to another passage of our author, in the second section of the Proemium to the Jugurthine War, where the same train of thought is again pursued, although he gives it somewhat a different turn in the piece last mentioned. The object, notwithstanding, of both these dissertations is to illustrate, in a striking manner, the pre-eminence of the mind over extrinsic advantage, or bodily endowments, and to show that it is by genius alone that we may aspire to a reputation which shall never die. "Igitur praeclara facies, magnae divitiae, adhuc vis corporis, et alia hujusmondi omnia, brevi dilabuntur: at ingenii egregia facinora, sicut anima, immortalia sunt".

[11] It is necessary to plan before beginning to act--Priusquam incipias, consulto--opus est. Most translators have rendered ***consulto*** "deliberation," or something equivalent; but it is ***planning*** or ***contrivance*** that is signified. Demosthenes, in his Oration ***de Pace***, reproaches the Athenians with acting without any settled plan: [Greek: Oi men gar alloi puntes anthropoi pro ton

pragmatonheiothasi chraesthai to Bouleuesthai, umeis oude meta ta pragmata.]

[12] To act with promptitude and vigor--***Mature facto opus est***. "Mature facto" seems to include the notions both of promptitude and vigor, of force as well as speed; for what would be the use of acting expeditiously, unless expedition be attended with power and effect?

[13] Each--***Utrumque***. The corporeal and mental faculties.

[14] The one requires the assistance of the other--Alterum alterius auxilio eget. "Eget," says Cortius, "is the reading of all the MSS." ***Veget***, which Havercamp and some others have adopted, was the conjecture of Palmerius, on account of ***indigens*** occurring in the same sentence. But ***eget*** agrees far better with consulto et--mature facto opus est, in the preceding sentence.

[15] II. Applied themselves in different ways--***Diversi***. "Modo et instituto diverso, diversa sequentes." ***Cortius***.

[16] At that period, however--***Et jam tum***. "Tunc temporis ***praecise***, at that time ***precisely***, which is the force of the particle ***jam***. as donatus shows. I have therefore written ***et jam*** separately. Virg. Aen. vii. 737. Late ***jam tum*** ditione premebat Sarrastes populos." ***Cortius***.

[17] Without covetousness--Sine cupiditate. "As in the famous golden age. See Tacit. Ann. iii. 28." ***Cortius***. See also Ovid. Met. i. 80, ***seq***. But "such times were never," as Cowper says.

[18] But after Cyrus in Asia, etc.--Postea vero quam in, Asia Cyrus, etc. Sallust writes as if he had supposed that kings were more

moderate before the time of Cyrus. But this can hardly have been the case. "The Romans," says De Brosses, whose words I abridge, "though not learned in antiquity, could not have been ignorant that there were great conquerors before Cyrus; as Ninus and Sesostris. But as their reigns belonged rather to the fabulous ages, Sallust, in entering upon a serious history, wished to confine himself to what was certain, and went no further back than the records of Herodotus and Thucydides." Ninus, says Justin. i. 1, was the first to change, through inordinate ambition, the ***veterem et quasi avitum gentibus morem***, that is, to break through the settled restraints of law and order. Gerlach agrees in opinion with De Brosses.

[19] Proof and experience--***Periculo atque negotiis***. Gronovius rightly interprets ***periculo*** "experiundo, experimentis," by experiment or trial. Cortius takes ***periculo atque negotiis*** for ***periculosis negotiis***, by hendyadys; but to this figure, as Kritzius remarks, we ought but sparingly to have recourse. It is better, he adds, to take the words in their ordinary signification, understanding by ***negotia*** "res graviores." Bernouf judiciously explains ***negotiis*** by "ipsa negotiorum tractatione," ***i. e.*** by the management of affairs, or by experience in affairs. Dureau Delamalle, the French translator, has "l'experience et la pratique." Mair has "trial and experience." which, I believe, faithfully expresses Sallust's meaning. Rose gives only "experience" for both words.

[20] And, indeed, if the intellectual ability, etc.--Quod si--animi virtus***, etc. "Quod si" can not here be rendered*** but if; it is rather equivalent to ***quapropter si***, and might be expressed by ***wherefore if, if therefore, if then, so that if***.

[21] Intellectual ability--***Animi virtus***. See the remarks on ***virtus***, above noted.

[22] Magistrates--*Imperatorum*. "Understand all who govern states, whether in war or in peace." *Bernouf*. Sallust calls the consuls *imperatores*, c. 6.

[23] Governments shifted from hand to hand--*aliud alio ferri*. Evidently alluding to changes in government.

[24] Less to the more deserving--Ad optimum quemque a minus bono. "From the less good to the best."

[25] Even in agriculture, etc.--Quae homines arant, navigant, aedificant, virtuti omnia parent. *Literally,* what men plow, sail, etc. Sallust's meaning is, that agriculture, navigation, and architecture, though they may seem to be effected by mere bodily exertion, are as much the result of mental power as the highest of human pursuits.

[26] Like travelers in a strange country--*Sicuti peregrinantes*. "Vivere nesciunt; igitur in vita quasi hospites sunt:" they know not how to use life, and are therefore, as it were, strangers in it. *Dietsch*. "*Peregrinantes*, qui, qua transeunt, nullum sui vestigium relinquunt;" they are as travelers who do nothing to leave any trace of their course. Pappaur.

[27] Of these I hold the life and death in equal estimation--Eorum ego vitam mortemque juxta aestimo. I count them of the same value dead as alive, for they are honored in the one state as much as in the other. "Those who are devoted to the gratification of their appetites," as Sallust says, "let us regard as inferior animals, not as men; and some, indeed, not as living, but as dead animals." Seneca, Ep. lx.

[28] III. Not without merit--**Haud absurdum**. I have borrowed this expression from Rose, to whom Muretus furnished "sua laude non caret." "The word ***absurdus*** is often used by the Latins as an epithet for sounds disagreeable to the ear; but at length it came to be applied to any action unbecoming a rational being." **Kunhardt**.

[29] Deeds must be adequately represented, etc.--Facta dictis sunt exaequanda. Most translators have regarded these words as signifying **that the subject must be equaled by the style**. But it is not of mere style that Sallust is speaking. "He means that the matter must be so represented by the words, that honorable actions may not be too much praised, and that dishonorable actions may not be too much blamed; and that the reader may at once understand what was done and how it was done." **Kunhardt**.

[30] Every one hears with acquiescence, etc.--Quae sibi--aequo animo accipit, etc. This is taken from Thucydides, ii. 35. "For praises spoken of others are only endured so far as each one thinks that he is himself also capable of doing any of the things he hears; but that which exceeds their own capacity, men at once envy and disbelieve." Dale's Translation: Bohn's Classical Library.

[31] Regards as fictitious and incredible--Veluti ficta, pro falsis ducit. Ducit pro falsis, he considers as false or incredible, ***veluti ficta***, as if invented.

[32] When a young man--**Adolescentulus**. "It is generally admitted that all were called ***adolescentes*** by the Romans, who were between the fifteenth or seventeenth year of their age and the fortieth. The diminutive is used in the same sense, but with a view to contrast more strongly the ardor and spirit of youth with the moderation, prudence, and experience of age. So Caesar is called ***adolescentulus***,

in c. 49, at a time when he was in his thirty-third year." **Dietsch**. And Cicero, referring to the time of his consulship, says, Defendi rempublicam adolescens, Philipp. ii. 46.

[33] To engage in political affairs--*Ad rempublicam*. "In the phrase of Cornelius Nepos, ***honoribus operam dedi***, I sought to obtain some share in the management of the Republic. All public matters were comprehended under the term ***Respublica***." **Cortius**.

[34] Integrity--***Virtute***. Cortius rightly explains this word as meaning *justice, equity*, and all other virtues necessary in those who manage the affairs of a state. Observe that it is here opposed to *avaritia*, not, as some critics would have it, to *largitio*.

[35] Was ensnared and infected--***Corrupta, tenebatur***. As ***obsessus tenetur***, Jug., c. 24.

[36] The same eagerness for honors, the same obloquy and jealousy, etc.--Honoris cupido eadem quae caeteros, fama atque invidia vexabat. I follow the interpretation of Cortius: "Me vexabat honoris cupido, et vexabat ***propterea*** etiam eadem, quae caeteros, fama atqua invidia." He adds, from a gloss in the Guelferbytan MS., that it is a ***zeugma***. "*Fama atque invidia*," says Gronovius, "is [Greek: *en dia duoin*], for *invidiosa et maligna fama*." Bernouf, with Zanchius and others, read *fama atque invidia* in the ablative case; and the Bipont edition has ***eadem qua--fama, etc.***; but the method of Cortius is, to me, by far the most straightforward and satisfactory. Sallust, observes De Brosses, in his note on this passage, wrote the account of Catiline's conspiracy shortly after his expulsion from the Senate, and wishes to make it appear that he suffered from calumny on the occasion; though he took no trouble, in the subsequent part of his life, to put such calumny to silence.

[37] IV. Servile occupations--agriculture or hunting--*Agrum colendo, aut venando, servilibus officiis intentum*. By calling agriculture and hunting **servilia officia**, Sallust intends, as is remarked by Graswinckelius, little more than was expressed in the saying of Julian the emperor, Turpe est sapienti, cum habeat animum, captare laudes ex corpore. "Ita ergo," adds the commentator, "agricultura et venatio servilio officia sunt, quum in solo consistant corporis usu, animum, vero nec meliorem nec prudentiorem reddant. Quia labor in se certe est illiberalis, ei praesertim cui facultas sit ad meliora." Symmachus (1 v. Ep. 66) and some others, whose remarks the reader may see in Havercamp, think that Sallust might have spoken of hunting and agriculture with more respect, and accuse him of not remembering, with sufficient veneration, the kings and princes that have amused themselves in hunting, and such illustrious plowmen as Curius and Cincinnatus. Sallust, however, is sufficiently defended from censure by the Abbe Thyvon, in a dissertation much longer than the subject deserves, and much longer than most readers are willing to peruse.

[38] Returning to those studies, etc.--*A quo incepto studio me ambitio mala detinuerat, eodem regressus*. "The study, namely, of writing history, to which he signifies that he was attached in c. 3." **Cortius**.

[39] In detached portions--**Carptim**. "Plin. Ep. viii., 47: Respondebis non posse perinde **carptim**, ut **contexta** placere: et vi. 22: Egit **carptim** et [Greek: **kata kephulaia**]," **Dietsch**.

[40] V. Of noble birth--**Nobili genere natus**. His three names were Lucius **Sergius** Catilina, he being of the family of the Sergii, for whose antiquity Virgil is responsible, Aen. v. 121: Sergestusque,

domus tenet a quo Sergia nomen. And Juvenal says, Sat. viii. 321: Quid, Catilino, tuis natalibus atque Cethegi Inveniet quisquam sublimius? His great grandfather, L. Sergius Silus, had eminently distinguished himself by his services in the second Punic war. See Plin. Hist. Nat. vii. 29. "Catiline was born A.U.C. 647, A.C. 107." *Dietsch*. Ammianus Marcellinus (lib. xxv.) says that he was the last of the Sergii.

[41] *Sedition--Discordia civilis*.

[42] And in such scenes he had spent his early years--Ibique juventutem suam exercuit. "It is to be observed that the Roman writers often used an adverb, where we, of modern times, should express ourselves more specifically by using a noun." *Dietsch* on c. 3, *ibique multa mihi advorsa fuere*. *Juventus* properly signified the time between thirty and forty-five years of age; *adolescentia* that between fifteen and thirty. But this distinction was not always accurately observed. Catiline had taken an active part in supporting Sylla, and in carrying into execution his cruel proscriptions and mandates. "Quis erat hujus (Syllae) imperii minister? Quis nisi Catilina jam in omne facinus manus exercens?" Sen. de Ira, iii. 18.

[43] Capable of pretending or dissembling whatever he wished --*Cujuslibet, rei simulator ac dissimulator*. "Dissimulation is the negative, when a man lets fall signs and arguments, that he is not that he is; simulation is the affirmative, when a man industriously and expressly feigns and pretends to be that he is not." Bacon, Essay vi.

[44] Abundance of eloquence--*Satis eloquentiae*. Cortius reads *loquentiae* "*Loquentia* is a certain facility of speech not necessarily attended with sound sense; called by the Greeks [Greek:

lalia]." ***Bernouf.*** "Julius Candidus used excellently to observe that *eloquentia* was one thing, and *loquentia* another; for eloquence is given to few, but what Candidus called *loquentia*, or fluency of speech, is the talent of many, and especially of the most impudent." Plin. Ep. v. 20. But *eloquentiae* is the reading of most of the MSS., and *loquentiae*, if Aulus Gellius (i. 15) was rightly informed, was a correction of Valerius Probus, the grammarian, who said that Sallust ***must*** have written so, as *eloquentiae* could not agree with ***sapientiae parum***. This opinion of Probus, the grammarian, who said that Sallust ***must*** have written so, as *eloquentiae* could not agree with ***sapientiae parum***. This opinion of Probus, however, may be questioned. May not Sallust have written *eloquentiae*, with the intention of signifying that Catiline had abundance of eloquence to work on the minds of others, though he wanted prudence to regulate his own conduct? Have there not been other men of whom the same may be said, as Mirabeau, for example? The speeches that Sallust puts into Catiline's mouth (c. 20, 58) are surely to be characterized rather as *eloquentia*, than *loquentia*. On the whole, and especially from the concurrence of MSS., I prefer to read *eloquentiae*, with the more recent editors, Gerlach, Kritz and Dietsch.

[45] Since the time of Sylla's dictatorship--Post dominationem Lucii Syllae. ***"The meaning is not the same as if it were*** finita dominatione ***but is the same as*** ab eo tempore quo dominari caeperat. In French, therefore, ***post*** should be rendered by ***depuis***, not, as it is commonly translated, ***apres***." ***Bernouf.*** As ***dictator*** was the title that Sylla assumed, I have translated ***dominatio***, "dictatorship". Rose, Gordon, and others, render it "usurpation".

[46] Power--***Regnum***. Chief authority, rule, dominion.

[47] Rendered thoroughly depraved--***Vexabant***. "Corrumpere et

pessundare studebant." ***Bernouf***. ***Quos vexabant***, be it observed, refers to ***mores***, as Gerlach and Kritz interpret, not to ***cives*** understood in ***civitatis***, which is the evidently erroneous method of Cortius.

[48] Conduct of our ancestors--***Instituta majorum***. The principles adopted by our ancestors, with regard both to their own conduct, and to the management of the state. That this is the meaning, is evident from the following account.

[49] VI. As I understand--***Sicuti ego accepi***. "By these words he plainly shows that nothing certain was known about the origin of Rome. The reader may consult Livy, lib. i.; Justin, lib. xliii.; and Dionys. Halicar., lib.i.; all of whom attribute its rise to the Trojans." ***Bernouf***.

[50] Aborigines--***Aborigines***. The original inhabitants of Italy; the same as ***indigenae***, or the [Greek: ***Autochthones***].

[51]: Almost incredible--***Incredibile memoratu***. "Non credi potest, si memoratur; superat omnem fidem." ***Pappaur***. Yet that which actually happened, can not be absolutely incredible; and I have, therefore, inserted ***almost***.

[52] Prepared with alacrity for there defense--***Festinare, parare***. "Made haste, prepared." "***Intenti ut festinanter pararent*** ea, quae defensioni aut bello usui essent." ***Pappaur***.

[53] Procured friendships rather by bestowing, etc;--Magisque dandis, quam accipiundis beneficiis amicitias parabant. Thucyd. ii., 40: [Greek: ***Ou paschontes eu, alla drontes, ktometha tous philous***]

[54] FATHERS--PATRES. "(Romulus) appointed that the direction of the state should be in the hands of the old men, who, from their authority, were called *Fathers*; from their age, *Senatus*." Florus, i. 1. *Senatus* from *senex*. "*Patres* ab honore--appellati." *Livy*.

[55] Two magistrates--*Binos imperatores*. The two consuls. They were more properly called *imperatores* at first, when the law, which settled their power, said "*Regio imperio* duo sunto" (Cic. de Legg. iii. 4), than afterward, when the people and tribunes had made encroachments on their authority.

[56] VII. Almost incredible--*Incredibile memoratu*. See above, c. 6.

[57] Able to bear the toils of war--*Laboris ac belli patiens*. As by *laboris* the labor of war is evidently intended, I have thought it better to render the words in this manner. The reading is Cortius'. Havercamp and others have "simul *ac belli* patiens erat, in castris *per laborem usu* militiam discebat;" but *per laborem usu* is assuredly not the hand of Sallust.

[58] Honor and true nobility--*Bonam famam magnamque nobilitatem*.

[59] VIII. Very great and glorious--*Satis amplae magnificaeque*. In speaking of this amplification of the Athenian exploits, he alludes, as Colerus observes, to the histories of Thucydides, Xenophen, and perhaps Herodotus; not, as Wasse seems to imagine, to the representations of the poets.

[60] There was never any such abundance of writers--Nunquam ea copia fuit. *I follow Kuhnhardt, who thinks* copia equivalent to *multitudo*. Others render it *advantage*, or something similar;

which seems less applicable to the passage. Compare c.28: *Latrones--**quorum**--magna copia **erat***.

[61] Chose to act rather than narrate--"For," as Cicero says, "neither among those who are engaged in establishing a state, nor among those carrying on wars, nor among those who are curbed and restrained under the rule of kings, is the desire of distinction in eloquence wont to arise." **Graswinckelius**.

[62] IX. Pressed by the enemy--***Pulsi***. In the words pulsi loco cedere ausi erant, loco is to be joined, as Dietsch observes, with cedere**, not, as Kritzius puts it, with** pulsi. "To retreat," adds Dietsch, "is disgraceful only to those qui ab hostibus se pelli patiantur**, who suffer themselves to be** repulsed by the enemy."

[63] X. When mighty princes had been vanquished in war--Perses, Antiochus, Mithridates, Tigranes, and others.

[64] To keep one thing concealed in the breast, and another ready on the tongue--Aliud clausum in pectore, aliud in lingua promptum,

[Greek: Echthros gar moi keinos homos Aidao pulaesin.
    Os ch' eteron men keuthei eni phresin, allo de Bazei.]

> Who dares think one thing, and another tell,
> My heart detests him as the gates of hell.
>   ***Pope***.

[65] XI. At first, however, it was ambition, rather than avarice, etc.--Sed primo magis ambitio quam avaritia animos hominum exercebat. Sallust has been accused of having made, in this passage, an assertion at variance with what he had said before (c.10), Igitur

primo pecuniae, deinde imperii cupido, crevit, and it will be hard to prove that the accusation is not just. Sir H. Steuart, indeed, endeavors to reconcile the passages by giving them the following "meaning", which, he says, "seems perfectly evident": "Although avarice was the first to make its appearance at Rome, yet, after both had had existence, it was ambition that, of the two vices, laid the stronger hold on the minds of men, and more speedily grew to an inordinate height". To me, however, it "seems perfectly evident" that the Latin can be made to yield no such "meaning". "How these passages agree," says Rupertus, "I do not understand: unless we suppose that Sallust, by the word *primo*, does not always signify order".

[66] Enervates whatever is manly in body or mind--Corpus virilemque animum effaeminat. That avarice weakens the mind, is generally admitted. But how does it weaken the body? The most satisfactory answer to this question is, in the opinion of Aulus Gellius (iii. 1), that those who are intent on getting riches devote themselves to sedentary pursuits, as those of usurers and money-changers, neglecting all such exercises and employments as strengthen the body. There is, however, another explanation by Valerius Probus, given in the same chapter of Aulus Gellius, which perhaps is the true one; namely, that Sallust, by **body and mind**, intended merely to signify **the whole man**.

[67] Having recovered the government--***Recepta republica***. Having wrested it from the hands of Marius and his party.

[68] All became robbers and plunderers--***Rapere omnes, trahere***. He means that there was a general indulgence in plunder among Sylla's party, and among all who, in whatever character, could profit by supporting it. Thus he says immediately afterward, "neque modum neque modestiam *victores* habere."

[69] which he had commanded in Asia--***Quem in Asia dustaverat***. I have here deserted Cortius, who gives ***in Asiam***, "into Asia," but this, as Bernouf justly observes, is incompatible with the frequentative verb ***ductaverat***.

[70] in public edifices and private dwellings--Privatim ac publice. I have translated this according to the notion of Burnouf. Others, as Dietsch and Pappaur, consider ***privatim*** as signifying ***each on his own account***, and ***publice***, in the name of the Republic.

[71] XII. A life of innocence was regarded as a life of ill-nature --***Innocentia pro malivolentia duci caepit***. "Whoever continued honest and upright, was considered by the unprincipled around him as their enemy; for a good man among the bad can never be regarded as of their party." ***Bernouf***.

[72] It furnishes much matter for reflection--***Operae pretium est***.

[73] Basest of mankind--***Ignavissumi mortales***. It is opposed to ***fortissumi viri***, which follows, "Qui nec fortiter nec bene quidquam fecere." ***Cortius***.

[74] XIII. Seas covered with edifices--***Maria constructa esse***.

Contracta pisces aequora sentiunt,
   Jactis in altum molibus, etc.   Hor. Od., iii. 1.

--The haughty lord, who lays
His deep foundations in the seas,
  And scorns earth's narrow bound;
The fish affrighted feel their waves

Contracted by his numerous slaves,
 Even in the vast profound.   *Francis*.

[75] To have made a sport of their wealth--Quibus mihi videntur ledibrio fuisse divitiae. "They spent their riches on objects which, in the judgment of men of sense, are ridiculous and contemptible." ***Cortius***.

[76] Luxury--***Cultus***. "Deliciarum in victu, luxuries of the table; for we must be careful not to suppose that apparel is meant." ***Cortius***.

[77] Cold--***Frigus***. It is mentioned by Cortius that this word is wanting in one MS.; and the English reader may possibly wish that it were away altogether. Cortius refers it to cool places built of stone, sometimes underground, to which the luxurious retired in the hot weather; and he cites Pliny, Ep., v. 6, who speaks of ***crytoporticus***, a gallery from which the sun was excluded, almost as if it were underground, and which, even in summer was cold nearly to freezing. He also refers to Ambros., Epist. xii., and Casaubon. Ad Spartian. Adrian., c. x., p. 87.

[78] XIV. Gaming--***Manu***. Gerlach, Dietsch, Kritzius, and all the recent editors, agree to interpret ***manu*** by ***gaming***.

[79] Assassins--***Parricidae***. "Not only he who had killed his father was called a ***parricide***, but he who had killed any man; as is evident from a law of Numa Pompilius: If any one unlawfully and knowingly bring a free man to death, let him be ***a parricide***." ***Festus*** sub voce ***Parrici***.

[80] Than from any evidence of the fact--Quam quod cuiquam id

compertum foret.

[81] XV. With a virgin of noble birth--*Cum virgine nobili*. Who this was is not known. The name may have been suppressed from respect to her family. If what is found in a fragment of Cicero be true, Catiline had an illicit connection with some female, and afterward married the daughter who was the fruit of the connection: Ex eodem stupro et uxorem et filiam invenisti; Orat. in Tog. Cand. (Oration xvi., Ernesti's edit.) On which words Asconius Pedianus makes this comment: "Dicitur Catilinam adulterium commisisse cum ea quae ci postea socrus fuit, et ex eo stupro duxisse uxorem, cum filia ejus esset. Haec Lucceius quoque Catilinae objecit in orationibus, quas in eum scripsit. Nomina harum mulierum nondum inveni." Plutarch, too (Life of Cicero, c. 10), says that Catiline was accused of having corrupted his own daughter.

[82] With a priestess of Vesta--*Cum sacerdote Vestae*. This priestess of Vesta was Fabia Terentia, sister to Terentia, Cicero's wife, whom Sallust, after she was divorced by Cicero, married. Clodius accused her, but she was acquitted, either because she was thought innocent, or because the interest of Catulus and others, who exerted themselves in her favor, procured her acquittal. See Orosius, vi. 3; the Oration of Cicero, quoted in the preceding note; and Asconius's commentary on it.

[83] Aurelia Orestilla--See c. 35. She was the sister or daughter, as De Brosses thinks, of Cneius Aurelius Orestis, who had been praetor, A.U.C. 677.

[84] A grown-up step-son--*Privignum adulta aetate*. A son of Catiline's by a former marriage.

[85] Desolate his tortured spirit--*Mentem exciteam vastabat*.

"Conscience desolates the mind, when it deprives it of its proper power and tranquillity, and introduces into it perpetual disquietude." *Cortius*. Many editions have ***vexabat***.

[86] XVI. He furnished false witnesses, etc. Testis signatoresque falsos commodare. "If any one wanted any such character, Catiline was ready to supply him from among his troop."***Bernouf***.

[87] Inoffensive persons, etc.--***Insontes, sicuti sontes.*** Most translators have rendered these words "innocent" and "guilty," terms which suggest nothing satisfactory to the English reader. The ***insontes*** are those who had given Catiline no cause of offens; the ***sontes*** those who had in some way incurred his displeasure, or become objects of his rapacity.

[88] Veterans of Sylla, etc.--Elsewhere called the colonists of Sylla; men to whom Sylla had given large tracts of land as rewards for their services, but who, having lived extravagantly, had fallen into such debt and distress, that, as Cicero said, nothing could relieve them but the resurrection of Sylla from the dead. Cic. ii. Orat. in Cat.

[89] Pompey was fighting in a distant part of the world--In extremis terris. Pompey was then conducting the war against Mithridates and Tigranes, in Pontus and Armenia.

[90] The senate was wholly off its guard--***Senatus nihil sane intentus***. The senate was ***regardless***, and unsuspicious of any danger.

[91] XVII. Lucius Caesar--He was a relation of Julius Caesar; and his sister was the wife of M. Antonius, the orator, and mother of Mark Antony, the triumvir.

[92] Publius Lentulus Sura--He was of the same family with Sylla, that of the Cornelii. He had filled the office of consul, but his conduct had been afterward so profligate, that the censors expelled him from the senate. To enable him to resume his seat, he had obtained, as a qualification, the office of praetor, which he held at the time of the conspiracy. He was called Sura, because, when he had squandered the public money in his quaestorship, and was called to account by Sylla for his dishonesty, he declined to make any defense, but said, "I present you the calf of my leg (*sura*);" alluding to a custom among boys playing at ball, of inflicting a certain number of strokes on the leg of an unsuccessful player. Plutarch, Life of Cicero, c.17.

[93] Publius Autronius--He had been a companion of Cicero in his boyhood, and his colleague in the quaestorship. He was banished in the year after the conspiracy, together with Cassius, Laeca, Vargunteius, Servius Sylla, and Caius Cornelius, under the Plautian law. De Brosses.

[94] Lucius Cassius Longinus.--He had been a competitor with Cicero for the consulship. Ascon. Ped., in Cic. Orat. in Tog. Cand. His corpulence was such that Cassius's fat (***Cassii adeps***) became proverbial. Cic. Orat. in Catil., iii. 7.

[95] Caius Cethegus--He also was one of the Cornelian family. In the civil wars, says De Brosses, he had first taken the side of Marius, and afterward that of Sylla. Both Cicero (Orat. in Catil., ii.7) and Sallust describe him as fiery and rash.

[96] Publius and Servius Sylla--These were nephews of Sylla the dictator. Publius, though present on this occasion, seems not to have joined in the plot, since, when he was afterward accused of having

been a conspirator, he was defended by Cicero and acquitted. See Cic. Orat. pro P. Sylla. He was afterward with Caesar in the battle of Pharsalia. Caes. de B.C., iii. 89.

[97] Lucius Vargunteius--"Of him or his family little is known. He had been, before this period, accused of bribery, and defended by Hortensius. Cic. pro P. Sylla, c. 2." **Bernouf.**

[98] Quintus Annius--He is thought by De Brosses to have been the same Annius that cut off the head of M. Antonius the orator, and carried it to Marius. Plutarch, Vit. Marii, c. 44.

[99] Marcus Porcius Laeca--He was one of the same *gens* with the Catones, but of a different family.

[100] Lucius Bestia--Of the Calpurnian *gens*. He escaped death on the discovery of the conspiracy, and was afterward aedile, and candidate for the praetorship, but was driven into exile for bribery. Being recalled by Caesar, he became candidate for the consulship, but was unsuccessful. **De Brosses**.

[101] Quintus Curius--He was a descendant of M. Curius Dentatus, the opponent of Pyrrhus. He was so notorious as a gamester and a profligate, that he was removed from the senate, A.U.C. 683. See c. 23. As he had been the first to give information of the conspiracy to Cicero, public honors were decreed him, but he was deprived of them by the influence of Caesar, whom he had named as one of the conspirators. Sueton. Caes. 17; Appian. De Bell. Civ., lib. ii.

[102] M. Fulvius Nobilior--"He was not put to death, but exiled, A.U.C. 699. Cic. ad Att. iv., 16." **Bernouf.**

[103] Lucius Statilius--of him nothing more is known than is told by

Sallust.

[104] Publius Gabinius Capito--Cicero, instead of Capito, calls him Cimber. Orat. in Cat., iii. 3. The family was originally from Gabii.

[105] Caius Cornelius--There were two branches of the **gens Cornelia**, one patrician, the other plebeian, from which sprung this conspirator.

[106] Municipal towns--***Municipiis***. "The ***municipia*** were towns of which the inhabitants were admitted to the rights of Roman citizens, but which were allowed to govern themselves by their own laws, and to choose their own magistrates. See Aul. Gell, xvi. 13; Beaufort, Rep. Rom., vol. v." **Bernouf**.

[107] Marcus Licinius Crassus--The same who, with Pompey and Caesar, formed the first triumvirate, and who was afterward killed in his expedition against the Parthians. He had, before the time of the conspiracy, held the offices of praetor and consul.

[108] XVIII. But previously, etc.--Sallust here makes a digression, to give an account of a conspiracy that was formed three years before that of Catiline.

[109] Publius Autronius and Publius Sylla--The same who are mentioned in the preceding chapter. They were consuls elect, and some editions have the words ***designati consules***, immediately following their names.

[110] Having been tried for bribery under the laws against it --***Legibus ambitus interrogati***. ***Bribery at their election***, is the meaning of the word ***ambitus***, for ***ambire***, as Cortius observes, is ***circumeundo favorem et suffragia quaerere***. De Brosses translates the passage thus: "Autrone et Sylla, convaincus d'avoir obtenu le consulat par corruption des suffrages, avaient ete punis selon la rigueur de la

loi". There were several very severe Roman laws against bribery. Autronius and Sylla were both excluded from the consulship.

[111] For extortion--*Pecuniarum repetundarum*. Catiline had been praetor in Africa, and, at the expiration of his office, was accused of extortion by Publius Clodius, on the part of the Africans. He escaped by bribing the prosecutor and judges.

[112] To declare himself a candidate within the legitimate number of days--Prohibitus erat consulatum petere, quod intra legitimos dies profiteri (se candidatum, says Cortius, citing Suet. Aug. 4) *nequiverit*. A person could not be a candidate for the consulship, unless he could declare himself free from accusation within a certain number of days before the time of holding the *comitia centuriata*. That number of days was *trinundinum spatium*, that is, the time occupied by three market-days, *tres nundinae*, with seven days intervening between the first and second, and between the second and third; or *seventeen days*. The *nundinae* (from *novem* and *dies*) were held, as it is commonly expressed, every ninth day; whence Cortius and others considered *trinundinum spatium* to be twenty-seven, or even thirty days; but this way of reckoning was not that of the Romans, who made the last day of *the first ennead* to be also the first day *of the second*. Concerning the *nundinae* see Macrob., Sat. i. 16. "Muller and Longius most erroneously supposed the *trinundinum* to be about thirty days; for that it embraced only seventeen days has been fully shown by Ernesti. Clav. Cic., sub voce; by Scheller in Lex. Ampl., p. 11, 669; by Nitschius Antiquitt. Romm. i. p. 623: and by Drachenborch (cited by Gerlach) ad Liv. iii. 35." **Kritzius**.

[113] Cneius Piso--Of the Calpurnian gens. Suetonius (Vit. Caes., c. 9) mentions three authors who related that Crassus and Caesar were both concerned in this plot; and that, if it had succeeded, Crassus was to

have assumed the dictatorship, and made Caesar his master of the horse. The conspiracy, as these writers state, failed through the remorse or irresolution of Crassus.

[114] Catiline and Autronius--After these two names, in Havercamp's and many other editions, follow the words ***circiter nonas Decembres***, ***i.e.***, about the fifth of December.

[115] On the first of January--***Kalendis Januariis***. On this day the consuls were accustomed to enter on their office. The consuls whom they were going to kill, Cotta and Torquatus, were those who had been chosen in the place of Antronius and Sylla.

[116] The two Spains--Hither and Thither Spain. ***Hispania Citerior*** and ***Ulterior***, as they were called by the Romans.

[117] XIX. Nor were the senate, indeed, unwilling, etc.--See Dio Cass. xxxvi. 27.

[118] XX. Just above mentioned--In c. 17.

[119] Favorable opportunity--***Opportuna res***. See the latter part of c. 16.

[120] Assert our claims to liberty--Nosmet ipsi vindicamus in libertatem.Unless we vindicate ourselves into liberty. See below, "En illa, illa, quam saepe optastis, libertas," etc.

[121] Kings and princes--***Reges tetrarchae***. ***Tetrarchs*** were properly those who had the government of the fourth part of the country; but at length, the signification of the word being extended, it was applied to any governors of any country who were possessed of supreme authority, and yet were not acknowledged as kings by the

Romans. See Hirt. Bell. Alex. c. 67: "Deiotarus, at that time ***tetrarch*** of almost all Gallograecia, a supremacy which the other ***tetrarchs*** would not allow to be granted him either by the laws or by custom, but indisputably acknowledged as king of Armenia Minor by the senate," etc. ***Dietsch.*** "Hesychius has, [Greek: Tetrarchas, basileis]. See Isidor., ix. 8; Alex. ab Alex., ii. 17." ***Colerus.*** "Cicero, Phil. II., speaks of Reges Tetrarchas Dynastasque. And Lucan has (vii. 46) Tetrarchae regesque tenent, magnique tyranni." ***Wasse.*** Horace also says,

  --Modo reges atque tetrarchas,
  Omnia magna loquens.

I have, with Rose, rendered the word ***princes***, as being the most eligible term.

[122] Insults--***Repulsas***. Repulses in standing for office.

[123] The course of events, etc.--***Caetera res expediet***.--"Of. Cic. Ep. Div. xiii. 26: ***explicare et expedire negotia***." Gerlach.

[124] Building over seas--See c. 13.

[125] Embossed plate--***Toreumata***. The same as ***vasa coelata***, sculptured vases, c. 11. Vessels ornamented in bas-relief; from [Greek: *toreuein*], ***sculpere***; see Bentley ad Hor. A. P., 441. "Perbona toreumata, in his pecula duo," etc. Cic. in Verr. iv. 18.

[126] XXI. What support or encouragement they had, and in what quarters.--***Quid ubique opis aut spei haberent; i.e.*** quid opis aut So c. 27, ***init.*** Quem ubique opportunum credebat, ***i.e.***, says Cortius, "quem, et ubi ***illum***, opportunum credebat".

[127] Abolition of their debts--***Tabulas novas.*** Debts were registered on tablets; and, when the debts were paid, the score was effaced, and the tablets were ready to be used ***as new.*** See Ernesti's Clav. in Cio.***sub voce***.

[128] Proscription of the wealthy citizens--Proscriptionem locupletium. The practice of proscription was commenced by Sylla, who posted up, in public places of the city, the names of those whom he doomed to death, offering rewards to such as should bring him their heads. Their money and estates he divided among his adherents, and Catiline excited his adherents with hopes of similar plunder.

[129] Another of his ruling passion--Admonebat--alium cupiditatis suae. Rose renders this passage, "Some he put in mind of their poverty, others of their amours." De Brosses renders it, "Il remontre a l'un sa pauvrete, a l'autre son ambition." Ruling passion***, however, seems to be the proper sense of*** cupiditatis; as it is said, in c. 14, "As the passions of each, according to his years, appeared excited, he furnished mistresses to some, bought horses and dogs for others", etc.

[130] XXII. They asserted--***Dictitare***. In referring this word to the circulators of the report, I follow Cortius, Gerlach, Kritzius, and Bernouf. Wasse, with less discrimination, refers it to Catiline. This story of the drinking of human blood is copied by Florus, iv 1, and by Plutarch in his Life of Cicero. Dio Cassius (lib. xxxvii.) says that the conspirators were reported to have killed a child on the occasion.

[131] XXIII. Quintus Curius--the same that is mentioned in c. 17.

[132] To promise her seas and mountains--*Maria montesque polliceri*. A proverbial expression. Ter. Phorm., i. 2, 18: Modo non montes auri pollicens. *Perc., iii. 65:* Et quid opus Cratero magnos promittere emontes.

[133] With greater arrogance than ever--*Ferocius quam solitus erat.*

[134] To Marcus Tullius Cicero--Cicero was now in his forty-third year, and had filled the office of quaestor, aedile, and praetor.

[135] A man of no family--*Novus homo.* A term applied to such as could not boast of any ancestor that had held any curule magistracy, that is, had been consul, praetor, censor, or chief aedile.

[136] XXIV. Manlius--He had been an officer in the army of Sylla, and, having been distinguished for his services, had been placed at the head of a colony of veterans settled about Faesulae: but he had squandered his property in extravagance. See Plutarch, Vit. Cic., Dio Cassius, and Appian.

[137] Faesulae--A town of Etruria, at the foot of the Appennines,

  At evening from the top of Fesole,
  Or in Valdarno to descry new lands, etc.
Par. L. i. 28.

[138] XXV. Sempronia--Of the same *gens* as the two Gracchi. She was the wife of Decimus Brutus.

[139] Sing, play, and dance--*Psallere, saltare.* As *psallo* signifies both to play on a musical instrument, and to sing to it while playing, I have thought it necessary to give both senses in the translation.

[140] By no means despicable--**Haud absurdum.** Compare, Bene dicere haud absurdum est, c. 8.

[141] She was distinguished, etc.--Multae facetiae, multusque lepos inerat. **Both** facetiae **and** lepos mean "agreeableness, humor, pleasantry," but *lepos* here seems to refer to diction, as in Cic. Orat. i. 7: **Magnus in jocando lepos.**

[142] XXVI. By an arrangement respecting their provinces--Pactione provinciae. This passage has been absurdly misrepresented by most translators, except De Brosses. Even Rose, who was a scholar, translated *pactione provinciae*, "by promising a province to his colleague." Plutarch, in his Life of Cicero, says that the two provinces, which Cicero and his colleague Antonius shared between them, were Gaul and Macedonia, and that Cicero, in order to retain Antonius in the interest of the senate, exchanged with him Macedonia, which had fallen to himself, for the inferior province of Gaul. See Jug., c. 27.

[143] Plots which he had laid for the consuls in the Campus Martius --*Insidiae quas consuli in campo fecerat*. I have here departed from the text of Cortius, who reads *consulibus*, thinking that Catiline, in his rage, might have extended his plots even to the consuls-elect. But *consuli*, there is little doubt, is the right reading, as it is favored by what is said at the beginning of the chapter, insidias parabat Ciceroni, *by what follows in the next chapter,* consuli insidias tendere, and by the words, sperans, si designatus foret, facile se ex voluntate Antonio usurum; for if Catiline trusted that he should be able to use his pleasure with Antonius, he could hardly think it necessary to form plots against his life. I have De Brosses on my side, who translates the phrase, *les pieges ou il comptait faire perir le consul*. The words in campo, which look extremely like an intruded gloss, I wonder that

Cortius should have retained. "***Consuli***," says Gerlach, "appears the more eligible, not only on account of ***consuli insidias tendere***, c. 27, but because nothing but the death of Cicero was necessary to make everything favorable for Catiline." Kritzius, Bernouf, Dietsch, Pappaur, Allen, and all the modern editors, read ***Consuli***. See also the end of c. 27: ***Si prius Ciceronem oppressisset***.] [note 144: Had ended in confusion and disgrace--***Aspera faedaque evenerant***. I have borrowed from Murphy.

[145] XXVII. Of Camerinum--Camertem. "That is, a native of Camerinum, a town on the confines of Umbria and Picenum. Hence the noun ***Camers***, as Cic. Pro. Syll., c. 19, ***in agro Camerti***." Cortius.

[146] Wherever he thought each would be most serviceable--Ubi quemque opportunum credebat. "Proprie reddas: quam, ***et ubi*** illum, ***opportunum credebat***," Cortius. See c. 23.

[147] When none of his numerous projects succeeded--Ubi multa agilanti nihil procedit.

[148] XXVIII. On that very night, and with but little delay--Ea nocte, paulo post. They resolved on going soon after the meeting broke up, so that they might reach Cicero's house early in the morning, which was the usual time for waiting on great men. Ingentem foribus domus alla superbis ***Mane*** salutantum totis vomit aedibus undam. Virg. Georg., ii. 461.

[149] XXIX. This is the greatest power which--is granted, etc. --Ea potestas per senatum, more Romano, magistratui maxima permittitur. ***Cortius,*** mira judicii peversitate, as Kritzius observes, makes *ea* the ablative case, understanding "decretione," "formula," or some such word; but, happily, no one has followed him.

[150] XXX. By the 27th of October--Ante diem VI. Kalendas Novembres. He means that they were in arms on or before that day.

[151] Quintus Marcius Rex--He had been proconsul in Cilicia, and was expecting a triumph for his successes.

[152] Quintus Metellus Creticus--He had obtained the surname of Creticus from having reduced the island of Crete.

[153] Both which officers, with the title of commanders, etc. --hi utrique ad urbem imperatores erant; impediti ne triumpharent calumnia paucorum quibus omnia honesta atque inhonesta vendere mos erat. "Imperator" was a title given by the army, and confirmed by the senate, to a victorious general, who had slain a certain number of the enemy. What the number was is not known. The general bore this title as an addition to his name, until he obtained (if it were granted him) a triumph, for which he was obliged to wait *ad urbem*, near the city, since he was not allowed to enter the gates as long as he held any military command. These *imperatores* had been debarred from their expected honor by a party who would sell *any thing honorable*, as a triumph, or *any thing dishonorable*, as a license to violate the laws.

[154] A hundred sestertia--two hundred sestertia--A hundred sestertia were about 807L. 5s. 10d. of our money.

[155] Schools of gladiators--*Gladiatoriae familiae*. Any number of gladiators under one teacher, or trainer (*lanista*), was called *familia*. They were to be distributed in different parts, and to be strictly watched, that they might not run off to join Catiline. See Graswinckelius, Rupertus, and Gerlach.

[156] The inferior magistrates--The aediles, tribunes, quaestors, and all others below the consuls, censors, and praetors. Aul. Cell., xiii. 15.

[157] XXXI. Dissipation--Lascivia. "Devotion to public amusements and gayety. The word is used in the same sense as in Lucretius, v.

Tum caput atque humeros planis redimire coronis.
Floribus et foliis, lascivia laeta monebat.

"Then sportive gayety prompted them to deck their heads and shoulders with garlands of flowers and leaves." Bernouf.

[158] Long tranquillity--**Diuturna quies**. "Since the victory of Sylla to the time of which Sallust is speaking, that is, for about twenty years, there had been a complete cessation from civil discord and disturbance" **Bernouf**.

[159] The Plautian law--**Lege Plautia**. "This law was that of M. Plautius Silanus, a tribune of the people, which was directed against such as excited a sedition in the state, or formed plots against the life of any individual." **Cyprianus Popma**. See Dr. Smith's Dict. of Gr. and Rom. Antiquities, sub Vis.

[160] Which he afterward wrote and published--Quam postea scriptam edidit. This was the first of Cicero's four Orations against Catiline. The epithet applied to it by Sallust, which I have rendered "splendid," is **luculentam**; that is, says Gerlach, "luminibus verborum et sententiarum ornatam," distinguished by much brilliancy of words and thoughts. And so say Kritzius, Bernouf, and Dietsch. Cortius, who is followed by Dahl, Langius, and Muller, makes the word equivalent merely to **lucid**, in the supposition that Sallust intended to bestow

on the speech, as on other performances of Cicero, only very cool praise. ***Luculentus***, however, seems certainly to mean something more than ***lucidus***.

[161] A mere adopted citizen of Rome--***Inquilinus civis urbis Romae***. "Inquilinus" means properly a lodger, or tenant in the house of another. Cicero was born at Arpinum, and is therefore called by Catiline a citizen of Rome merely by adoption or by sufferance. Appian, in repeating this account (Bell. Civ., ii. 104), says, [Greek: Ingkouilinon, phi raemati kalousi tous enoikountas en allotriais oikiais.]

[162] Traitor--***Parricidam***. See c. 14. "An oppressor or betrayer of his country is justly called a parricide; for our country is the common parent of all. Cic. ad Attic." ***Wasse***.

[163] Since I am encompassed, by enemies, he exclaimed, etc.--"It was not on this day, nor indeed to Cicero, that this answer was made by Catiline. It was a reply to Cato, uttered a few days before the comitia for electing consuls, which were held on the 22d day of October. See Cic. pro Muraeno, c. 25. Cicero's speech was delivered on the 8th of November. Sallust is, therefore, in error on this point, as well as Florus and Valerius Maximus, who have followed him." ***Bernouf***. From other accounts we may infer that no reply was made to Cicero by Catiline on this occasion. Plutarch, in his Life of Cicero, says that Catiline, before Cicero rose, seemed desirous to address the senate in defense of his proceedings, but that the senators refused to listen to him. Of any answer to Cicero's speech, on the part of Catiline, he makes no mention. Cicero himself, in his second Oration against Catiline, says that Catiline ***could not endure his voice***, but, when he was ordered to go into exile, "paruit, quievit," obeyed and submitted in silence. And in his Oration, c. 37, he says, "That

most audacious of men, Catiline, when he was accused by me in the senate, was dumb."

[164] XXXII. With directions to address him, etc.--Cum mandatis hujuscemodi. The communication, as Cortius observes, was not an epistle, but a verbal message.

[165] XXXIII. To have the benefit of the law--***Lege uti***. The law here meant was the Papirian law, by which it was provided, contrary to the old law of the Twelve Tables, that no one should be confined in prison for debt, and that the property of the debtor only, not his person, should be liable for what he owed. Livy (viii. 28) relates the occurrence which gave rise to this law, and says that it ruptured one of the strongest bonds of credit.

[166] The praetor--The ***praetor urbanus***, or city praetor, who decided all causes between citizens, and passed sentence on debtors.

[167] Relieved their distress by decrees--Decretis suis inopiae opitulati sunt. In allusion to the laws passed at various times for diminishing the rate of interest.

[168] Silver--was paid with brass--***Agentum aere solutum est***. Thus a ***sestertius***, which was of silver, and was worth four ***asses***, was paid with one ***as***, which was of brass; or the fourth part only of the debt was paid. See Plin. H. N. xxxiii. 3; and Velleius Paterculus, ii. 23; who says, ***quadrantem solvi***, that ***a quarter*** of their debts were paid by the debtors, by a law of Valerius Flaccus, when he became consul on the death of Marius.

[169] Often--have the commonalty--seceded, etc.--"This happened three times: 1. To the Mons Sacer, on account of debt; Liv. ii. 32. 2.

To the Aventine, and thence to the Mons Sacer, through the tyranny of Appius Claudius, the decemvir; Liv. iii. 50. 3. To the Janiculum, on account of debt; Liv. Epist. xi." ***Bernouf.***

[170] XXXIV. That such had always been the kindness, etc.--Ea, mansuetudine atque misericordia senatum populumque Romanum, semper fuisse. "That the senate, etc., had always been of such kindness." I have deserted the Latin for the English idiom.

[171] XXXV. The commencement of this letter is different in different editions. In Havercamp it stands thus: Egregiatua fides, re cognita, grata mihi, magnis in meis periculis, fiduciam commendationi meae tribuit. ***Cortius corrected it as follows:*** Egregia tua fides, re cognita, gratam in magnis periculis fiduciam commendationi meae tribuit. Cortius's reading has been adopted by Kritzius, Bernouf, and most other editors. Gerlach and Dietsch have recalled the old text. That Cortius's is the better; few will deny; for it can hardly be supposed that Sallust used ***mihi, meis***, and ***meae*** in such close succession. Some, however, as Rupertus and Gerlach, defend Havercamp's text, by asserting, from the phrase ***earum exemplam infra scriptum,*** that this is a true copy of the letter, and that the style is, therefore, not Sallust's, but Catiline's. But such an opinion is sufficiently refuted by Cortius, whose remarks I will transcribe: "Rupertus," says he, "quod in promptu erat, Catilinae culpam tribuit, qui non eo, quo Crispus, stilo scripserit. Sed cur oratio ejus tam apta et composita supra, c. 20 refertur? At, inquis, hic ipsum litterarum exemplum exhibetur. At vide mihi exemplum litterarum Lentuli, c. 44; et lege Ciceronem, qui idem exhibet, et senties sensum magis quam verba referri. Quare inanis haec quidem excusatio." Yet it is not to be denied that ***grata mihi*** is the reading of all the manuscripts.

[172] Known--by experience.--***Re cognita.*** "Cognita" be it observed, ***tironum gratia,*** is the nominative case. "Catiline had experienced the friendship of Catulus in his affair with Fabia Terentia; for it was by his means that he escaped when he was brought to trial, as is related by Orosius." ***Bernouf.***

[173] Recommendation--***Commendationi.*** His recommendation of his affairs, and of Orestilla, to the care of Catulus.

[174] Formal defense--***Defensionem.*** Opposed to ***satisfactionem***, which follows, and which means a private apology or explanation. "***Defensio***, a defense, was properly a statement or speech to be made against an adversary, or before judges; ***satisfactio*** was rather an excuse or apology made to a friend, or any other person, in a private communication." ***Cortius.***

[175] Though conscious of no guilt--***Ex nulla conscientia de culpa***. This phrase is explained by Cortius as equivalent to "Propter conscientam denulla culpa," or "inasmuch as I am conscious of no fault." "***De culpa***, he adds, is the same as ***culpae***; so in the ii. Epist. to Caesar, c. 1: Neque ***de futuro*** quisquam satix callidus; and c. 9: ***de illis*** potissimum jactura fit."

[176] To make no formal defense--to offer you some explanation --***Defensionem--parare; satisfactionem--proponere***. "Parare," says Cortius, "is applied to a defense which might require some study and premeditation; ***proponere*** to such a statement as it was easy to make at once".

[177] On my word of honor--***Me dius fidius***, sc. juvet. So may the god of faith help me, as I speak truth. But who is the god of faith? ***Dius***, say some, is the same as ***Deus*** (Plautus has ***Deus*** fidius,

Asin i. 1, 18); and the god here meant is probably Jupiter (*sub dio* being equivalent to *sub Jove*); so that ***Dius fidius*** (***fidius*** being an adjective from *fides*) will be the [Greek: ***Zeus pistios***] of the Greeks. "***Me dius fidius***" will therefore be, "May Jupiter help me!" This is the mode of explication adopted by Gerlach, Bernouf, and Dietsch. Others, with Festus (sub voce ***Medius fidius***) make *fidius* equivalent to ***filius***, because the ancients, according to Festus, often used D for L, and ***dius fidius*** will then be the same as [Greek: ***Dios***] or Jovis filius, or Hercules, and ***medius fidius*** will be the same as ***mehercules*** or ***mehercule***. Varro de L. L. (v. 10, ed. Sprengel) mentions a certain Aelius who was of this opinion. Against this derivation there is the quantity of ***fidius***, of which the first syllable is short: ***Quaerebam Nonas Sanco fidone referrem***, Ov. Fast. vi. 213. But if we consider ***dius*** the same as ***deus***, we may as well consider ***dius fidius*** to be the god Hercules as the god Jupiter, and may thus make ***medius fidius*** identical with ***mehercules***, as it probably is. "Tertullian, de Idol. 20, says that ***medius fidius*** is a form of swearing by Hercules." Schiller's Lex. sub ***Fidius***. This point will be made tolerably clear if we consider (with Varro, v. 10, and Ovid, ***loc. cit.***) Dius Fidius to be the same with the Sabine Sancus, or Semo Sancus, and Semo Sancus to be the same with Hercules.

[178] You may receive as true--***Veram licet cognoscas***. Some editions, before that of Cortius, have quae--licet vera mecum recognoscas; which was adopted from a quotation of Servius ad Aen. iv. 204. But twenty of the best MSS., according to Certius, have ***veram licet cognoscas***.

[179] Robbed of the fruit of my labor and exertion--Fructu laboris industriaeque meae privatus. "The honors which he sought he elegantly calls the ***fruit*** of his labor, because the one is obtained

by the other." ***Cortius***.

[180] Post of honor due to me--***Statum dignitatis***. The consulship.

[181] On my own security--***Meis nominibus***. "He uses the plural," says Herzogius, "because he had not borrowed once only, or from one person, but oftentimes, and from many." No other critic attempts to explain this point. For ***alienis nominibus***, which follows, being in the plural, there is very good reason. My translation is in conformity with Bernouf's comment.

[182] Proscribed--***Alienatum***. "Repulsed from all hope of the consulship." ***Bernouf***.

[183] Adopted a course--***Spes--secutus sum***. "***Spem sequi*** is a phrase often used when the direction of the mind to any thing, action, or course of conduct, and the subsequent election and adoption of what appears advantageous, is signified." ***Cortius***.

[184] Protection--***Fidei***.

[185] Intreating you, by your love for your own children, to defend her from injury--***Eam ab injuria defendas, per liberos tuos rogatus***. "Defend her from injury, being intreated [to do so] by [or for the sake of] your own children."

[186] XXXVI. In the neighborhood of Arretium--***In agro Arretino***. Havercamp, and many of the old editions, have ***Reatino***; "but," says Cortius, "if Catiline went the direct road to Faesulae, as is rendered extremely probable by his pretense that he was going to Marseilles, and by the assertion of Cicero, made the day after his departure, that he was on his way to join Manlius, we must certainly read ***Arretino***."

Arretium (now *Arezzo*) lay in his road to Faesulae; Reate was many miles out of it.

[187] In an extremely deplorable condition--***Multo maxime miserabile***. *Multe* is added to superlatives, like *longe*. So c. 52, multo pulcherrimam eam nos haberemus. Cortius gives several other instances.

[188] Notwithstanding the two decrees of the senate--Duobus senati decretis. ***I have translated it*** "the two decrees," with Rose. One of the two was that respecting the rewards mentioned in c. 30; the other was that spoken of in c. 36., allowing the followers of Catiline to lay down their arms before a certain day.

[189] XXXVII. Endeavor to exalt the factious--***Malos extollunt***. They strive to elevate into office those who resemble themselves.

[190] Poverty does not easily suffer loss--Egestas facile habetur sine damna He that has nothing, has nothing to lose. Petron. Sat., c. 119: ***Inops audacia tuta est***.

[191] Had become disaffected--Praeceps abierat. Had grown demoralized, sunk in corruption, and ready to join in any plots against the state. So Sallust says of Sempronia, ***praeceps abierat***, c. 25.

[192] In the first place--Primum omnium. "These words refer, not to ***item*** and ***postremo in the same sentence, but to*** deinde at the commencement of the next." ***Bernouf***.

[193] Civil rights had been curtailed--Jus libertatis imminutum erat. "Sylla, by one of his laws, had rendered the children of proscribed persons incapable of holding any public office; a law unjust, indeed, but which, having been established and acted upon for

more than twenty years, could not be rescinded without inconvenience to the government. Cicero, accordingly, opposed the attempts which were made, in his consulship, to remove this restriction, as he himself states in his Oration against Piso, c. 2." **Bernouf.** See Vell. Patere., ii., 28; Plutarch, Vit. Syll.; Quintil., xi. 1, where a fragment of Cicero's speech, *De Proscriptorum Liberis*, is preserved. This law of Sylla was at length abrogated by Julius Caesar, Suet. J. Caes. 41; Plutarch Vit. Caes.; Dio Cass., xli. 18.

[194] This was an evil--to the extent to which it now prevailed--Id adeo malum multos post annos in civitatem reverterat. "Adeo, says Cortius, "*in particula elegantissima*" Allen makes it equivalent to *eo usque*.

[195] XXXVIII. The powers of the tribunes--had been fully restored --*Tribunicia potestas restituta*. Before the time of Sylla, the power of the tribunes had grown immoderate, but Sylla diminished and almost annihilated it, by taking from them the privileges of holding any other magistracy after the tribunate, of publicly addressing the people, of proposing laws, and of listening to appeals. But in the consulship of Cotta, A.U.C. 679, the first of these privileges had been restored; and in that of Pompey and Crassus, A.U.C. 683, the tribunes were reinstated in all their former powers.

[196] Having obtained that high office--*Summam potestatem nacti*. Cortius thinks these words spurious.

[197] XXXIX. Free from harm--*Innoxii*. In a passive sense.

[198] Overawing others--with threats of impeachment--Caeteros judiciis terrere. "Accusationibus et judiciorum periculis." **Bernouf.**

[199] His father ordered to be put to death--*Parens necari jussit*. "His father put him to death, not by order of the consuls, but by his own private authority; nor was he the only one who, at the same period, exercised similar power." Dion. Cass., lib. xxxvii. The father observed on the occasion, that, "he had begotten him, not for Catiline against his country, but for his country against Catiline". Val. Max., v.8. The Roman laws allowed fathers absolute control over the lives of their children.

[200] XL. Certain deputies of the Allobroges--*Legatos Allobrogum*. Plutarch, in his Life of Cicero, says that there were then at Rome *two deputies* from this Gallic nation, sent to complain of oppression on the part of the Roman governors.

[201] As Brutus was then absent from Borne--Nam tum Brutus ab Roma, aberat. From this remark, say Zanchius and Omnibonus, it is evident that Brutus was not privy to the conspiracy. "What sort of woman *Sempronia* was, has been told in c. 25. Some have thought that she was the wife of Decimus Brutus; but since Sallust speaks of her as being in the decay of her beauty at the time of the conspiracy, and since Brutus, as may be seen in Caesar (B. G. vii., sub fin.), was then very young, it is probable that she had only an illicit connection with him, but had gained such an ascendency over his affections, by her arts of seduction, as to induce him to make her his mistress, and to allow her to reside in his house." *Beauzee*. I have, however, followed those who think that Brutus was the husband of Sempronia. Sallust (c. 24), speaking of the woman, of whom Sempronia was one, says that Catiline credebat posse--viros earum vel adjungere sibi, vel interficere. The truth, on such a point, is of little importance.

[202] XLI. To be expected from victory--*In spe victoriae*.

[203] Certain rewards--*Certa praemia*. "Offered by the senate to those who should give information of the conspiracy. See c. 30." **Kuhnhardt**.

[204] Quintus Fabius Sanga--"A descendent of that Fabius who, for having subdued the Allobroges, was surnamed Allobrogicus." **Bernouf**. Whole states often chose patrons as well as individuals.

[205] XLII. There were commotions--*Motus erat*. "*Motus* is also used by Cicero and Livy in the singular number for *seditiones* and *tumultus*. No change is therefore to be made in the text." **Gerlach**. "Motus bellicos intelligit, *tumultus*; ut Flor., iii. 13." **Cortius**.

[206] Having brought several to trial--Complures--caussa cognita. "Caussum cognoscere is the legal phrase for examining as to the authors and causes of any crime." **Dietsch**.

[207] Caius Muraena in Further Gaul--*In Ulteriore Gallia C. Muraena*. All the editions, previous to that of Cortius, have in citeriore Gallia. "But C. Muraena," says the critic, "commanded in Gallia Transalpina, or Ulterior Gaul, as appears from Cic. pro Muraena, c. 41. To attribute such an error to a lapse or memory in Sallust, would be absurd. I have, therefore, confidently altered *citeriore* into *ulteriore*." The praise of having first discovered the error, however, is due, not to Cortius, but to Felicius Durantinus, a friend of Rivius, in whose note on the passage his discovery is recorded.

[208] XLIII. The excellent consul--*Optimo consuli*. With the exception of the slight commendation bestowed on his speech, *luculentam* atque *utilem reipublicae*, c. 31, this is the only

epithet of praise that Sallust bestows on the consul throughout his narrative. That it could be regarded only as frigid eulogy, is apparent from a passage in one of Cicero's letters to Atticus (xii. 21), in which he speaks of the same epithet having been applied to him by Brutus: "Brutus thinks that he pays me a great compliment when he calls me an excellent consul (optimum consulem); but what enemy could speak more coldly of me?"

[209] Twelve places of the city, convenient for their purpose--Duodecim--opportuna loca. Plutarch, in his Life of Cicero, says a hundred places. Few narratives lose by repetition.

[210] In order that, during the consequent tumult--***Quo tumultu***. "It is best," says Dietsch, "to take ***quo*** as the ***particula finalis*** (to the end that), and ***tumultu*** as the ablative of the instrument".

[211] Delay--***Dies prolatando***. By putting off from day to day.

[212] XLIV. Soon to visit their country--***Semet eo brevi venturum***. "It is plain that the adverb relates to what precedes (***ad cives***); and that Cassius expresses an intention to set out for Gaul." ***Dietsch***.

[213] Remember that you are a man--***Memineris te virum***. Remember that you are a man, and ought to act as one. Cicero, in repeating this letter from memory (Orat. in Cat., iii. 5), gives the phrase, Cura ut vir sis.

[214] XLV. The praetors--***Praetoribus*** urbanis, the praetors of the city.

[215] The Milvian Bridge--***Ponte Mulvio***. Now ***Ponte Molle***.

[216] Of the object with which they were sent--Rem--cujus gratia

mittebantur.

[217] From each side of the bridge--*Utrinque*. "Utrinque," observes Cortius, "glossae MSS. exponunt ex utraque parte pontis," and there is little doubt that the exposition is correct. No translator, however, before myself, has availed himself of it.

[218] XLVI. The box with the letters--*Scrinium cum literis. Litterae* may be rendered either *letter* or *letters*. There is no mention made previously of more letters than that of Lentulus to Catiline, c. 44. But as it is not likely that the deputies carried a box to convey only one letter, I have followed other translators by putting the word in the plural. The oath of the conspirators, too, which was a written document, was probably in the box.

[219] XLVII. His letter--*Litteris.* His own letter to Catiline, c. 44. So *praeter litteras* a little below.

[220] What object he had had in view, etc.--Quid, aut qua de causa, consilli habuisset. What design he had entertained, and from what motive *he had entertained it*.

[221] To prevaricate.--*Fingere alia.* "To pretend other things than what had reference to the conspiracy." *Bernouf.*

[222] On the security of the public faith--*Fide publica.* "Cicero pledged to him the public faith, with the consent of the senate; or engaged, in the name of the republic, that his life should be spared, if he would but speak the truth." *Bernouf.*

[223] That Cinna and Sylla had ruled already--Cinnam atque Syllam antea. "Had ruled," or something similar, must be supplied. Cinna

had been the means of recalling Marius from Africa, in conjunction with whom he domineered over the city, and made it a scene of bloodshed and desolation.

[224] Their seals--*Signa sua*. "Leurs cachets, leurs sceaux." Bernouf. The Romans tied their letters round with a string, the knot of which they covered with wax, and impressed with a seal. To open the letter it was necessary to cut the string: "*nos linum incidimus*." Cic. Or. in Cat. iii. 5. See also C. Nep. Panc. 4, and Adam's Roman Antiquities. The seal of Lentulus had on it a likeness of one of his ancestors; see Cicero, *loc. cit.*

[225] In private custody--*In liberis custodiis.* Literally, in "free custody," but "private custody" conveys a better notion of the arrangement to the mind of the English reader. It was called *free* because the persons in custody were not confined in prison. Plutarch calls it [Greek: *adeomon phylakin*] as also Dion., cap. lviii. 3. See Tacit. Ann. vi. 8. It was adopted in the case of persons of rank and consideration.

[226] XLVIII. If the public faith were pledged to him--Si fides publica data, esset. See c. 47.

[227] And to facilitate the escape of those in custody--Et illi facilius e periculo eriperentur.

[228] A man of such power--*Tanta vis hominis*. So great power of the man.

[229] Liberty of speaking--*Potestatem*. "Potestatem loquendi." *Cyprianus Popma*. As it did not appear that he spoke the truth, the pledge which the senate had given him, on condition that he spoke the

truth, went for nothing; he was not allowed to continue his evidence, and was sent to prison.

[230] As was his custom--*More suo*. Plutarch, in his Life of Crassus, relates that frequently when Pompey, Caesar, and Cicero, had refused to undertake the defense of certain persons, as being unworthy of their support, Crassus would plead in their behalf; and that he thus gained great popularity among the common people.

[231] XLIX. Piso, as having been attacked by him, when he was on, etc.--Piso oppugnatus in judicio repetundarum propter cujusdam Transpadani supplicium injustum. Such is the reading and punctuation of Cortius. Some editions insert *pecuniarum* before *repetundarum*, and some a comma after it. I have interpreted the passage in conformity with the explanation of Kritzius, which seems to me the most judicious that has been offered. *Oppugnatus*, says he, is equivalent to *gravitur vexatus*, or violently assailed; and Piso was thus assailed by Caesar on account of his unjust execution of the Gaul; the words *in judicio repetundarum* merely mark the time when Caesar's attack was made. While he was on his trial for one thing, he was attacked by Caesar for another. Gerlach, observing that the words *in judicio* are wanting in one MS., would emit them, and make *oppugnatus* govern *pecuniarum repetundarum*, as if it were *accusatus*; a change which would certainly not improve the passage. The Galli Transpadani seem to have been much attached to Caesar; see Cic. Ep. ad Att., v. 2; ad Fam. xvi. 12.

[232] Comparatively a youth--*Adolescentalo*. Caesar was then in the thirty-third, or, as some say, the thirty-seventh year of his age. See the note on this word, c. 3.

[233] By magnificent exhibitions in public--*Publice maximis muneribus*.

Shows of gladiators.

[234] L. In various directions throughout the city--Variis itineribus --in vicis. Going hither and thither through the streets.

[235] Slaves--*Familiam*. "Servos suos, qui proprie *familia*," Cortius. *Familia* is a number of *famuli*.

[236] A full senate, however, had but a short time before, etc.--The senate had already decreed that they were enemies to their country; Cicero now calls a meeting to ascertain what sentence should be passed on them.

[237] On this occasion--moved--*Tunc--decreverat*. The *tunc* (or, as most editors have it, *tum*) must be referred to the second meeting or the senate, for it does not appear that any proposal concerning the punishment of the prisoners was made at the first meeting. There would be no doubt on this point, were it not for the pluperfect tense, *decreverat*. I have translated it as the perfect. We must suppose that Sallust had his thoughts on Caesar's speech, which was to follow, and signifies that all this business had been done before Caesar addressed the house. Kritzius thinks that the pluperfect was referred by Sallust, not to Caesar's speech, but to the decree of the senate which was finally made; but this is surely a less satisfactory method of settling the matter. Sallust often uses the pluperfect, where his reader would expect the perfect; see, for instance, *concusserat*, at the beginning of c. 24.

[238] That he would go over to the opinion of Tiberius Nero--Pedibus in sententian Tib. Neronis--iturum. Any question submitted to the senate was decided by the majority of votes, which was ascertained either by *numeratio*, a counting of the votes, or by *discessio*,

when those who were of one opinion, at the direction of the presiding magistrate, passed over to one side of the house, and those who were of the contrary opinion, to the other. See Aul. Gell. xiv. 7; Suet. Tib. 31; Adam's Rom. Ant.; Dr. Smith's Dictionary, Art. **Senatus**.

[239] LI. It becomes all men, etc.--The beginning of this speech, attributed to Caesar, is imitated from Demosthenes, [Greek: Peri ton hen Chersonaeso pragmaton: Edei men, o andres Athaenaioi, tous legontas apantas en umin maete pros echthran poieisthai logon maedena, maete pros charin]. "It should be incumbent on all who speak before you, O Athenians, to advance no sentiment with any view either to enmity or to favor."

[240] I consent to extraordinary measures--***Novum consilium adprobo***. "That is, I consent that you depart from the usage of your ancestors, by which Roman citizens were protected from death." ***Bernouf***.

[241] Whatever can be devised--***Omnium ingenia***.

[242] Studied and impressive language--Composite atque magnifice. Composite, *in language nicely put together; elegantly.* Magnifice, in striking or imposing terms. **Composite** is applied to the speech of Caesar, by Cato, in the following chapter.

[243] Such I know to be his character, such his discretion--Eos mores, eam modestiam viri cognovi. *I have translated* modestiam, discretion, which seems to be the proper meaning of the word. Beauzee renders it ***prudence***, and adds a note upon it, which may be worth transcription. "I translate ***modestia***," says he, "by ***prudence***, and think myself authorized to do so. ***Sic definitur a Stoicis***, says Cicero (De Off. i. 40), ut modestia sit sicentia earum rerum, quae agentur, aut dicentur, loco suo collocandarum; and shortly afterward,

Sic fit ut modestia scientia sit opportunitatis idoneorum ad agendum temporum. And what is understood in French by prudence? It is, according to the Dictionary of the Academy, 'a virtue by which we discern and practice what is proper in the conduct of life.' This is almost a translation of the words of Cicero".

[244] That--death is a relief from suffering, not a torment, etc. --This Epicurean doctrine prevailed very much at Rome in Caesar's, and afterward. We may very well suppose Caesar to have been a sincere convert to it. Cato alludes to this passage in the speech which follows; as also Cicero, in his fourth Oration against Catiline, c. 4. See, for opinions on this point, the first book of Cicero's Tusculan Questions.

[245] The Porcian Law--**Lex Porcia**. A law proposed by P. Porcius Loeca, one of the tribunes, A.U.O. 454, which enacted that no one should bind, scourge or kill a Roman citizen. See Liv., x. 9; Cic. pro. Rabir., 3, 4: Verr., v 63; de Rep., ii, 31.

[246] Other laws--**Aliae leges**. So Caesar says below, "Tum lex Porcia aliaeque paratae, quibus legibus auxilium damnatis permissum;" what other laws these were is uncertain. One of them, however, was the Sempronian law, proposed by Caius Gracchus, which ordained that sentence should not be passed on the life of a Roman citizen without the order of the people. See Cic. pro Rabir. 4. So "O lex Porcia legesque Semproniae!" Cic. in. Verr., v. 63.

[247] Parricides--See c. 14, 32.

[248] The course of events--**Dies**. "Id est, temporis momentum (*der veraenderte Zeitpunkt*)." **Dietsch**. Things change, and that which is approved at one period, is blamed at another. **Tempus** and **dies** are sometimes joined (Liv., xxii. 39, ii. 45), as if not only

time in general, but particular periods, as *from day to day*, were intended.

[249] All precedents productive of evil effects--***Omnia mala exempla***. Examples of severe punishments are meant.

[250] Any new example of severity, etc.--Novum illud exemplum ab dignis et idoneis ad indignos et non idoneos transferetur. Gerlach, Kritzius, Dietsch, and Bernouf, agree to giving to this passage the sense which is given in the translation. ***Digni*** and ***idonei*** are here used in a bad sense, for ***digni et idonei qui poena afficiantur***, deserving and fit objects for punishment.

[251] When they had conquered the Athenians--At the conclusion of the Peloponnesian war.

[252] Damasippus--"He, in the consulship of Caius Marius, the younger, and Cneius Carbo, was city praetor, and put to death some of the most eminent senators, a short time before the victory of Sylla. See Vell. Paterc. ii. 26." ***Bernouf***.

[253] Ensigns of authority--***Insignia magistratum***. "The fasces and axes of the twelve lictors, the robe adorned with purple, the curule chair, and the ivory scepter. For the Etrurians, as Dionysius Halicarnassensis relates, having been subdued, in a nine years' war, by Tarquinius Priscus, and having obtained peace on condition of submitting to him as their sovereign, presented him with the *insignia* of their own monarchs. See Strabo, lib. V.; Florus, i. 5," ***Kuhnhardt***.

[254] Best able to bear the expense--***Maxime opibus valent***. Are possessed of most resources.

Conspiracy of Catiline and The Jurgurthine War 101

[255] LII. The rest briefly expressed their assent, etc.--*Caeteri verbo, alius alii, varie assentiebantur. Verbo assentiebantur* signifies that they expressed their assent merely by a word or two, as ***assentior Silano, assentior Tiberio Neroni, aut Caesari***, the three who had already spoken. ***Varie***, "in support of their different proposals."

[256] My feelings, Conscript Fathers, are extremely different, etc.--***Longe mihi alia mens est, P. C.***, etc. The commencement of Cato's speech is evidently copied from the beginning of the third Olynthiac of Demosthenes: [Greek: Ouchi tauta paristatai moi ginoskein, o andres Athaenaioi, otan te eis ta pragmata apoblepso kai otan pros tous logous ous akouo tous men gar logous peri tou timoraesasthai Philippon oro gignomenous, ta de pragmata eis touto proaekonta oste opos mae peisometha autoi proteron kakos skepsasthai deon.] "I am by no means affected in the same manner. Athenians, when I review the state of our affairs, and when I attend to those speakers who have now declared their sentiments. They insist that we should punish Philip; but our affairs, situated as they now appear, warn us to guard against the dangers with which we ourselves are threatened." ***Leland***.

[257] Their altars and their homes--***Aris atque focis suis***. "When ***arae*** and ***foci*** are joined, beware of supposing that they are to be distinguished as referring the one (arae) to the public temples, and the other (***foci***) to private dwellings. Both are to be understood of private houses, in which the ***ara*** belonged to the Dii Penates, ***and was placed in the*** impluvium in the inner part of the house; the ***focus*** was dedicated to the ***lares***, and was in the hall." Ernesti, Clav. Cic., sub. v. ***Ara***. Of the commentators on Sallust, Kritzius is, I believe, the only one who has concurred in this notion

of Ernesti; Langins and Dietsch (with Cortius) adhere to the common opinion that *arae* are the public altars. Dietsch refers, for a complete refutation of Ernesti, to G. A. B. Hertzberg de Diis Romanorum Penatibus, Halae, 1840, p. 64; a book which I have not seen. Certainly, in the observation of Cicero ad Att., vii. 11, "Non est respublica in parietibus, sed in aris et focis," *arae* must be considered (as Schiller observes) to denote the public altars and national religion. See Schiller's Lex. v. *Ara*.

[258] In vain appeal to justice--*Frusta judicia implores. Judicia*, trials, to procure the inflictions of legal penalties.

[259] Could not easily pardon the misconduct, etc.--Haud facile alterius lubidini malefacta condonabam. "Could not easily forgive the licentiousness of another its evil deeds."

[260] Yet the republic remained secure; its own strength, etc. --*Tamen respublica firma, opulentia neglegentiam tolerabat*. This is Cortius's reading; some editors, as Havercamp, Kritzius, and Dietsch, insert *erat* after *firma*. Whether *opulentia* is the nominative or ablative, is disputed. "*Opulentia*," says Allen, "casum sextum intellige, et repete *respublica* (ad *tolerabat*)." "*Opulentia*," says Kritzius, "melius nominativo capiendum videtur; nam quae sequuntur verba novam enunciationem efficiunt." I have preferred to take it as a nominative.

[261] We have lost the real names of things, etc.--Imitated from Thucydides, iii. 32: [Greek: Kai taen eiothuian axiosin ton onomaton es ta erga antaellaxan tae dikaiosei. Tolma men gar alogistos, andria philetairos enomisthae, mellasis te promaethaes, deilia euprepaes to de sophron. Tou anandrou proschaema, kai to pros apan syneton, epi pan argon.] "The ordinary meaning of words was changed by them as they

thought proper. For reckless daring was regarded as courage that was true to its friends; prudent delay, as specious cowardice; moderation, as a cloak for unmanliness; being intelligent in every thing, as being useful for nothing." ***Dale's*** translation; Bohn's Classical Library.

[262] Elegant language--***Composite***. See above, c. 51.

[263] In a most excellent condition--***Multo pulcherrumam.*** See c. 36.

[264] For of allies and citizens, etc.--Imitated from Demosthenes, Philipp. III.4.

[265] I advise you to have mercy upon them--Misereamini censeo, i.e., ***censeo*** ut misereanum, spoken ironically. Most translators have taken the words in the sense of "You would take pity on them, I suppose," or something similar.

[266] Unless this be the second time that he has made war upon his country--"Cethegus first made war on his country in conjunction with Marius." ***Bernouf***. Whether Sallust alludes to this, or intimates (as Gerlach thinks) that he was engaged in the first conspiracy, is doubtful.

[267] Is ready to devour us--***Faucibus urget***. Cortius, Kritzius, Gerlach, Burnouf, Allen, and Dietsch, are unanimous in interpreting this as a metaphorical expression, alluding to a wild beast with open jaws ready to spring upon its prey. They support this interpretation by Val. Max., v. 3: "Faucibus apprehensam rempublicam;" Cic. pro. Cluent., 31: "Quum faucibus premetur;" and Plaut. Casin. v. 3,4, "Manifesto faucibus teneor." Some, editors have read ***in faucibus***, and understood the words as referring to the jaws or narrow passes of Etruria, where Catiline was with his army.

[268] LIII. All the senators of consular dignity, and a great part of the rest--***Consulares omnes, itemque senatus magna pars***. "As the consulars were senators, the reader would perhaps expect Sallust to have said ***reliqui senatus*** but ***itemque*** is equivalent to et praeter eos.*"* Dietsch.

[269] That they had carried on wars--***Bella gesta***. That wars had been carried on ***by them***.

[270] As if the parent stock were exhausted--Sicuti effoeta parentum. This is the reading of Cortius, which he endeavors to explain thus: "Ac sicuti ***effoeta parens***, inter parentes, sese habere solet, ut nullos amplius liberas proferat, sic Roma sese habuit, ubi multis tempestatibus nemo virtute magnus fuit." "***Est***," he adds, "or ***solet esse***, or ***sese habere solet***, may very well be understood from the ***fuit*** which follows." But all this only serves to show what a critic may find to say in defense of a reading to which he is determined to adhere. All the MSS., indeed, have ***parentum***, except one, which has ***parente***. Dietsch thinks that some word has been lost between ***effoeta*** and ***parentum***, and proposes to read sicuti effoeta aetate parentum, with the sense, as if the age of the parents were too much exhausted to produce strong children. Kritzius, from a suggestion of Cortius (or rather of his predecessor, Rupertus), reads ***effoetae parentum*** (the effoetae agreeing with Romae which follows), considering the sense to be the same as as ***effoetae parentis***--as ***divina dearum*** for ***divina dea***, etc. Gerlach retains the rending of Cortius, and adopts his explanation (4to. ed., 1827), but says that the ***explicatio*** may seem ***durior***, and that it is doubtful whether we ought not to have recourse to the ***effoeta parente*** of the old critics. Assuredly if we retain ***parentum***, ***effoetae*** is the only reading that we can well put with it. We may compare with it ***loca nuda gignentium***,

(Jug. c. 79), i.e. "places bare of objects producing any thing." Gronovius know not what to do with the passage, called it locus intellectus nemini, *and at last decided on understanding* virtute with *effoetae parentum*, which, *pace tarti viri*, and although Allen has followed him, is little better than folly. The concurrence of the majority of manuscripts in giving *parentum* makes the scholar unwilling to set it aside. However, as no one has explained it satisfactorily even to himself, I have thought it better, with Dietsch, to regard it a *scriptura non ferenda*, and to acquiesce, with Glareanus, Rivius, Burnouf, and the Bipont edition, in the reading *effoeta parente*.

[271] LIV. Though attained by different means--*Sed alia alii*. "Alii alia *gloria*," for *altera alteri*. So Livy, i. 21: Duo reges, alius alia via.

[272] Simplicity--*Pudore*. The word here seems to mean the absence of display and ostentation.

[273] With the temperate--*Cum innocente*. "That is cum integro et abstinente. *For* innocentia *is used for* abstinentia, and opposed to *avaritia*. See Cic. pro Lego Manil., c. 13." *Burnouf.*

[274] LV. The triumvirs--*Triumviros*. The *triumviri capitales*, who had the charge of the prison and of the punishment of the condemned. They performed their office by deputy, Val. Max., v. 4. 7.

[275] The Tullian dungeon--*Tullianum*. "Tullianum" is an adjective, with which *robur* must be understood, as it was originally constructed, wholly or partially, with oak. See Festus, sub voce *Robum* or *Robur*: his words are *arcis robustis includebatur*, of which the sense is not very clear. The prison at Rome was built by

Ancus Marcius, and enlarged by Servius Tullius, from whom this part of it had its name; Varro de L. L., iv. 33. It is now transformed into a subterranean chapel, beneath a small church erected over it, called **San Pietro in Carcere**. De Brosses and Eustace both visited it; See Eustace's Classical Tour, vol. i. p. 260, in the **Family Library**. See also Wasse's note on this passage.

[276] A vaulted roof connected with stone arches--Camera lapideis fornicibus vincta. *"That* camera was a roof curved in the form of a *testudo*, is generally admitted; see Vitruv. vii. 3; Varr., R. R. iii. 7, init." **Dietsch**. The roof is now arched in the usual way.

[277] Certain men, to whom orders had been given--Quibus praeceptum erat. The editions of Havercamp, Gerlach, Kritzius, and Dietsch, have **vindices rerum capitalium, quibus**, etc. Cortius ejected the first three words from his text, as an intruded gloss. If the words be genuine, we must consider these **vindices** to have been the deputies, or lictors, of the "triumvirs" mentioned above.

[278] LVI. As far as his numbers would allow--**Pro numero militum**. He formed his men into two bodies, which he called legions, and divided each legion, as was usual, into ten cohorts, putting into each cohort as many men as he could. The cohort of a full legion consisted of three maniples, or six hundred men; the legion would then be six thousand men. But the legions were seldom so large as this; they varied at different periods, from six thousand to three thousand; in the time of Polybius they were usually four thousand two hundred. See Adam's Rom. Ant., and Lipsius de Mil. Rom Dial. iv.

[279] From his confederates--**Ex sociis**. "Understand, not only the leaders in the conspiracy, but those who, in c. 35, are said to

have set out to join Catiline, though not at that time exactly implicated in the plot." **Kritzius**. It is necessary to notice this, because Cortius erroneously supposes "sociis" to mean the allies of Rome. Dahl, Longius, Mueller, Burnouf, Gerlach, and Dietsch, all interpret in the same manner as Kritzius.

[280] Hoped himself shortly to find one--Sperabat propediem sese habiturum. Other editions, as those of Havercamp, Gerlach, Kritzius, Dietsch, and Burnouf, have the words *magnas copias* before *sese*. Cortius struck them out, observing that *copiae* occurred too often in this chapter, and that in one MS. they were wanting. One manuscript, however, was insufficient authority for discarding them; and the phrase suits much better with what follows, si Romae socii incepta patravissent, if they are retained.

[281] Slaves--of whom vast numbers, etc.--Servitia--cujus magnae copiae. "Cujus," says Priscian (xvii. 20, vol. ii., p. 81, cd. Krehl), "is referred *ad rem*, that is *cujus rei servitiorum*." **Servorum** or *hominum genus*, is, perhaps, rather what Sallust had in his mind, as the subject of his relation. Gerlach adduces as an expression most nearly approaching to Sallust's, Thucyd., iii. 92; [Greek: Kai dorieis, hae maetropolis ton Lakedaimonion].

[282] Impolitic--*Alienum suis rationibus*. Foreign to his views; inconsistent with his policy.

[283] LVII. In his hurried march into Gaul--*In Galliam properanti*. These words Cortius inclosed in brackets, pronouncing them as a useless gloss. But all editors have retained them as genuine, except the Bipont and Burnouf, who wholly omitted them.

[284] As he was pursuing, though with a large army, yet through

plainer ground, and with fewer hinderances; the enemy in retreat--Utpote qui magna exercitu, locis aequioribus, expeditus, in fuga sequeretur. It would be tedious to notice all that has been written upon this passage of Sallust. All the editions, before that of Cortius, had ***expeditos, in fugam***, some joining ***expeditos*** with ***locis aequioribus***, and some with ***in fugam***. ***Expeditos in fugam*** was first condemned by Wasse, no negligent observer of phrases, who said that no expression parallel to it could be found in any Latin writer. Cortius, seeing that the ***expedition***, of which Sallust is speaking, is on the part of Antonius, not of Catiline, altered ***expeditos***, though found in all the manuscripts, into ***expeditus***; and ***in fugam***, at the same time, into ***in fuga***; and in both these emendations he has been cordially followed by the subsequent editors, Gerlach, Kritzius, and Dietsch. I have translated ***magno exercitu***, "***though*** with a large army," although, according to Dietsch and some others, we need not consider a large army as a cause of slowness, but may rather regard it as a cause of speed; since the more numerous were Metellus's forces, the less he would care how many he might leave behind through fatigue, or to guard the baggage; so that he might be the more ***expeditus***, unincumbered. With ***sequeretur*** we must understand ***hostes***. The Bipont, Burnouf's, which often follows it, and Havercamp's, are now the only editions of any note that retain ***expeditos in fugam***.

[285] LVIII. That a spiritless army can not be rendered active, etc.--Neque ex ignavo strenuum, neque fortem ex timido exercitum oratione imperatoris fieri. I have departed a little from the literal reading, for the sake of ease.

[286] That on your own right hands depend, etc.--In dextris portare. "That you carry in your right hands."

[287] Those same places--*Eadem illa*. "Coloniae atque municipia portas claudent." ***Burnouf***.

[288] They contend for what but little concerns them--Illis supervacaneum est pugnare. It is but of little concern to the great body of them personally: they may fight, but others will have the advantages of their efforts.

[289] We might, etc.--*Licuit nobis*. The editions vary between ***nobis*** and ***robis***; but most, with Cortius, have ***nobis***.

[290] LIX. In the rear--*In subsidio*. Most translators have rendered this, "as a body of reserve;" but such can not well be the signification. It seems only to mean the part behind the front: Catiline places the eight cohorts *in front*, and the rest of his force *in subsidio*, to support the front. ***Subsidia***, according to Varro (de L. L., iv. 16) and Festus (v. ***Subsidium***), was a term applied to the Triarii, because they ***subsidebant***, or sunk down on one knee, until it was their turn to act. See Sheller's Lex. v. ***Subsidium***. "Novissimi ordines ita dicuntur." ***Gerlach***. In subsidiis***, which occurs a few lines below, seems to signify*** in lines in the rear*; as in Jug. 49,* triplicibus subsidiis aciem intruxit, i.e. with three lines behind the front. "Subsidium ea pars aciei vocabatur quae reliquis submitti posset; Caes. B. G., ii. 25." ***Dietsch***.

[291] All the ablest centurions--***Centuriones omnes lectos***. "***Lectos*** you may consider to be the same as ***eximios, praestantes***, centurionum praestantissimum quemque." ***Kritzius***. Cortius and others take it for a participle, ***chosen***.

[292] Veterans--***Evocatos***. Some would make this also a participle,

because, say they, it can not signify *evocati*, or called-out veterans, since, though there were such soldiers in a regular Roman army, there could be none so called in the tumultuary forces of Catiline. But to this it is answered that Catiline had imitated the regular disposition of a Roman army, and that his veterans might consequently be called *evocati*, just as if they had been in one; and, also that *evocatus* as a participle would be useless; for if Catiline removed (*subducit*) the centurions, it is unnecessary to add that he called them out, "*Evocati* erant, qui expletis stipendiis non poterant in delectu scribi, sed precibus imperatoris permoti, aut in gratiam ejus, militiam resumebant, homines longo uso militiae peritissimi. Dio., xiv. p. 276. [Greek: Ek touton de ton anoron kai to ton Haeouokaton hae Ouokaton systaema (ous Anaklaetous an tis Ellaenisas, hoti pepaumenoi taes strateias, ep' autein authis aneklaethmsan, ouomaseien) enomisthae.] Intelligit itaque ejusmodi homines veteranos, etsi non proprie erant tales evocati, sed sponte castra Catilinae essent secuti." **Cortius**.

[293] Into the foremost ranks--*In primam aciem*. Whether Sallust means that he ranged them with the eight cohorts, or only in the first line of the *subsidia*, is not clear.

[294] A certain officer of Faesulae--*Faesulanum quemdam*. "He is thought to have been that P. Furius, whom Cicero (Cat., iii. 6, 14) mentions as having been one of the colonists that Sylla settled at Faesulae, and who was to have been executed, if he had been apprehended, for having been concerned in corrupting the Allobrogian deputies." **Dietsch**. Plutarch calls this officer Furius.

[295] His freedmen--*Libertis*. "His own freedmen, whom he probably had about him as a body-guard, deeming them the most attached of his adherents. Among them was, possibly, that Sergius, whom we find

from Cic. pro Domo, 5, 6, to have been Catiline's armor bearer." ***Dietsch***.

[296] The colonists--***Colonis***. "Veterans of Sylla, who had been settled by him as colonists in Etruria, and who had now been induced to join Catiline." ***Gerlach***. See c. 28.

[297] By the eagle--***Propter aquilam***. See Cic. in Cat., i. 9.

[298] Being lame--***Pedibus aeger***. It has been common among translators to render ***pedibus aeger*** afflicted with the gout, though a Roman might surely be lame without having the gout. As the lameness of Antonius, however, according to Dion Cassius (xxxvii. 39), was only pretended, it may be thought more probable that he counterfeited the gout than any other malady. It was with this belief, I suppose, that the writer of a gloss on one of the manuscripts consulted by Cortius, interpreted the words, ***ultroneam passus est podogram***, "he was affected with a voluntary gout." Dion Cassius says that he preferred engaging with Antonius, who had the larger army, rather than with Metellus, who had the smaller, because he hoped that Antonius would designedly act in such a way as to lose the victory.

[299] To meet the present insurrection--***Tumulti causa***. Any sudden war or insurrection in Italy or Gaul was called ***tumultus***. See Cic. Philipp. v. 12.

[300] Their temples and their homes--***Aris atque focis suis***. See c. 52.

[301] LX. In a furious charge--***Infestis siqnis***.

[302] Offering but partial resistance--***Alios alibi resistentes***.

Not making a stand in a body, but only some in one place, and some in another.

[303] Among the first, etc.--*In primis pugnantes cadunt*. Cortius very properly refers *in primis* to *cadunt*.

CHRONOLOGY OF THE CONSPIRACY OF CATILINE.

EXTRACTED FROM DE BROSSES.

A.U.C 685.--COSS. L. CAECILIUS METELLUS, Q. MARCIIS REX.--Catiline is Praetor.

686.--C. CALPURNIUS PISO, M. ACILIUS GLABRIO.--Catiline Governor of Africa.

687.--L. VOLCATIUS TULLUS, M. AEMILIUS LEPIDUS.--Deputies from Africa accuse Catiline of extortion, through the agency of Clodius. He is obliged to desist from standing for the consulship, and forms the project of the first conspiracy. See Sall. Cat., c. 18.

688.--L. MANLIUS TORQUATUS, L. AURELIUS COTTA.--*Jan*. 1: Catiline's project of the first conspiracy becomes known, and he defers the execution of it to the 5th of February, when he makes an unsuccessful attempt to execute it. *July* 17: He is acquitted of extortion, and begins to canvass for the consulship for the year 690.

689.--L. JULIUS CAESAR, C. MARCIUS FIGULUS THERMUS.--*June* 1: Catiline convokes the chiefs of the second conspiracy. He is disappointed in his views on the consulship.

690--M. TULLIUS CICERO, C. ANTONIUS HYBRIDA.--*Oct*. 19: Cicero lays the affair of the conspiracy before the senate, who decree plenary powers to the consuls for defending the state. *Oct*. 21: Silanus and Muraena are elected consuls for the next year, Catiline, who was a candidate, being rejected. *Oct*. 22: Catiline is accused under the Plautian Law *de vi*. Sall. Cat., c. 31. **Oct**. 24: Manlius takes up arms in Etruria. **Nov**. 6: Catiline assembles the chief conspirators, by the agency of Porcius Laeca Sall. Cat., c. 27. **Nov**. 7: Vargunteius and Cornelius undertake to assassinate Cicero. Sall. Cat., c. 28. **Nov**. 8: Catiline appears in the senate; Cicero delivers his first Oration against him; he threatens to extinguish the flame raised around him in a general destruction, and quits Rome. Sall. Cat., c. 31. **Nov**. 9: Cicero delivers his second Oration against Catiline, before an assembly of the people, convoked by order of the senate. **Nov**. 20, **or thereabouts**: Catiline and Manlius are declared public enemies. Soon after this the conspirators attempt to secure the support of the Allobrogian deputies. **Dec**. 3: About two o'clock in the morning the Allobroges are apprehended. Toward evening Cicero delivers his third Oration against Catiline, before the people. **Dec**. 5. Cicero's fourth Oration against Catiline, before the senate. Soon after, the conspirators are condemned to death, and great honors are decreed by the senate to Cicero. 691.--D. JUNIUS SILANUS, L. LICINIUS MURAENA--*Jan*. 5: Battle of Pistoria, and death of Catiline.

*   *   *   *   *

    The narrative of Sallust terminates with the account of the battle of Pistoria. There are a few other particulars connected with the history of the conspiracy, which, for the sake of the English reader, it may not be improper to add.

    When the victory was gained, Antonius caused Catiline's head to be cut off, and sent it to Rome by the messengers who carried the news. Antonius himself was honored, by a public decree, with the title of ***Imperator***, although he had done little to merit the distinction, and although the number of slain, which was three thousand, was less than that for which the title was generally given. See Dio Cass. xxxvii., 40, 41.

    The remains of Catiline's army, after the death of their leader, continued to make efforts to raise another insurrection. In August, eight months after the battle, a party, under the command of Lucius Sergius, perhaps a relative or freedman of Catiline, still offered resistance to the forces of the government in Etruria. **Rel-**

iquiae conjuratorum, cum L. Sergio, tumultuantur in Hetruria. Fragm. Act. Diurn. The responsibility of watching these marauders was left to the proconsul Metellus Celer. After some petty encounters, in which the insurgents were generally worsted, Sergius, having collected his force at the foot of the Alps, attempted to penetrate into the country of the Allobroges, expecting to find them ready to take up arms; but Metellus, learning his intention, pre-occupied the passes, and then surrounded and destroyed him and his followers.

At Rome, in the mean time, great honors were paid to Cicero. A thanksgiving of thirty days was decreed in his name, an honor which had previously been granted to none but military men, and which was granted to him, to use his own words, because **he had delivered the city from fire, the citizens from slaughter, and Italy from war**. "If my thanksgiving," he also observes, "be compared with those of others, there will be found this difference, that theirs were granted them for having managed the interests of the republic successfully, but that mine was decreed to me for having preserved the republic from ruin." See Cic. Orat. iii., in Cat., c. 6. Pro Sylla, c. 30. In Pison. c. 3. Philipp. xiv., 8. Quintus Catulus, then **princeps senatus**, and Marcus

> Roma parentem,
> Roma patrem patriae Ciceronem libera dixit.

Juv. Sat., viii. 244.

Of the inferior conspirators, who did not follow Sergius, and who were apprehended at Rome, or in other parts of Italy, after the death of the leaders in the plot, some were put to death, chiefly on the testimony of Lucius Vettius, one of their number, who turned informer against the rest. But many whom he accused were acquitted; others, supposed to be guilty, were allowed to escape.

THE JUGURTHINE WAR

THE ARGUMENT.

The Introduction, I.-IV. The author's declaration of his design, and prefatory account of Jugurtha's family, V. Jugurtha's character, VI. His talents excite apprehensions in his uncle Micipsa, VII. He is sent to Numantia. His merits, his favor with Scipio, and his popularity in the army, VIII. He receives commendation and advice from Scipio and is adopted by Micipsa, who resolves that Jugurtha, Adherbal, and Hiempsal, shall, at his death, divide his kingdom equally between them, IX. He is addressed by Micipsa on his death-bed, X. His proceedings, and those of Adherbal and Hiempsal, after the death of Micipsa, XI. He murders Hiempsal, XII. He defeats Adherbal, and drives him for refuge to Rome. He dreads the vengeance of the senate, and sends embassadors to Rome, who are confronted with those of Adherbal in the senate-house, XIII. The speech of Adherbal, XIV. The reply of Jugurtha's embassadors, and the opinions of the senators, XV. The prevalence of Jugurtha's money, and the partition of the kingdom between him and Adherbal, XVI. A description of Africa, XVII. An account of its inhabitants, and of its principal divisions at the commencement of the Jugurthine war, XVIII., XIX. Jugurtha invades Adherbal's part of the kingdom, XX. He defeats Adherbal, and besieges him in Cirta, XXI. He frustrates the intentions of the Roman deputies, XXII. Adherbal's distresses, XXIII. His letter to the senate, XXIV. Jugurtha disappoints a second Roman deputation, XXV. He takes Cirta, and puts Adherdal to death, XXVI. The senate determine to make war upon him, and commit the management of it to Calpurnius, XXVII. He sends an ineffectual embassy to the senate. His dominions are vigorously invaded by Calpurnius, XXVIII. He bribes Calpurnius, and makes a treaty with him, XXIX.

His proceedings are discussed at Rome, XXX. The speech of Memmius concerning them, XXXI. The consequences of it, XXXII. The arrival of Jugurtha at Rome, and his appearance before the people, XXXIII., XXXIV. He procures the assassination of Massiva, and is ordered to quit Italy, XXXV. Albinus, the successor of Calpurnius, renews the war. He returns to Rome, and leaves his brother Aulus to command in his absence, XXXVI. Aulus miscarries in the siege of Suthul, and concludes a dishonorable treaty with Jugurtha, XXXVII, XXXVIII. His treaty is annulled by the senate. His brother, Albinus, resumes the command, XXXIX. The people decree an inquiry into the conduct of those who had treated with Jugurtha, XL. Consideration on the popular and senatorial factions, XLI., XLII. Metellus assumes the conduct of the war, XLIII. He finds the army in Numidia without discipline, XLIV. He restores subordination, XLV. He rejects Jugurtha's offers of submission, bribes his deputies, and marches into the country, XLVI. He places a garrison in Vacca, and seduces other deputies of Jugurtha, XLVII. He engages with Jugurtha, and defeats him. His lieutenant, Rutilius, puts to flight Bomilcar, the general of Jugurtha, XLVIII.-LIII. He is threatened with new opposition. He lays waste the country. His stragglers are cut off by Jugurtha, LIV. His merits are celebrated at Rome. His caution. His progress retarded, LV. He commences the siege of Zama, which is reinforced by Jugurtha. His lieutenant, Marius, repulses Jugurtha at Sicca, LVI. He is joined by Marius, and prosecutes the siege. His camp is surprised, LVII., LVIII. His struggles with Jugurtha, and his operations before the town, LIX., LX. He raises the siege, and goes into winter quarters. He attaches Bomilcar to his interest, LXI. He makes a treaty with Jugurtha, who breaks it, LXII. The ambition of Marius. His character. His desire of the consulship, LXIII. His animosity toward Metellus. His intrigues to supplant him, LXIV, LXV. The Vaccians surprise the Roman garrison, and kill all the Romans but Turpilius, the governor, LXVI., LXVII. Metellus recovers Vacca, and puts Turpilius to death, LXVIII., LXIX. The conspiracy of Bomilcar, and Nabdalsa against Jugurtha, and the discovery of it. Jugurtha's disquietude, LXX.-LXXII. Metellus makes preparations for a second campaign. Marius returns to Rome, and is chosen consul, and appointed to command the army in Numidia, LXXIII. Jugurtha's irresolution. Metellus defeats him, LXXIV. The flight of Jugurtha to Thala. The march of Metellus in pursuit of him, LXXV. Jugurtha abandons Thala, and Metellus takes possession of it, LXXVI. Metellus receives a deputation from Leptis, and sends a detachment thither, LXXVII. The situation of Leptis, LXXVIII. The history of the Philaeni, LXXIX. Jugurtha collects an army of Getulians, and gains the support of Bocchus, King of Mauritania. The two kings proceed toward Cirta, LXXX., LXXXI. Metellus marches against them, but hearing that Marius is appointed to succeed him, contents himself with endeavoring to alienate Bocchus from Jugurtha, and protracting the war rather than prosecuting it, LXXXII., LXXXIII. The preparations of Marius for his departure. His disposition toward the nobility. His popularity, LXXXIV. His speech to the people, LXXXV. He completes his levies, and arrives in Africa, LXXXVI. He opens the campaign, LXXXVII. The reception of Metellus in Rome. The successes and plans of Marius. The applications of Bocchus, LXXXVIII. Marius marches against Capsa, and takes it, LXXXIX-XCI. He gains possession of a fortress which the Numidians thought impregnable, XCII.-XCIV. The arrival of Sylla in the camp. His character, XCV. His arts to obtain the favor of Marius and the soldiers, XCVI. Jugurtha and Bocchus attack Marius, and are vigorously opposed, XCVII., XCVIII. Marius surprises them in the night, and routs them with great slaughter, XCIX. Marius prepares to go into winter quarters. His vigilance, and maintenance of discipline, C. He fights a second battle with Jugurtha and Bocchus, and gains a second victory over them, CI. He arrives at Cirta. He receives a deputation from Bocchus, and sends Sylla and Manlius to confer with him, CII. Marina undertakes an expedition Bocchus prepares to send ambassadors to Rome, who being stripped by robbers, takes refuge in the Roman camp, and are entertained by Sylla during the absence of Marius, CIII. Marius returns. The ambassadors set out for Rome. The answer which they receive from the senate, CIV. Bocchus desires a conference with Sylla; Sylla arrives at the camp of Bocchus, CV.-CVII. Negotiations between Sylla and Bocchus, CVIII., CIX. The address of Bocchus to Sylla, CX. The reply of Sylla. The subsequent transactions between them. The resolution of Bocchus to betray Jugurtha, and the execution of it, CXI-CXIII. The triumph of Marius, CXIV.

I. Mankind unreasonably complain of their nature, that, being weak and short-lived, it is governed by chance rather than intellectual power;[1] for, on the contrary, you will find, upon reflection, that there is nothing more noble or excellent, and that to nature is wanting rather human industry than ability or time.

The ruler and director of the life of man is the mind, which, when it pursues glory in the path of true merit, is sufficiently powerful, efficient, and worthy of honor,[2] and needs no assistance from fortune, who can neither bestow integrity, industry, or other good qualities, nor can take them away. But if the mind, ensnared by corrupt passions, abandons itself[3] to indolence and sensuality, when it has indulged for a season in pernicious gratifications, and when bodily strength, time, and mental vigor, have been wasted in sloth, the infirmity of nature is accused, and those who are themselves in fault impute their delinquency to circumstances.[4]

If man, however, had as much regard for worthy objects, as he has spirit in the pursuit of what is useless,[5] unprofitable, and even perilous, he would not be governed by circumstances more than he would govern them, and would attain to a point of greatness, at which, instead of being mortal,[6] he would be immortalized by glory.

II. As man is composed of mind and body, so, of all our concerns and pursuits, some partake the nature of the body, and some that of the mind. Thus beauty of person, eminent wealth, corporeal strength, and all other things of this kind, speedily pass away; but the illustrious achievements of the mind are, like the mind itself, immortal.

Of the advantages of person and fortune, as there is a beginning, there is also an end; they all rise and fall,[7] increase and decay. But the mind, incorruptible and eternal, the ruler of the human race, actuates and has power over all things,[8] yet is itself free from control.

The depravity of those, therefore, is the more surprising, who, devoted to corporeal gratifications, spend their lives in luxury and indolence, but suffer the mind, than which nothing is better or greater in man, to languish in neglect and inactivity; especially when there are so many and various mental employments by which the highest renown may be attained.

III. Of these occupations, however, civil and military offices,[9] and all administration of public affairs, seem to me at the present time, by no means to be desired; for neither is honor conferred on merit, nor are those, who have gained power by unlawful means, the more secure or respected for it. To rule our country or subjects[10] by force, though we may have the ability, and may correct what is wrong, is yet an ungrateful undertaking; especially as all changes in the state lead to[11] bloodshed, exile, and other evils of discord; while to struggle in ineffectual attempts, and to gain nothing, by wearisome exertions, but public hatred, is the extreme of madness; unless when a base and pernicious spirit, perchance, may prompt a man to sacrifice his honor and liberty to the power of a party.

IV. Among other employments which are pursued by the intellect, the recording of past events is of pre-eminent utility; but of its merits I may, I think, be silent, since many have spoken of them, and since, if I were to praise my own occupation, I might be considered as presumptuously[12] praising myself. I believe, too, that there will be some, who, because I have resolved to live unconnected with political affairs, will apply to my arduous and useful labors the name of idleness; especially those who think it an important pursuit to court the people, and gain popularity by entertainments. But if such persons will consider at what periods I obtained office, what sort of men[13] were then unable to obtain it, and what description of persons have subsequently entered the senate,[14] they will think, assuredly, that I have altered my sentiments rather from prudence than from indolence, and that more good will arise to the state from my retirement, than from the busy efforts of others.

I have often heard that Quintus Maximus,[15] Publius Scipio,[16] and many other illustrious men of our country, were accustomed to observe, that, when they looked on the images of their ancestors, they felt their minds irresistibly excited to the pursuit of honor.[17] Not, certainly, that the wax,[18] or the shape, had any such influence; but, as they called to mind their forefathers' achievements, such a flame was kindled in the breasts of those eminent persons, as could not be extinguished till their own merit had equaled the fame and glory of their ancestors.

But, in the present state of manners, who is there, on the contrary, that does not rather emulate his forefathers in riches and extravagance, than in virtue and labor? Even men of humble birth,[19] who formerly used to surpass the nobility in merit, pursue power and honor rather by intrigue and dishonesty, than by honorable qualifications; as if the praetorship, consulate, and all other offices of the kind, were noble and dignified in themselves, and not to be estimated according to the worth of those who fill them.

But, in expressing my concern and regret at the manners of the state, I have proceeded with too great freedom, and at too great length. I now return to my subject.

V. I am about to relate the war which the Roman people carried on with Jugurtha, King of the Numidians; first, because it was great, sanguinary, and of varied fortune; and secondly, because then, for the first time, opposition was offered to the power of the nobility; a contest which threw every thing, religious and civil, into confusion,[20] and was carried to such a height of madness, that nothing but war, and the devastation of Italy, could put an end to civil dissensions.[21] But before I fairly commence my narrative, I will take a review of a few preceding particulars, in order that the whole subject may be more clearly and distinctly understood.

In the second Punic war, in which Hannibal, the leader of the Carthaginians, had weakened the power of Italy more than any other enemy[22] since the Roman name became great,[23] Masinissa, King of the Numidians, being received into alliance by Publius Scipio, who, from his merits was afterward surnamed Africanus, had performed for us many eminent exploits in the field. In return for which services, after the Carthaginians were subdued, and after Syphax,[24] whose power in Italy was great and extensive, was taken prisoner, the Roman people presented to Masinissa, as a free gift, all the cities and lands that they had captured. Masinissa's friendship for us, accordingly, remained faithful and inviolate; his reign[25] and his life ended together. His son, Micipsa, alone succeeded to his kingdom; Mastanabal and Gulussa, his two brothers, having been carried off by disease. Micipsa had two sons, Adherbal and Hiempsal, and had brought up in his house, with the same care as his own children, a son of his brother Mastanabal, named Jugurtha, whom Masinissa, as being the son of a concubine, had left in a private station.

VI. Jugurtha, as he grew up, being strong in frame, graceful in person, but, above all, vigorous in understanding, did not allow himself to be enervated by pleasure and indolence, but, as is the usage of his country, exercised himself in riding, throwing the javelin, and contending in the race with his equals in age; and, though he excelled them all in reputation, he was yet beloved by all. He also passed much of his time in hunting; he was first, or among the first, to wound the lion and other beasts; he performed very much, but spoke very little of himself.

Micipsa, though he was at first gratified with these circumstances, considering that the merit of Jugurtha would be an honor to his kingdom, yet, when he reflected that the youth was daily increasing in popularity, while he himself was advanced in age, and his children but young, he was extremely disturbed at the state of things, and revolved it frequently in his mind. The very nature of man, ambitious of power, and eager to gratify its desires, gave him reason for apprehension, as well as the opportunity afforded by his own age and that of his children, which was sufficient, from the prospect of such a prize, to lead astray even men of moderate desires. The affection of the Numidians, too, which was strong toward Jugurtha, was another cause for alarm; among whom, if he should cut off such a man, he feared that some insurrection or war might arise.

VII. Surrounded by such difficulties, and seeing that a man, so popular among his countrymen, was not to be destroyed either by force or by fraud, he resolved, as Jugurtha was of an active disposition, and eager for military reputation, to expose him to dangers in the field, and thus make trial of fortune. During the Numantine war,[26] therefore, when he was sending supplies of horse and foot to the Romans, he gave him the command of the Numidians, whom he dispatched into Spain, hoping that he would certainly perish, either by an ostentatious display of his bravery, or by the merciless hand of the enemy. But this project had a very different result from that which he had expected. For when Jugurtha, who was of an active and penetrating intellect, had learned the disposition of Publius Scipio, the Roman general, and the character of the enemy, he quickly rose, by great exertion and vigilance, by modestly submitting to orders, and frequently exposing himself to dangers, to such a degree of reputation, that he was greatly beloved by our men, and extremely dreaded by the Numantines. He was indeed, what is peculiarly difficult, both brave in action, and wise in counsel; qualities, of which the one, from forethought, generally produces fear, and the other, from confidence, rashness. The general, accordingly, managed almost every difficult matter by the aid of Jugurtha, numbered him among his friends, and grew daily more and more attached to him, as a man whose advice and whose efforts were never useless. With such merits were joined generosity of disposition, and readiness of wit, by which he united to himself many of the Romans in intimate friendship.

VIII. There were at that time, in our army, a number of officers, some of low, and some of high birth, to whom wealth was more attractive than virtue or honor; men who were attached to certain parties, and of consequence in their own country; but, among the allies, rather distinguished than respected. These persons inflamed the mind of Jugurtha, of itself sufficiently aspiring, by assuring him, "that if

Micipsa should die, he might have the kingdom of Numidia to himself; for that he was possessed of eminent merit, and that anything might be purchased at Rome."

When Numantia, however, was destroyed, and Scipio had determined to dismiss the auxiliary troops, and to return to Rome, he led Jugurtha, after having honored him, in a public assembly, with the noblest presents and applauses, into his own tent; where he privately admonished him "to court the friendship of the Romans rather by attention to them as a body, than by practicing on individuals;[27] to bribe no one, as what belonged to many could not without danger be bought from a few; and adding that, if he would but trust to his own merits, glory and regal power would spontaneously fall to his lot; but, should he proceed too rashly, he would only, by the influence of his money, hasten his own ruin."

IX. Having thus spoken, he took leave of him, giving him a letter, which he was to present to Micipsa, and of which the following was the purport: "The merit of your nephew Jugurtha, in the war against Numantia, has been eminently distinguished; a fact which I am sure will afford you pleasure. He is dear to us for his services, and we shall strive, with our utmost efforts, to make him equally dear to the senate and people of Rome. As a friend, I sincerely congratulate you; you have a kinsman worthy of yourself, and of his grandfather Masinissa."

Micipsa, when he found, from the letter of the general, that what he had already heard reported was true, being moved, both by the merit of the youth and by the interest felt for him by Scipio, altered his purpose, and endeavored to win Jugurtha by kindness. He accordingly, in a short time,[28] adopted him as his son, and made him, by his will, joint-heir with his own children.

A few years afterward, when, being debilitated by age and disease, he perceived that the end of his life was at hand, he is said, in the presence of his friends and relations, and of Adherbal and Hiempsal his sons, to have spoken with Jugurtha in the following manner:

X. "I received you, Jugurtha, at a very early age, into my kingdom,[29] at a time when you had lost your father, and were without prospects or resources, expecting that, in return for my kindness, I should not be less loved by you than by my own children, if I should have any. Nor have my anticipations deceived me; for, to say nothing of your other great and noble deeds, you have lately, on your return from Numantia, brought honor and glory both to me and my kingdom; by your bravery, you have rendered the Romans, from being previously our friends, more friendly to us than ever; the name of our family is revived in Spain; and, finally, what is most difficult among mankind, you have suppressed envy by preeminent merit.[30]

And now, since nature is putting a period to my life, I exhort and conjure you, by this right hand, and by the fidelity which you owe to my kingdom,[31] to regard these princes, who are your cousins by birth, and your brothers by my generosity, with sincere affection; and not to be more anxious to attach to yourself strangers, than to retain the love of those connected with you by blood. It is not armies, or treasures,[32] that form the defenses of a kingdom, but friends, whom you can neither command by force nor purchase with gold; for they are acquired only by good offices and integrity. And who can be a greater friend than one brother to another?[33] Or what stranger will you find faithful, if you are at enmity with your own family? I leave you a kingdom, which will be strong if you act honorably, but weak, if you are ill-affected to each other; for by concord even small states are increased, but by discord, even the greatest fall to nothing.

But on you, Jugurtha, who are superior in age and wisdom, it is incumbent, more than on your brothers, to be cautious that nothing of a contrary tendency may arise; for, in all disputes, he that is the stronger, even though he receive the injury, appears, because his power is greater, to have inflicted it. And do you, Adherbal and Hiempsal, respect and regard a kinsman of such a character; imitate his virtues, and make it your endeavor to show that I have not adopted a better son[34] than those whom I have begotten."

XI. To this address, Jugurtha, though he knew that the king had spoken insincerely,[35] and though he was himself revolving thoughts of a far different nature, yet replied with good feeling, suitable to the occasion. A few days afterward Micipsa died.

When the princes had performed his funeral with due magnificence, they met together to hold a discussion on the general condition of their affairs. Hiempsal, the youngest, who was naturally violent, and who had previously shown contempt for the mean birth of Jugurtha, as being inferior on his mother's side, sat down on the right hand of Adherbal, in order to prevent Jugurtha from being the middle one of the three, which is regarded by the Numidians as the seat of honor.[36] Being urged by his brother, however, to yield to superior age, he at length removed, but with reluctance, to the other seat.[37]

In the course of this conference, after a long debate about the administration of the kingdom, Jugurtha suggested, among other measures, "that all the acts and decrees made in the last five years should be annulled, as Micipsa, during that period, had been enfeebled by age, and scarcely sound in intellect."

Hiempsal replied, "that he was exceedingly pleased with the proposal, since Jugurtha himself, within the last three years, had been adopted as joint-heir to the throne." This repartee sunk deeper into the mind of Jugurtha than any one imagined. From that very time, accordingly, being agitated with resentment and jealousy, he began to meditate and concert schemes, and to think of nothing but projects for secretly cutting off Hiempsal. But his plans proving slow in operation, and his angry feelings remaining unabated, he resolved to execute his purpose by any means whatsoever.

XII. At the first meeting of the princes, of which I have just spoken, it had been resolved, in consequence of their disagreement, that the treasures should be divided among them, and that limits should be set to the jurisdiction of each. Days were accordingly appointed for both these purposes, but the earlier of the two for the division of the money. The princes, in the mean time, retired into separate places of abode in the neighborhood of the treasury. Hiempsal, residing in the town of Thirmida, happened to occupy the house of a man, who, being Jugurtha's chief lictor,[38] had always been liked and favored by his master. This man, thus opportunely presented as an instrument, Jugurtha loaded with promises, and induced him to go to his house, as if for the purpose of looking over it, and provide himself with false keys to the gates; for the true ones used to be given to Hiempsal, adding, that he himself, when circumstances should call for his presence, would be at the place with a large body of men. This commission the Numidian speedily executed, and, according to his instructions, admitted Jugurtha's men in the night, who, as soon as they had entered the house, went different ways in quest of the prince; some of his attendants they killed while asleep, and others as they met them; they searched into secret places, broke open those that were shut, and filled the whole premises with uproar and tumult. Hiempsal, after a time, was found concealed in the hut of a maid-servant,[39] where, in his alarm and ignorance of the locality, he had at first taken refuge. The Numidians, as they had been ordered, brought his head to

Jugurtha.

XIII The report of so atrocious an outrage was soon spread through Africa. Fear seized on Adherbal, and on all who had been subject to Micipsa. The Numidians divided into two parties, the greater number following Adherbal, but the more warlike, Jugurtha; who, accordingly, armed as large a force as he could, brought several cities, partly by force and partly by their own consent, under his power, and prepared to make himself sovereign of the whole of Numidia. Adherbal, though he had sent embassadors to Rome, to inform the senate of his brother's murder and his own circumstances, yet, relying on the number of his troops, prepared for an armed resistance. When the matter, however, came to a contest, he was defeated, and fled from the field of battle into our province,[40] and from thence hastened to Rome.

Jugurtha, having thus accomplished his purposes,[41] and reflecting, at leisure, on the crime which he had committed, began to feel a dread of the Roman people, against whose resentment he had no hopes of security but in the avarice of the nobility, and in his own wealth. A few days afterward, therefore, he dispatched embassadors to Rome, with a profusion of gold and silver, whom he directed, in the first place, to make abundance of presents to his old friends, and then to procure him new ones; and not to hesitate, in short; to effect whatever could be done by bribery.

When these deputies had arrived at Rome, and had sent large presents, according to the prince's direction, to his intimate friends,[42] and to others whose influence was at that time powerful, so remarkable a change ensued, that Jugurtha, from being an object of the greatest odium, grew into great regard and favor with the nobility; who, partly allured with hope, and partly with actual largesses, endeavored, by soliciting the members of the senate individually, to prevent any severe measures from being adopted against him. When the embassadors accordingly, felt sure of success, the senate, on a fixed day, gave audience to both parties[43]. On that occasion, Adherbal, as I have understood, spoke to the following effect:

XIV. "My father Micipsa, Conscript Fathers, enjoined me, on his death-bed, to look upon the kingdom of Numidia as mine only by deputation;[44] to consider the right and authority as belonging to you; to endeavor, at home and in the field, to be as serviceable to the Roman people as possible; and to regard you as my kindred and relatives:[45] saying that, if I observed these injunctions. I should find, in your friendship, armies, riches, and all necessary defenses of my realm. By these precepts I was proceeding to regulate my conduct, when Jugurtha, the most abandoned of all men whom the earth contains, setting at naught your authority, expelled me, the grandson of Masinissa, and the hereditary[46] ally and friend of the Roman people, from my kingdom and all my possessions.

Since I was thus to be reduced to such an extremity of wretchedness, I could wish that I were able to implore your aid, Conscript Fathers, rather for the sake of my own services than those of my ancestors; I could wish, indeed, above all, that acts of kindness were due to me from the Romans, of which I should not stand in need; and, next to this,[47] that, if I required your services, I might receive them as my due. But as integrity is no defense in itself, and as I had no power to form the character of Jugurtha,[48] I have fled to you, Conscript Fathers, to whom, what is the most grievous of all things, I am compelled to become a burden before I have been an assistance.

Other princes have been received into your friendship after having been conquered in war, or have solicited an alliance with you in circumstances of distress; but our family commenced its league with the Romans in the war with Carthage, at a time when their faith was a greater object of attraction than their fortune. Suffer not, then, O Conscript Fathers, a descendent of that family to implore aid from you in vain. If I had no other plea for obtaining your assistance but my wretched fortune; nothing to urge, but that, having been recently a king, powerful by birth, by character, and by resources, I am now dishonored, afflicted,[49] destitute, and dependent on the aid of others, it would yet become the dignity of Rome to protect me from injury, and to allow no man's dominions to be increased by crime. But I am driven from those very territories which the Roman people gave to my ancestors, and from which my father and grandfather, in conjunction with yourselves, expelled Syphax and the Carthaginians. It is what you bestowed that has been wrested from me; in my wrongs you are insulted.

Unhappy man that I am! Has your kindness, O my father Micipsa, come to this, that he whom you made equal with your children, and a sharer of your kingdom, should become, above all others,[50] the destroyers of your race? Shall our family, then, never be at peace? Shall we always be harassed with war, bloodshed, and exile? While the Carthaginians continued in power, we were necessarily exposed to all manner of troubles; for the enemy were on our frontiers; you, our friends, were at a distance; and all our dependence was on our arms. But after that pest was extirpated, we were happy in the enjoyment of tranquillity, as having no enemies but such as you should happen to appoint us. But lo! on a sudden, Jugurtha, stalking forth with intolerable audacity, wickedness, and arrogance, and having put to death my brother, his own cousin, made his territory, in the first place, the prize of his guilt; and next, being unable to ensnare me with similar stratagems, he rendered me, when under your rule I expected any thing rather than violence or war, an exile, as you see, from my country and my home, the prey of poverty and misery, and safer any where than in my own kingdom.

I was always of opinion, Conscript Fathers, as I had often heard my father observe, that those who cultivated your friendship might indeed have an arduous service to perform, but would be of all people the most secure. What our family could do for you, it has done; it has supported you in all your wars; and it is for you to provide for our safety in time of peace. Our father left two of us, brothers; a third, Jugurtha, he thought would be attached to us by the benefits conferred upon him; but one of us has been murdered, and I, the other, have scarcely escaped the hand of lawlessness.[51] What course can I now take? Unhappy that I am, to what place, rather than another, shall I betake myself? All the props of our family are extinct; my father, of necessity, has paid the debt of nature; a kinsman, whom least of all men it became, has wickedly taken the life of my brother; and as for my other relatives, and friends, and connections, various forms of destruction have overtaken them. Seized by Jugurtha, some have been crucified, and some thrown to wild beasts, while a few, whose lives have been spared, are shut up in the darkness of the dungeon, and drag on, amid suffering and sorrow, an existence more grievous than death itself.

If all that I have lost, or all that, from being friendly, has become hostile to me,[52] remained unchanged, yet, in case of any sudden calamity, it is of you that I should still have to implore assistance, to whom, from the greatness of your empire, justice and injustice in general should be objects of regard. And at the present time, when I am exiled from my country and my home, when I am left alone, and destitute of all that is suitable to my dignity, to whom can I go, or to whom shall: I appeal, but to you? Shall I go to nations and kings, who, from our friendship with

Rome, are all hostile to my family? Could I go, indeed, to any place where there are not abundance of hostile monuments of my ancestors? Will any one, who, has ever been at enmity with you, take pity upon me?

Masinissa, moreover, instructed us, Conscript Fathers, to cultivate no friendship but that of Rome, to adopt no new leagues or alliances, as we should find, in your good-will, abundance of efficient support; while, if the fortune of your empire should change, we must sink together with it. But, by your own merits, and the favor of the gods, you are great and powerful; the whole world regards you with favor and yields to your power; and you are the better able, in consequence, to attend to the grievances of your allies. My only fear is, that private friendship for Jugurtha, too little understood, may lead any of you astray; for his partisans, I hear, are doing their utmost in his behalf, soliciting and importuning you individually, to pass no decision against one who is absent, and whose cause is yet untried; and saying that I state what is false, and only pretend to be an exile, when I might, if I pleased, have remained still in my kingdom. But would that I could see him,[53] by whose unnatural crime I am thus reduced to misery, pretending as I now pretend; and would that, either with you or with the immortal gods, there may at length arise some regard for human interests; for then assuredly will he, who is now audacious and triumphant in guilt, be tortured by every kind of suffering, and pay a heavy penalty for his ingratitude to my father, for the murder of my brother, and for the distress which he has brought upon myself.

And now, O my brother, dearest object of my affection, though thy life has been prematurely taken from thee, and by a hand that should have been the last to touch it, yet I think thy fate a subject for rejoicing rather than lamentation, for, in losing life, thou hast not been cut off from a throne, but from flight, expatriation, poverty, and all those afflictions which now press upon me. But I, unfortunate that I am, cast from the throne of my father into the depths of calamity, afford an example of human vicissitudes, undecided what course to adopt, whether to avenge thy wrongs, while I myself stand in need of assistance, or to attempt the recovery of my kingdom, while my life or death depends on the aid of others.[54]

Would that death could be thought an honorable termination to my misfortunes, that I might not seem to live an object of contempt, if, sinking under my afflictions, I tamely submit to injustice. But now I can neither live with pleasure, nor can die without disgrace.[55] I implore you, therefore, Conscript Fathers, by your regard for yourselves,[56] for your children, and for your parents, and by the majesty of the Roman people, to grant me succor in my distress, to arrest the progress of injustice, and not to suffer the kingdom of Numidia, which is your own property, to sink into ruin[57] through villainy and the slaughter of our family."

XV. When the prince had concluded his speech, the embassadors of Jugurtha, depending more on their money than their cause, replied, in a few words, "that Hiempsal had been put to death by the Numidians for his cruelty; that Adherbal, commencing war of his own accord, complained, after he was defeated, of being unable to do injury; and that Jugurtha entreated the senate not to consider him a different person from what he had been known to be at Numantia, nor to set the assertions of his enemy above his own conduct."

Both parties then withdrew from the senate-house, and the senate immediately proceeded to deliberate. The partisans of the embassadors, with a great many others, corrupted by their influence, expressed contempt for the statements of Adherbal, extolled with the highest encomiums the merits of Jugurtha, and exerted themselves as strenuously, with their interest and eloquence, in defense of the guilt and infamy of another, as they would have striven for their own honor. A few, however, on the other hand, to whom right and justice were of more estimation than wealth, gave their opinion that Adherbal should be assisted, and the murder of Hiempsal severely avenged. Of all these the most forward was Aemilius Scaurus,[58] a man of noble birth and great energy, but factious, and ambitious of power, honor, and wealth; yet an artful concealer of his own vices. He, seeing that the bribery of Jugurtha was notorious and shameless, and fearing that, as in such cases often happens, its scandalous profusion might excite public odium, restrained himself from the indulgence of his ruling passion.[59]

XVI. Yet that party gained the superiority in the senate, which preferred money and interest to justice. A decree was made, "that ten commissioners should divide the kingdom, which Micipsa had possessed, between Jugurtha and Adherbal." Of this commission the leading person was Lucius Opimius,[60] a man of distinction, and of great influence at that time in the senate, from having in his consulship, on the death of Caius Gracchus and Marcus Fulvius Flaccus, prosecuted the victory of the nobility over the plebeians with great severity.

Jugurtha, though he had already counted Scaurus among his friends at Rome, yet received him with the most studied ceremony, and, by presents and promises, wrought on him so effectually, that he preferred the prince's interest to his own character, honor, and all other considerations. The rest of the commissioners he assailed in a similar way, and gained over most of them; by a few only integrity was more regarded than lucre. In the division of the kingdom, that part of Numidia which borders on Mauretania, and which is superior in fertility and population, was allotted to Jugurtha; of the other part, which, though better furnished with harbors and buildings, was more valuable in appearance than in reality, Adherbal became the possessor.

XVII. My subject seems to require of me, in this place, a brief account of the situation of Africa, and of those nations in it with whom we have had war or alliances. But of those tracts and countries, which, from their heat, or difficulty of access, or extent of desert, have been but little visited, I can not possibly give any exact description. Of the rest I shall speak with all possible brevity.

In the division of the earth, most writers consider Africa as a third part; a few admit only two divisions, Asia and Europe,[61] and include Africa in Europe. It is bounded, on the west, by the strait connecting our sea with the ocean;[62] on the east, by a vast sloping tract, which the natives call the Catabathmos.[63] The sea is boisterous, and deficient in harbors; the soil is fertile in corn, and good for pasturage, but unproductive of trees. There is a scarcity of water both from rain and from landsprings. The natives are healthy, swift of foot, and able to endure fatigue. Most of them die by the gradual decay of age,[64] except such as perish by the sword or beasts of prey; for disease finds but few victims. Animals of a venomous nature they have in great numbers.

Concerning the original inhabitants of Africa, the settlers that afterward joined them, and the manner in which they intermingled, I shall offer the following brief account, which, though it differs from the general opinion, is that which was interpreted to me from the Punic volumes said to have belonged to King Hiempsal[65], and which the inhabitants of that country believe to be consistent with fact. For the truth of the statement, however, the writers themselves must be responsible.

XVIII. Africa, then, was originally occupied by the Getulians and Libyans,[66] rude and uncivilized tribes, who subsisted on the flesh of wild animals, or, like cattle, on the herbage of the soil. They were controlled neither by customs, laws, nor the authority of any ruler; they wandered about, without fixed habitations, and slept in the abodes to which night drove them. But after Hercules, as the Africans think, perished in Spain, his army, which was composed of various nations,[67] having lost its leader, and many candidates severally claiming the command of it, was speedily dispersed. Of its constituent troops, the Medes, Persians, and Armenians,[68] having sailed over into Africa, occupied the parts nearest to our sea.[69] The Persians, however, settled more toward the ocean,[70] and used the inverted keels of their vessels for huts, there being no wood in the country, and no opportunity of obtaining it, either by purchase or barter, from the Spaniards; for a wide sea, and an unknown tongue, were barriers to all intercourse. These, by degrees, formed intermarriages with the Getulians; and because, from constantly trying different soils, they were perpetually shifting their abodes, they called themselves NUMIDIANS. [71] And to this day the huts of the Numidian boors, which they call *mapalia*, are of an oblong shape, with curved roofs; resembling the hulls of ships.

The Medes and Armenians connected themselves with the Libyans, who dwelled near the African sea; while the Getulians lay more to the sun,[72] not far from the torrid heats; and these soon built themselves towns,[73] as, being separated from Spain only by a strait, they proceeded to open an intercourse with its inhabitants. The name of Medes the Libyans gradually corrupted, changing it, in their barbarous tongue, into Moors.[74]

Of the Persians[75] the power rapidly increased; and at length, the children, through excess of population, separating from the parents, they took possession, under the name of Numidians, of those regions bordering on Carthage which are now called Numidia. In process of time, the two parties,[76] each assisting the other, reduced the neighboring tribes, by force or fear, under their sway; but those who had spread toward our sea, made the greater conquests: for the Lybians are less warlike than the Getulians[77] At last nearly all lower Africa[78] was occupied by the Numidians; and all the conquered tribes were merged in the nation and name of their conquerors.

XIX. At a later period, the Phoenicians, some of whom wished to lessen their numbers at home, and others, ambitious of empire, engaged the populace, and such as were eager for change, to follow them, founded Hippo,[79] Adrumetum,

Leptis,[80] and other cities, on the sea-coast; which, soon growing powerful, became partly a support, and partly an honor, to their parent state. Of Carthage I think it better to be silent, than to say but little; especially as time bids me hasten to other matters.

Next to the Catabathmos,[81] then, which divides Egypt from Africa, the first city along the sea-coast[82] is Cyrene, a colony of Theraeans;[83] after which are the two Syrtes,[84] with Leptis[85] between them; then the Altars of the Philaeni,[86] which the Carthaginians considered the boundary of their dominion on the side of Egypt; beyond these are the other Punic towns. The other regions, as far as Mauretania, the Numidians occupy; the Moors are nearest to Spain. To the south of Numidia,[87] as we are informed, are the Getulians, of whom some live in huts, and others lead a vagrant and less civilized life; beyond these are the Ethiopians; and further on, regions parched by the heat of the sun.

At the time of the Jugurthine war, most of the Punic towns, and the territories which Carthage had lately possessed,[88] were under the government of Roman praetors; a great part of the Getulians, and Numidia as far as the river Mulucha, were subject to Jugurtha; while the whole of the Moors were governed by Bocchus, a king who knew nothing of the Romans but their name, and who, before this period, was as little known to us, either in war or peace. Of Africa and its inhabitants I have now said all that my narrative requires.

XX. When the commissioners, after dividing the kingdom, had left Africa, and Jugurtha saw that, contrary to his apprehensions, he had obtained the object of his crimes; he then being convinced of the truth of what he had heard from his friends at Numantia, "that all things were purchasable at Rome," and being also encouraged by the promises of those whom he had recently loaded with presents, directed his views to the domain of Adherbal. He was himself bold and warlike, while the other, at whose destruction he aimed, was quiet, unfit for arms, of a mild temper, a fit subject for injustice, and a prey to fear rather than an object of it. Jugurtha, accordingly, with a powerful force, made a sudden irruption into his dominions, took several prisoners, with cattle and other booty, set fire to the buildings, and made hostile demonstrations against several places with his cavalry. He then retreated, with all his followers, into his own kingdom, expecting that Adherbal, roused by such provocation, would avenge his wrongs by force, and thus furnish a pretext for war. But Adherbal, thinking himself unable to meet Jugurtha in the field, and relying on the friendship of the Romans more than on the Numidians, merely sent embassadors to Jugurtha to complain of the outrage; and, although they brought back but an insolent reply, yet he resolved to endure any thing rather than have recourse to war, which, when he attempted it before, had ended in his defeat. By such conduct the eagerness of Jugurtha was not at all allayed; for he had now, indeed, in imagination, possessed himself of all Adherbal's dominions. He therefore renewed hostilities, not, as before, with a predatory band, but at the head of a large army which he had collected, and openly aspired to the sovereignty of all Numidia. Wherever he marched, he ravaged the towns and the fields, drove off booty, and raised confidence in his own men and dismay among the enemy.

XXI. Adherbal, when he found that matters had arrived at such a point, that he must either abandon his dominions, or defend them by force of arms, collected an army from necessity, and advanced to meet Jugurtha. Both armies took up[89] their position near the town of Cirta[90], at no great distance from the sea; but, as evening was approaching, encamped without coming to an engagement. But when the night was far advanced, and twilight was beginning to appear[91], the troops of Jugurtha, at a given signal, rushed into the camp of the enemy, whom they routed and put to flight, some half asleep and others resuming their arms. Adherbal, with a few of his cavalry, fled to Cirta; and, had there not been a number of Romans[92] in the town, who repulsed his Numidian pursuers from the walls, the war between the two princes would have been begun and ended on the same day.

Jugurtha proceeded to invest the town, and attempted to storm it with the aid of mantelets, towers, and every kind of machines; being anxious above all things, to take it before the embassadors could arrive at Rome, who, he was informed, had been dispatched thither by Adherbal before the battle was fought. But as soon as the senate heard of their contention, three young men[93] were sent as deputies into Africa, with directions to go to both of the princes, and to announce to them, in the words of the senate and people of Rome, "that it was their will and resolution that they should lay down their arms, and settle their disputes rather by arbitration than by the sword; since to act thus would be to the honor both of the Romans and themselves."

XXII. These deputies soon arrived in Africa, using the greater dispatch, because, while they were preparing for their journey, a report was spread at Rome of the battle which had been fought, and of the siege of Cirta; but this report told much less than the truth[94] Jugurtha, having given them an audience, replied, "that nothing was of greater weight with him, nothing more respected, than the authority of the senate; that it had been his endeavor, from his youth, to deserve the esteem of all men of worth; that he had gained the favor of Publius Scipio, a man of the highest eminence, not by dishonorable practices, but by merit; that, for the same good qualities, and not from want of heirs to the throne, he had been adopted by Micipsa; but that, the more honorable and spirited his conduct had been, the less could his feelings endure injustice; that Adherbal had formed designs against his life on discovering which, he had counteracted his malice; that the Romans would act neither justly nor reasonably, if they withheld from him the common right of nations;[96] and, in conclusion, that he would soon send embassadors to Rome to explain the whole of his proceedings." On this understanding, both parties separated. Of addressing Adherbal the deputies had no opportunity.

XXIII. Jugurtha, as soon as he thought that they had quitted Africa, surrounded the walls of Cirta, which, from the nature of its situation, he was unable to take by assault, with a rampart and a trench; he also erected towers, and manned them with soldiers; he made attempts on the place, by force or by stratagem, day and night; he held out bribes, and some times menaces, to the besieged; he roused his men, by exhortations, to efforts of valor, and resorted, with the utmost perseverance, to every possible expedient.

Adherbal, on the other hand, seeing that his affairs were in a desperate condition, that his enemy was determined on his ruin, that there was no hope of succor, and that the siege, from want of provisions, could not long be protracted, selected from among those who had fled with him to Cirta, two of his most resolute supporters, whom he induced, by numerous promises, and an affecting representation of his distress, to make their way in the night, through the enemy's lines, to the nearest point of the coast, and from thence to Rome.

XXIV. The Numidians, in a few days executed their commission; and a letter from Adherbal was read in the senate, of which the following was the purport:

"It is not through my own fault, Conscript Fathers, that I so often send requests to you; but the violence of Jugurtha compels me; whom so strong a desire for my destruction has seized, that he pays no regard[96] either to you or to the immortal gods; my blood he covets beyond every thing. Five months, in consequence, have I, the ally and friend of the Roman people, been besieged with an armed force; neither the remembrance of my father Micipsa's benefits, nor your decrees, are of any avail for my relief; and whether I am more closely pressed by the sword, or by famine, I am unable to say.

From writing further concerning Jugurtha, my present condition deters me; for I have experienced, even before,[97] that little credit is given to the unfortunate. Yet I can perceive that his views extend further than to myself, and that he does not expect to possess, at the same time, your friendship and my kingdom; which of the two he thinks the more desirable, must be manifest to every one. For, in the first place, he murdered my brother Hiempsal; and, in the next, expelled me from my dominions; which, however, may be regarded as our own wrongs, and as having no reference to you. But now he occupies your kingdom with an army; he keeps me, whom you appointed a king over the Numidians, in a state of blockade; and in what estimation he holds the words of your embassadors, my perils may serve to show. What then is left, except your arms, that can make an impression upon him?

I could wish, indeed, that what I now write, as well as the complaints which I lately made before the senate, were false, rather than that my present distresses should confirm the truth of my statements. But since I am born to be an example of Jugurtha's villainy, I do not now beg a release from death or distress, but only from the tyranny of an enemy, and from bodily torture. Respecting the kingdom of Numidia, which is your own property, determine as you please, but if the memory of my grandfather Masinissa is still cherished by you, deliver me, I entreat you, by the majesty of your empire, and by the sacred ties of friendship, from the inhuman hands of Jugurtha."

XXV. When this letter was read, there were some who thought that an army should be dispatched into Africa, and relief afforded to Adherbal, as soon as possible; and that the senate, in the mean time, should give judgment on the conduct of Jugurtha, in not having obeyed the embassadors. But by the partisans of Jugurtha, the same that had before supported his cause, effectual exertions were made to prevent any decree from being passed; and thus the public interest, as is too frequently the case, was defeated by private influence.

An embassy was, however, dispatched into Africa, consisting of men of advanced years, and of noble birth, and who had filled the highest offices of the state; among whom was Marcus Scaurus, already mentioned, a man who had held the consulship, and who was at that time chief of the senate[98]. These embassadors, as their business was an affair of public odium, and as they were urged by the entreaties of the Numidians, embarked in three days; and having soon arrived at Utica, sent a letter from thence to Jugurtha, desiring him "to come to the province as quickly as possible, as they were deputed by the senate to meet him."

Jugurtha, when he found that men of eminence, whose influence at Rome he knew to be powerful, were come to put a stop to his proceedings, was at first perplexed, and distracted between fear and cupidity. He dreaded the displeasure of the senate, if he should disobey the embassadors; while his eager spirit, blinded by the lust of power, hurried him on to complete the injustice which he had begun. At length the evil incitements of ambition prevailed[99]. He accordingly drew his army round the city of Cirta, and endeavored, with his utmost efforts, to force an entrance; having the strongest hopes, that, by dividing the attention of the enemy's troops, he should be able, by force or artifice, to secure an opportunity of success. When his attempts, however, were unavailing, and he found himself unable, as he had designed, to get Adherbal into his power before he met the embassadors, fearing that, by further delay, he might irritate Scaurus, of whom he stood in great dread, he proceeded with a small body of cavalry into the Province. Yet, though serious menaces were repeated to him in the name of the senate, because he had not desisted from the siege, nevertheless, after spending a long time in conference, the embassadors departed without making any impression upon him.

XXVI. When news of this result was brought to Cirta, the Italians[100], by whose exertions the city had been defended, and who trusted that, if a surrender were made, they would be able, from respect to the greatness of the Roman power, to escape without personal injury, advised Adherbal to deliver himself and the city to Jugurtha, stipulating only that his life should be spared, and leaving all other matters to the care of the senate. Adherbal, though he thought nothing less trustworthy than the honor of Jugurtha, yet, knowing that those who advised could also compel him if he resisted, surrendered the place according to their desire. Jugurtha immediately proceeded to put Adherbal to death with torture, and massacred all the inhabitants that were of age, whether Numidians or Italians, as each fell in the way of his troops.

XXVII. When this outrage was reported at Rome, and became a matter of discussion in the senate, the former partisans of Jugurtha applied themselves, by interrupting the debates and protracting the time, sometimes exerting their interest, and sometimes quarreling with particular members, to palliate the atrocity of the deed. And had not Caius Memmius, one of the tribunes of the people elect, a man of energy, and hostile to the power of the nobility, convinced the people of Rome that an attempt was being made, by the agency of a small faction, to have the crimes of Jugurtha pardoned, it is certain that the public indignation against him would have passed off under the protraction of the debates; so powerful was party interest, and the influence of Jugurtha's money. When the senate, however, from consciousness of misconduct, became afraid of the people, Numidia and Italy, by the Sempronian law,[101] were appointed as provinces to the succeeding consuls, who were declared to be Publius Scipio Nasica[102], and Lucius Bestia Calpurnius[103]. Numidia fell to Calpurnius, and Italy to Scipio. An army was then raised to be sent into Africa; and pay, and all other necessaries of war, were decreed for its use.

XXVIII. When Jugurtha received this news, which was utterly at variance with his expectations, as he had felt convinced that all things were purchasable at Rome, he sent his son, with two of his friends, as deputies to the senate, and directed them, like those whom he had sent on the murder of Hiempsal, to attack every body with bribes. Upon the approach of these deputies to Rome, the senate was consulted by Bestia, whether they would allow them to be admitted within the gates; and the senate decreed, "that, unless they came to surrender Jugurtha's kingdom and himself, they must quit Italy within the ten following days." The consul directed this decree to be communicated to the Numidians, who consequently returned home without effecting their object.

Calpurnius, in the mean time, having raised an army, chose for his officers men of family and intrigue, hoping that whatever faults he might commit, would be screened by their influence; and among these was Scaurus, of whose disposition and character we have already spoken. There were, indeed, in our consul Calpurnius, many excellent qualities, both mental and personal, though avarice interfered with the exercise of them; he was patient of labor, of a penetrating intellect, of great foresight, not inexperienced in war, and extremely vigilant against danger and surprise.

The troops were conducted through Italy to Rhegium, from thence to Sicily, and from Sicily into Africa; and Calpurnius's first step, after collecting provisions, was to invade Numidia with spirit, where he took many prisoners, and several towns, by force of arms.

XXIX. But when Jugurtha began, through his emissaries, to tempt him with bribes, and to show the difficulties of the war which he had undertaken to conduct, his mind, corrupted with avarice, was easily altered. His accomplice, however, and manager in all his schemes, was Scaurus; who, though he had at first, when most of his party were corrupted, displayed violent hostility to Jugurtha, yet was afterward seduced, by a vast sum of money, from integrity and honor to injustice and perfidy. Jugurtha, however, at first sought only to purchase a suspension of hostilities, expecting to be able, during the interval, to make some favorable impression, either by bribery or by interest, at Rome; but when he heard that Scaurus was co-operating with Calpurnius, he was elated with great hopes of regaining peace, and resolved upon a conference with them in person respecting the terms of it. In the mean time, for the sake of giving confidence [104] to Jugurtha, Sextus the quaestor was dispatched by the consul to Vaga, one of the prince's towns; the pretext for his journey being the receiving of corn, which Calpurnius had openly demanded from Jugurtha's emissaries, on the ground that a truce was observed through their delay to make a surrender. Jugurtha then, as he had determined, paid a visit to the consul's camp, where, having made a short address to the council, respecting the odium cast upon his conduct, and his desire for a capitulation, he arranged other matters with Bestia and Scaurus in secret; and the next day, as if by an evident majority of voices[105], he was formally allowed to surrender. But, as was demanded in the hearing of the council, thirty elephants, a considerable number of cattle and horses, and a small sum of money, were delivered into the hands of the quaestor. Calpurnius then returned to Rome to preside at the election of magistrates[106], and peace was observed throughout Numidia and the Roman army.

XXX. When rumor had made known the affairs transacted in Africa, and the mode in which they had been brought to pass, the conduct of the consul became a subject of discussion in every place and company at Rome. Among the people there was violent indignation; as to the senators, whether they would ratify so flagitious a proceeding, or annul the act of the consul, was a matter of doubt. The influence of Scaurus, as he was said to be the supporter and accomplice of Bestia, was what chiefly restrained the senate from acting with justice and honor. But Caius Memmius, of whose boldness of spirit, and hatred to the power of the nobility, I have already spoken, excited the people by his harangues, during the perplexity and delay of the senators, to take vengeance on the authors of the treaty; he exhorted them not to abandon the public interest or their own liberty; he set before them the many tyrannical and violent proceedings of the nobles, and omitted no art to inflame the popular passions. But as the eloquence of Memmius, at that period, had great reputation and influence I have thought proper to give in full[107] one out of many of his speeches; and I take, in preference to others, that which he delivered in the assembly of the people, after the return of Bestia, in words to the following effect:

XXXI. "Were not my zeal for the good of the state, my fellow-citizens, superior to every other feeling, there are many considerations which would deter me from appearing in your cause; I allude to the power of the opposite party, your own tameness of spirit, the absence of all justice, and, above all, the fact that integrity is attended with more danger than honor. Indeed, it grieves me to relate, how, during the last fifteen years[108], you have been a sport to the arrogance of an oligarchy; how dishonorably, and how utterly unavenged, your defenders have perished[109]; and how your spirit has become degenerate by sloth and indolence; for not even now, when your enemies are in your power, will you rouse yourselves to action, but continue still to stand in awe of those to whom you should be a terror.

Yet, notwithstanding this state of things, I feel prompted to make an attack on the power of that faction. That liberty of speech[110], therefore, which has been left me by my father, I shall assuredly exert against them; but whether I shall use it in vain, or for your advantage, must, my fellow-citizens, depend upon yourselves. I do not, however, exhort you, as your ancestors have often done, to rise in arms against injustice.

There is at present no need of violence, no need of secession; for your tyrants must work their fall by their own misconduct.

After the murder of Tiberius Gracchus, whom they accused of aspiring to be king, persecutions were instituted against the common people of Rome; and after the slaughter of Caius Gracchus and Marcus Fulvius, many of your order were put to death in prison. But let us leave these proceedings out of the question; let us admit that to restore their rights to the people, was to aspire to sovereignty; let us allow that what can not be avenged without shedding the blood of citizens, was done with justice. You have seen with silent indignation, however, in past years, the treasury pillaged; you have seen kings, and free people, paying tribute to a small party of Patricians, in whose hands were both the highest honors and the greatest wealth; but to have carried on such proceedings with impunity, they now deem but a small matter; and, at last, your laws and your honor, with every civil and religious obligation[111], have been sacrificed for the benefit of your enemies. Nor do they, who have done these things, show either shame or contrition, but parade proudly before your faces, displaying their sacerdotal dignities, their consulships, and some of them their triumphs, as if they regarded them as marks of honor, and not as fruits of their dishonesty. Slaves, purchased with money[112], will not submit to unjust commands from their masters; yet you, my fellow-citizens, who are born to empire, tamely endure oppression.

But who are these that have thus taken the government into their hands? Men of the most abandoned character, of blood-stained hands, of insatiable avarice, of enormous guilt, and of matchless pride; men by whom integrity, reputation, public spirit[113], and indeed every thing, whether honorable or dishonorable, is converted to a means of gain. Some of them make it their defense that they have killed tribunes of the people; others, that they have instituted unjust prosecutions; others, that they have shed your blood; and thus, the more atrocities each has committed, the greater is his security; while your oppressors, whom the same desires, the same aversions, and the same fears, combine in strict union (a union which among good men is friendship, but among the bad confederacy in guilt), have excited in you, through your want of spirit, that terror which they ought to feel for their own crimes.

But if your concern to preserve your liberty were as great as their ardor to increase their power of oppression, the state would not be distracted as it is at present; and the marks of favor which proceed from you[114], would be conferred, not on the most shameless, but on the most deserving. Your forefathers, in order to assert their rights and establish their authority, twice seceded in arms to Mount Aventine;

and will not you exert yourselves, to the utmost of your power, in defense of that liberty which you received from them? Will you not display so much the more spirit in the cause, from the reflection that it is a greater disgrace to lose[115] what has been gained, than not to have gained it at all?

But some will ask me, 'What course of conduct, then, would you advise us to pursue?' I would advise you to inflict punishment on those who have sacrificed the interests of their country to the enemy; not, indeed, by arms, or any violence (which would be more unbecoming, however, for you to inflict than for them to suffer), but by prosecutions, and by the evidence of Jugurtha himself, who, if he has really surrendered, will doubtless obey your summons; whereas, if he shows contempt for it, you will at once judge what sort of a peace or surrender it is, from which springs impunity to Jugurtha for his crimes, immense wealth to a few men in power, and loss and infamy to the republic.

But perhaps you are not yet weary of the tyranny of these men; perhaps these times please you less than those[116] when kingdoms, provinces, laws, rights, the administration of justice, war and peace, and indeed every thing civil and religious, was in the hands of an oligarchy; while you, that is, the people of Rome, though unconquered by foreign enemies, and rulers of all nations around, were content with being allowed to live; for which of you had spirit to throw off your slavery? For myself, indeed, though I think it most disgraceful to receive an injury without resenting it, yet I could easily allow you to pardon these basest of traitors, because they are your fellow-citizens, were it not certain that your indulgence would end in your destruction. For such is their presumption, that to escape punishment for their misdeeds will have but little effect upon them, unless they be deprived, at the same time, of the power of doing mischief; and endless anxiety will remain for you, if you shall have to reflect that you must either be slaves or preserve your liberty by force of arms.

Of mutual trust, or concord, what hope is there? They wish to be lords, you desire to be free; they seek to inflict injury, you to repel it; they treat your allies as enemies, your enemies as allies. With feelings so opposite, can peace or friendship subsist between you? I warn, therefore, and exhort you, not to allow such enormous dishonesty to go unpunished. It is not an embezzlement of the public money[117] that has been committed; nor is it a forcible extortion of money from your allies;

offenses which, though great, are now, from their frequency, considered as nothing; but the authority of the senate, and your own power, have been sacrificed to the bitterest of enemies, and the public interest has been betrayed for money, both at home and abroad; and unless these misdeeds be investigated, and punishment be inflicted on the guilty, what remains for us but to live the slaves of those who committed them? For those who do what they will with impunity are undoubtedly kings.[118]

I do not, however, wish to encourage you, O Romans, to be better satisfied at finding your fellow-citizens guilty than innocent, but merely to warn you not to bring ruin on the good, by suffering the bad to escape. It is far better, in any government, to be unmindful of a service than of an injury; for a good man, if neglected, only becomes less active; but a bad man, more daring. Besides, if the crimes of the wicked are suppressed,[119] the state will seldom need extraordinary support from the virtuous."

XXXII. By repeating these and similar sentiments, Memmius prevailed on the people to send Lucius Cassius,[120] who was then praetor, to Jugurtha, and to bring him, under guarantee of the public faith[121], to Rome, in order that, by the prince's evidence, the misconduct of Scaurus and the rest, whom they charged with having taken bribes, might more easily be made manifest.

During the course of these proceedings at Rome, those whom Bestia had left in Numidia in command of the army, following the example of their general, had been guilty of many scandalous transactions. Some, seduced by gold, had restored Jugurtha his elephants; others had sold him his deserters; others had ravaged the lands of those at peace with us; so strong a spirit of rapacity, like the contagion of a pestilence, had pervaded the breasts of all.

Cassius, when the measure proposed by Memmius had been carried, and while all the nobility were in consternation, set out on his mission to Jugurtha, whom, alarmed as he was, and despairing of his fortune, from a sense of guilt, he admonished "that since he had surrendered himself to the Romans, he had better make trial of their mercy than their power." He also pledged his own word, which Jugurtha valued not less than that of the public, for his safety. Such, at that period, was the reputation of Cassius.

XXXIII. Jugurtha, accordingly, accompanied Cassius to Rome, but without any mark of royalty, and in the garb, as much as possible, of a suppliant[122]; and, though he felt great confidence on his own part, and was supported by all those through whose power or villainy he had accomplished his projects, he purchased, by a vast bribe, the aid of Caius Baebius, a tribune of the people, by whose audacity he hoped to be protected against the law, and against all harm.

An assembly of the people being convoked, Memmius, although they were violently exasperated against Jugurtha, (some demanding that he should be cast into prison, others that, unless he should name his accomplices in guilt, he should be put to death, according to the usage of their ancestors, as a public enemy), yet, regarding rather their character than their resentment, endeavored to calm their turbulence and mitigate their rage; and assured them that, as far as depended on him, the public faith should not be broken. At length, when silence was obtained, he brought forward Jugurtha, and addressed them. He detailed the misdeeds of Jugurtha at Rome and in Numidia, and set forth his crimes toward his father and brothers; and admonished the prince, "that the Roman people, though they were well aware by whose support and agency he had acted, yet desired further testimony from himself; that, if he disclosed the truth, there was great hope for him in the honor and clemency of the Romans; but if he concealed it, he would certainly not save his accomplices, but ruin himself and his hopes forever."

XXXIV. But when Memmius had concluded his speech, and Jugurtha was expected to give his answer, Caius Baebius, the tribune of the people, whom I have just noticed as having been bribed, enjoined the prince to hold his peace[123]; and though the multitude, who formed the assembly, were desperately enraged, and endeavored to terrify the tribune by outcries, by angry looks, by violent gestures, and by every other act to which anger prompts[124], his audacity was at last triumphant. The people, mocked and set at naught, withdrew from the place of assembly; and the confidence of Jugurtha, Bestia, and the others, whom this investigation had alarmed, was greatly augmented. XXXV. There was at this period in Rome a certain Numidian named Massiva, a son of Gulussa and grandson of Masinissa, who, from having been, in the dissensions among the princes, opposed to Jugurtha, had been obliged, after the surrender of Cirta and the murder of Adherbal, to make his escape out of Africa. Spurius Albinus, who was consul with Quintus Minucius Rufus the year after Bestia, prevailed upon this man, as he was of the family of Masinissa, and as odium and terror hung over Jugurtha for his crimes, to petition the senate for the kingdom of Numidia. Albinus, being eager for the conduct of a war, was desirous that affairs should be disturbed[125], rather than sink into tranquillity; especially as, in the division of the provinces, Numidia had fallen to himself, and Macedonia to Minucius.

When Massiva proceeded to carry these suggestions into execution, Jugurtha, finding that he had no sufficient support in his friends, as a sense of guilt deterred some, and evil report or timidity others, from coming forward in his behalf, directed Bomilcar, his most attached and faithful adherent, to procure by the aid of money, by which he had already effected so much, assassins to kill Massiva; and to do it secretly if he could; but, if secrecy should be impossible, to cut him off in any way whatsoever. This commission Bomilcar soon found means to execute; and, by the agency of men versed in such service, ascertained the direction of his journeys, his hours of leaving home, and the times at which he resorted to particular places [126], and, when all was ready, placed his assassins in ambush. One of their number sprung upon Massiva, though with too little caution, and killed him; but being himself caught, he made, at the instigation of many, and especially of Albinus the consul, a full confession. Bomilcar was accordingly committed for trial, though rather on the principles of reason and justice than in accordance with the law of nations[127], as he was in the retinue of one who had come to Rome on a pledge of the public faith for his safety. But Jugurtha, though clearly guilty of the crime, did not cease to struggle against the truth, until he perceived that the infamy of the deed was too strong for his interest or his money. For which reason, although, at the commencement of the proceedings[128], he had given fifty of his friends as bail for Bomilcar, yet, thinking more of his kingdom than of the sureties, he sent him off privately into Numidia; for he feared that if such a man should be executed, his other subjects would be deterred from obeying him[129]. A few days after, he himself departed, having been ordered by the senate to quit Italy. But, as he was going from Rome, he is said, after frequently looking back on it in silence, to have at last exclaimed, "That it was a venal city, and would soon perish, if it could but find a purchaser!"[130]

XXXVI. The war being now renewed, Albinus hastened to transport provisions, money, and other things necessary for the army, into Africa, whither he himself soon followed, with the hope that, before the time of the comitia, which was not far distant, he might be able, by an engagement, by capitulation, or by some other method, to bring the contest to a conclusion.

Jugurtha, on the other hand, tried every means of protracting the war, continually inventing new causes for delay; at one time he promised to surrender, at another he feigned distrust; he retreated when Albinus attacked him, and then, lest his men should lose courage, attacked in return, and thus amused the consul with alternate procrastinations of war and of peace.

There were some, at that time, who thought that Albinus understood Jugurtha's object, and who believed that so ready a protraction of the war, after so much haste at the commencement, was to be attributed less to tardiness than to treachery. However this might be, Albinus, when time passed on, and the day of the comitia approached, left his brother Aulus in the camp as propraetor[131], and returned to Rome.

XXXVII. The republic, at this time, was grievously distracted by the contentions of the tribunes. Two of them, Publius Lucullus and Lucius Annius, were struggling against the will of their colleagues, to prolong their term of office; and this dispute put off the comitia throughout the year[132]. In consequence of this delay, Aulus, who, as I have just said, was left as propraetor in the camp, conceiving hopes either of finishing the war, or of extorting money from Jugurtha by the terror of his army, drew out his troops in the month of January, from their winter-quarters into the field, and by forced marches, during severe weather, made his way to the town of Suthul, where Jugurtha's treasures were deposited. And though this place, both from the inclemency of the season, and from its advantageous situation, could neither be taken nor besieged; for around its walls, which were built on the edge of a steep hill[133], a marshy plain, flooded by the rains of winter, had been converted into a lake; yet Aulus, either as a feint to strike terror into Jugurtha, or blinded by avarice, began to move forward his vineae[134], to cast up a rampart, and to hasten all necessary preparations for a siege.

XXXVIII. Jugurtha, seeing the propraetor's vanity and ignorance, artfully strengthened his infatuation; he sent him, from time to time, deputies with submissive messages, while he himself, as if desirous to escape, led his army away through woody defiles and cross-roads. At length he succeeded in alluring Aulus, by the prospect of a surrender on conditions, to leave Suthul, and pursue him, as if in full retreat, into the remoter parts of the country. Meanwhile, by means of skillful emissaries, he tampered night and day with our men, and prevailed on some of the officers, both of infantry and cavalry, to desert to him at once, and upon others to quit their posts at a given signal, that their defection might thus be less observed[135]. Having prepared matters according to his wishes, he suddenly surrounded the camp of Aulus, in the dead of night, with a vast body of Numidians. The Roman soldiers were alarmed with an unusual disturbance; some of them seized their arms, others hid themselves, others encouraged those that were afraid; but consternation prevailed every where; for the number of the enemy was great, the sky was thick with clouds and darkness, the danger was indiscernible, and it was uncertain whether it were safer to flee or to remain. Of those whom I have just mentioned as being bribed, one cohort of Ligurians, with two troops of Thracian horse, and a few common soldiers, went over to Jugurtha; and the chief centurion[136] of the third legion allowed the enemy an entrance at the very post which he had been appointed to defend, and at which all the Numidians poured into the camp. Our men fled disgracefully, the greater part having thrown away their arms, and took possession of a neighboring hill. Night, and the spoils of the camp, prevented the enemy from making full use of this victory. On the following day, Jugurtha, coming to a conference with Aulus, told him, "that though he held him hemmed in by famine and the sword, yet that, being mindful of human vicissitudes, he would, if they would make a treaty with him, allow them to depart uninjured; only that they must pass under the yoke, and quit Numidia within ten days." These terms were severe and ignominious; but, as death was the alternative[137], peace was concluded as Jugurtha desired.

XXXIX. When this affair was made known at Rome, consternation and dismay pervaded the city; some were concerned for the glory of the republic; others, ignorant of war, trembled for their liberty. But all were indignant at Aulus, and especially those who had been distinguished in the field, because, with arms in his hands, he had sought safety in disgrace rather than in resistance. The consul Albinus, apprehending, from the delinquency of his brother, odium and danger to himself, consulted the senate on the treaty which had been made, but, at the same time, raised recruits for the army, sent for auxiliaries to the allies and Latins, and made general preparations for war. The senate, as was just, decreed, "that no treaty could be made without their own consent and that of the people."

The consul, though he was hindered by the influence of the tribunes from taking with him the force which he had raised, set out in a few days for the province of Africa, where the whole army, being withdrawn, according to the agreement, from Numidia, had gone into winter-quarters. When he arrived there, although he longed to pursue Jugurtha, and diminish the odium that had fallen on his brother, yet, when he saw the state of the troops, whom, besides the flight and relaxation of discipline, licentiousness, and debauchery had corrupted, he determined, under all the circumstances of the case[138], to attempt nothing.

XL. At Rome, in the mean time, Caius Mamilius Limetanus, one of the tribunes, proposed that the people should pass a bill for instituting an inquiry into the conduct of those by whose influence Jugurtha had set at naught the decrees of the senate, as well as of those who, whether as embassadors or commanders, had received money from him, or who had restored to him his elephants and deserters, or had made any compacts with the enemy relative to peace or war. To this bill some, who were conscious of guilt, and others, who apprehended danger from the jealousy of parties, secretly raised obstructions through the agency of friends, and especially of men among the Latins and Italian allies[139], since they could not openly resist it, without admitting that these and similar practices met their approbation. But as to the people, it is incredible what eagerness they displayed, and with what spirit they approved, voted, and passed the bill, though rather from hatred to the nobility, against whom these severe measures were directed, than from concern for the republic; so violent was the fury of party.

While the rest of the delinquents were in trepidation, Marcus Scaurus [140], whom I have previously noticed as Bestia's lieutenant, contrived, amid the exultation of the populace, the dismay of his own party, and the continued agitation in the city, to have himself elected one of the three commissioners who were appointed by the bill of Mamilius to carry it into execution. But the investigation, notwithstanding, was conducted [141] with great rigor and violence, under the influence of common rumor and popular caprice; for the insolence of success, which had often distinguished the nobility, on this occasion characterized the people.

XLI. The prevalence of parties among the people, and of factions in the senate, and of all evil practices attendant on them, had its origin at Rome, a few years before, during a period of tranquillity, and amid the abundance of all that mankind regarded as desirable. For, before the destruction of Carthage, the senate and people managed the affairs of the republic with mutual moderation and forbearance; there were no contests among the citizens for honor or ascendency; but the dread of an enemy kept the state in order. When that fear, however, was removed from their minds, licentiousness and pride, evils which prosperity loves to foster, immediately began to prevail; and thus peace, which they had so eagerly desired in adversity, proved, when they had obtained it, more grievous and fatal than adversity itself. The patricians carried their authority, and the people their liberty, to excess; every man took, snatched, and seized[142] what he could. There was a complete division into two factions, and the republic was torn in pieces between them. Yet the nobility still maintained an ascendency by conspiring together; for the strength of the people, being disunited and dispersed among a multitude, was less able to exert itself. Things were accordingly directed, both at home and in the field, by the will of a small number of men, at whose disposal were the treasury, the provinces, offices, honors, and triumphs; while the people were oppressed with military service and with poverty, and the generals divided the spoils of war with a few of their friends. The parents and children of the soldiers,[143] meantime, if they chanced to dwell near a powerful neighbor, were driven from their homes. Thus avarice, leagued with power, disturbed, violated, and wasted every thing, without moderation or restraint; disregarding alike reason and religion, and rushing headlong, as it were, to its own destruction. For whenever any arose among the nobility[144], who preferred true glory to unjust power, the state was immediately in a tumult, and civil discord spread with as much disturbance as attends a convulsion of the earth.

XLII. Thus when Tiberius and Caius Gracchus, whose forefathers had done much to increase the power of the state in the Punic and other wars, began to vindicate the liberty of the people, and to expose the misconduct of the few, the nobility, conscious of guilt, and seized with alarm, endeavored, sometimes by means of the allies and Latins[145], and sometimes by means of the equestrian order, whom the hope of coalition with the patricians had detached from the people, to put a stop to the proceedings of the Gracchi; and first they killed Tiberius, and a few years after Caius, who pursued the same measures as his brother, the one when he was tribune, and the other when he was one of a triumvirate for settling colonies; and with them they cut off Marcus Fulvius Flaccus. In the Gracchi, indeed, it must be allowed that, from their ardor for victory, there was not sufficient prudence. But to a reasonable man it is more agreeable to submit[146] to injustice than to triumph over it by improper means. The nobility, however, using their victory with wanton extravagance, exterminated numbers of men by the sword or by exile, yet rather increased, for the time to come, the dread with which they were regarded, than their real power. Such proceedings have often ruined powerful states; for of two parties, each strives to suppress the other by any means whatever, and take vengeance with undue severity on the vanquished.

But were I to attempt to treat of the animosities of parties, and of the morals of the state, with minuteness of detail, and suitably to the vastness of the subject, time would fail me sooner than matter. I therefore return to my subject.

XLIII. After the treaty of Aulus, and the disgraceful flight of our army, Quintus Metellus and Marcus Silanus, the consuls elect, divided the provinces between them; and Numidia fell to Metellus, a man of energy, and, though an opponent of the popular party, yet of a character uniformly irreproachable[147]. He, as soon as he entered on his office, regarded all other things as common to himself and his colleague[148], but directed his chief attention to the war which he was to conduct. Distrusting, therefore, the old army, he began to raise new troops, to procure auxiliaries from all parts, and to provide arms, horses, and other military requisites, besides provisions in abundance, and every thing else which was likely to be of use in a war varied in its character, and demanding great resources. To assist in accomplishing these objects, the allies and Latins, by the appointment of the senate, and different princes[149] of their own accord, sent supplies; and the whole state exerted itself in the cause with the greatest zeal. Having at length prepared and arranged every thing according to his wishes, Metellus set out for Numidia, attended with sanguine expectations on the part of his fellow-citizens, not only because of his other excellent qualities, but especially because his mind was proof against gold; for it was through the avarice of our commanders, that, down to this period, our affairs in Numidia had been ruined, and those of the enemy rendered prosperous.

XLIV. When he arrived in Africa, the command of the army was resigned to him by Albinus, the proconsul[150]; but it was an army spiritless and unwarlike;

incapable of encountering either danger or fatigue; more ready with the tongue than with the sword; accustomed to plunder our allies, while itself was the prey of the enemy; unchecked by discipline, and void of all regard to its character. The new general, accordingly, felt more anxiety from the corrupt morals of the men, than confidence or hope from their numbers. He determined, however, though the delay of the comitia had shortened his summer campaign, and though he knew his countrymen to be anxious for the result of his proceedings, not to commence operations, until, by a revival of the old discipline, he had brought the soldiers to bear fatigue. For Albinus, dispirited by the disaster of his brother Aulus and his army, and having resolved not to leave the province during the portion of the summer that he was to command, had kept the soldiers, for the most part, in a stationary camp[151], except when stench, or want of forage, obliged them to remove. But neither had the camp been fortified[152], nor the watches kept, according to military usage; every one had been allowed to leave his post when he pleased. The camp-followers, mingled with the soldiers, wandered about day and night, ravaging the country, robbing the houses, and vying with each other in carrying off cattle and slaves, which they exchanged with traders for foreign wine[153] and other luxuries; they even sold the corn, which was given them from the public store, and bought bread from day to day; and, in a word, whatever abominations, arising from idleness and licentiousness, can be expressed or imagined, and even more, were to be seen in that army.

XLV. But I am assured that Metellus, in these difficult circumstances, no less than in his operations against the enemy, proved himself a great and wise man; so just a medium did he observe between an affectation of popularity and an excessive enforcement of discipline. His first measure was to remove incentives to idleness, by a general order that no one should sell bread, or any other dressed provisions, in the camp; that no sutlers should follow the army; and that no common soldier should have a servant, or beast of burden, either in a camp or on a march. He made the strictest regulations, too, with regard to other things.[154] He moved his camp daily, exercising the soldiers by marches across the country; he fortified it with a rampart and a trench, exactly as if the enemy had been at hand; he placed numerous sentinels[155] by night, and went the rounds with his officers; and, when the army was on the march; he would be at one time in the front, at another in the rear, and at another in the center, to see that none quitted their ranks, that the men kept close to their standards, and that every soldier carried his provisions and his arms. Thus by preventing rather than punishing irregularities, he in a short time rendered his army effective.

XLVI. Jugurtha, meantime, having learned from his emissaries how Metellus was proceeding, and having heard, when he was in Rome, of the integrity of the consul's character, began to despair of his plans, and at length actually endeavored to effect a capitulation. He therefore sent deputies to the consul with proposals of submission, stipulating only for his own life and that of his children, and offering to surrender every thing else to the Romans. But Metellus had already learned by experience, that the Numidians were a faithless race, of unsettled disposition, and fond of change; and he accordingly applied himself to each of the deputies separately, and after gradually sounding them, and finding them proper instruments for his purpose, prevailed on them, by large promises, to deliver Jugurtha into his hands; bringing him alive, if they could, or dead, if to take him alive was impracticable. In public, however, he directed that such an answer should be given to the king as would be agreeable to his wishes.

A few days afterward, he led the army, which was now vigorous and resolute, into Numidia, where, instead of any appearance of war, he found the cottages full of people, and the cattle and laborers in the fields, while the officers of Jugurtha came from the towns and villages[156] to meet him, offering to supply him with corn, to convey provisions for him, and to do whatever might be required of them. Metellus, notwithstanding, made no diminution in the caution with which he marched, but kept as much upon the defensive as if an enemy had been at hand; and he dispatched scouts to explore the country, thinking that these signs of submission were but pretense, and that the Numidians were watching an opportunity for treachery. He himself, with some light-armed cohorts, and a select body of slingers and archers, advanced always in the front; while Caius Marius, his lieutenant-general, at the head of the cavalry, had charge of the rear. The auxiliary horse, distributed among the tribunes of the legions and prefects of the cohorts, he placed on the flanks, so that, with the aid of the light troops mixed with them, they might repel the enemy whenever an approach should be made. For such was the subtlety of Jugurtha, and such his knowledge of the country and the art of war, that it was doubtful whether he was more formidable absent or present, offering peace or threatening hostilities.

XLVII. There lay, not far from the route which Metellus was pursuing, a city of the Numidians named Vaga, the most celebrated place for trade in the whole kingdom, in which many Italian merchants were accustomed to reside and traffic. Here the consul, to try the disposition of the inhabitants, and, should they allow him, to take advantage of the situation of the place[157], established a garrison, and ordered the people to furnish him with corn, and other necessaries for war; thinking, as circumstances indeed suggested, that the concourse of merchants, and frequent arrival of supplies[158], would add strength to his army, and further the plans which he had already formed.

In the midst of these proceedings, Jugurtha, with extraordinary earnestness[159], sent deputies to sue for peace, offering to resign every thing to Metellus, except his own life and that of his children. These, like the former, the consul first reduced to treachery, and then sent back; the peace which Jugurtha asked, he neither granted nor refused, but waited, during these delays, the performance of the deputies' promises. XLVIII. Jugurtha, on comparing the words of Metellus with his actions, perceived that he was assailed with his own artifices; for though peace was offered him in words, a most vigorous war was in reality pursued against him; one of his strongest cities was wrested from him; his country was explored by the enemy, and the affections of his subjects alienated. Being compelled, therefore, by the necessity of circumstances, he resolved to try the fortune of a battle. Having, with this view, informed himself of the exact route of the enemy, and hoping for success from the advantage of the ground, he collected as large a force of every kind as he could, and, marching by cross-roads, got in advance of Metellus' army.

There was, in that part of Numidia, of which, on the division of the kingdom, Adherbal had become possessor, a river named Muthul, flowing from the south; and, about twenty miles from it, was a range of mountains running parallel with the stream[160], wild and uncultivated; but from the center of it stretched a kind of hill, reaching to a vast distance, covered with wild olives, myrtles, and other trees, such as grow in a dry and sandy soil. The plain, which lay between the mountains and the Muthul, was uninhabited from want of water, except the parts bordering on the river, which were planted with trees, and full of cattle and inhabitants.

XLIX. On this hill, which I have just mentioned, stretching in a transverse direction[161], Jugurtha took post with his line drawn out to a great length. The command of the elephants, and of part of the infantry, he committed to Bomilcar, and gave him instructions how to act. He himself, with the whole of the cavalry and the choicest of the foot, took his station nearer to the range of mountains. Then, riding round among the several squadrons and battalions, he exhorted and conjured them to call to mind their former prowess and triumphs, and to defend themselves and their country from Roman rapacity; saying that they would have to engage with those whom they had already conquered and sent under the yoke, and that, though their commander was changed, there was no alteration in their spirit. He added, that he had provided for his men every thing becoming a general; that he had chosen the higher ground, where they, being well acquainted with the country[162], would contend with adversaries ignorant of it; nor would they engage, inferior in numbers and skill, with a larger or more experienced force; and that they should, therefore, be ready, when the signal should be given, to fall vigorously on the Romans, as that day would either crown[163] all their labors and victories, or be a prelude to the most grievous calamities. He also addressed himself, individually, to any one whom he had rewarded with money or honors for military desert, reminding him of his favors, and pointing him out as an example to the rest; and finally he excited all his men, some in one way and some in another, by threats or entreaties, according to the different dispositions of each.

Metellus, who was still ignorant of the enemy's position, was now seen[164] descending the mountain with his army. He was at first doubtful what the strange appearance before him indicated; for the Numidians, both cavalry and infantry, had taken post among the wood, not entirely concealing themselves, by reason of the lowness of the trees, yet rendering it uncertain[165] what they were, as both themselves and their standards were screened as well by the nature of the ground as by artifice; but soon perceiving that there were men in ambush, he halted awhile, and, having altered the arrangement of his troops, he drew up those in the right wing, which was nearest to the enemy, in three lines[166]; he distributed the slingers and archers among the infantry, posted all the cavalry on the flanks, and having made a brief address, such as time permitted, to his men, he led them down, with the front changed into a flank[167], toward the plain.

L. But when he observed that the Numidians remained quiet, and did not offer to descend from the hill, he became apprehensive that his army, from the season of the year and the scarcity of water, might be overcome with thirst, and therefore sent Rutilius, one of his lieutenant-generals, with the light-armed cohorts and a detachment of cavalry, toward the river, to secure ground for an encampment, expecting that the enemy, by frequent charges and attacks on his flank, would endeavor to impede his march, and, as they despaired of success in arms, would try the effect of fatigue and thirst on his troops.

He then continued to advance by degrees, as his circumstances and the ground permitted, in the same order in which he had descended from the range of mountains. He assigned Marius his post behind the front line[168], and took on himself the command of the cavalry on the left wing, which, on the march, had become the van[169].

When Jugurtha perceived that the rear of the Roman army had passed his first line, he took possession of that part of the mountain from which Metellus had descended, with a body of about two thousand infantry, that it might not serve the enemy, if they were driven back, as a place of retreat, and afterward as a post of defense; and then, ordering the signal to be given, suddenly commenced his attack. Some of his Numidians made havoc in the rear of the Romans, while others assailed them on the right and left wings; they all advanced and charged furiously, and every where threw the consul's troops into confusion. Even those of our men who made the stoutest resistance, were baffled by the enemy's versatile method of fighting, and wounded from a distance, without having the power of wounding in return, or of coming to close combat; for the Numidian cavalry, as they had been previously instructed by Jugurtha, retreated whenever a troop of Romans attempted to pursue them, but did not keep in a body, or collect themselves into one place, but dispersed as widely as possible. Thus, being superior in numbers, if they could not deter the Romans from pursuing, they surrounded them, when disordered, on the rear or flank, or, if the hill seemed more convenient for retreat than the plain, the Numidian horses, being accustomed to the brushwood, easily made their way among it, while the difficulty of the ascent, and want of acquaintance with the ground, impeded those of the Romans.

LI. The aspect of the whole struggle[170] was indeed various, perplexing, direful, and lamentable; the men, separated from their comrades, were partly fleeing, partly pursuing; neither standards nor ranks were regarded, but wherever danger pressed, there they made a stand and defended themselves; arms and weapons, horses and men, enemies, and fellow-countrymen, were all mingled in confusion; nothing was done by direction or command, but chance ordered every thing. Though the day, therefore, was now far advanced, the event of the contest was still uncertain. At last, however, when all were faint with exertion and the heat of the day, Metellus, observing that the Numidians were less vigorous in their charges, drew his troops together by degrees, restored order among them, and led four cohorts of the legions against the enemy's infantry, of whom a great number, overcome with fatigue, had seated themselves on the high ground. He at the same time entreated and exhorted his men not to lose courage, nor to suffer a flying enemy to be victorious; adding that they had neither camp nor citadel to which they could flee, but that their only dependence was on their arms. Nor was Jugurtha, in the mean time, inactive; he rode round among his troops, cheered them, renewed the contest, and, at the head of a select body, made every possible effort for victory; supporting his own men, charging such of the enemy as wavered, and repressing with missiles such as he saw remaining unshaken.

LII. Thus did these two commanders, both eminent men, maintain the contest against each other. In personal ability they were equal, but in circumstances unequal. Metellus had resolute troops, but a disadvantageous position; Jugurtha had every thing in his favor except men. At last the Romans, seeing that they had no place of refuge, that the enemy allowed no opportunity for a regular engagement, and that the evening was fast approaching, forced their way, according to the orders which were given, up the hill. The Numidians were thus driven from their position, routed, and put to flight; a few of them were slain, but their speed, and the enemy's ignorance of the country[171], saved the greater number of them.

Meanwhile Bomilcar, who, as I have said before, was appointed by Jugurtha over the elephants and a part of the infantry, having seen Rutilius pass by him, led down his men gradually into the plain, and while Rutilius hastened to the river, to which he had been dispatched, quietly drew them up in such order as circumstances required; not omitting, at the same time, to watch every movement of the enemy. When he learned that Rutilius had taken his position, and seemed free from apprehension of danger, and heard, at the same time, an increasing noise where Jugurtha was engaged, fearing lest the lieutenant-general, taking the alarm, should go to the support of his countrymen in difficulties, he, in order to intercept his march, increased the extent of his lines, which, from distrust of the bravery of his men, he had previously condensed, and advanced in this order toward Rutilius' camp.

LIII. The Romans, on a sudden, observed a vast cloud of dust, which, as the ground, thickly covered with brushes, obstructed their view, they at first supposed to be only sand raised by the wind; but at length, when they saw that it continued uniform, and approached nearer and nearer as the line advanced, they understood the real cause of it, and, hastily seizing their arms, drew up, as their commander directed, before the camp. When the enemy came up, both sides rushed to the encounter with loud shouts. But the Numidians maintained the contest only as long as they trusted for support to their elephants; for, when they saw the animals entangled in the boughs of the trees, and dispersed or surrounded by the enemy, they betook themselves to flight, and most of them, having thrown away their arms, escaped, by favor of the hill, or of the night, which was now coming on, without injury. Of the elephants, four were taken, and the rest, to the number of forty, were killed.

The Romans, though fatigued and exhausted[172] with their march, the construction of their camp, and the engagement, yet, as Metellus was longer in coming than they expected, advanced to meet him in regular and steady order. The subtlety of the Numidians, indeed, allowed them neither rest nor relaxation. But as the two parties drew together, in the obscurity of the night, each occasioned, by a noise like that of enemies approaching, alarm and trepidation in the other; and, had not parties of horse, sent forward from both sides, ascertained the truth, a fatal disaster was on the point of happening from the mistake. However, in place of fear, joy quickly succeeded; the soldiers met with mutual congratulations, relating their adventures, or listening to those of others, and each extolling his own achievements to the skies. For thus it is with human affairs; in success, even cowards may boast; while defeat lowers the character even of heroes.

LIV. Metellus remained four days in the same camp. He carefully provided for the recovery of the wounded, rewarded, in military fashion, such as had distinguished themselves in the engagements, and praised and thanked them all in a public address; exhorting them to maintain equal resolution in their future labors, which would be less arduous, as they had fought sufficiently for victory, and would now have to contend only for spoil. In the mean time he dispatched deserters, and other eligible persons, to ascertain where Jugurtha was, or what he was doing; whether he had but few followers, or a large army; and how he conducted himself under his defeat. The prince, he found, had retreated to places full of wood, well defended by nature, and was there collecting an army, which would be more numerous indeed than the former, but inactive and inefficient, as being composed of men better acquainted with husbandry and cattle than with war. This had happened from the circumstance, that, in case of flight, none of the Numidian troops, except the royal cavalry, follow their king; the rest disperse, wherever inclination leads them; nor is this thought any disgrace to them as soldiers, such being the custom of the people.

Metellus, therefore, seeing that Jugurtha's spirit was still unsubdued; that a war was being renewed, which could only be conducted[173] according to the prince's pleasure; and that he was struggling with the enemy on unequal terms, as the Numidians suffered a defeat with less loss than his own men gained a victory, he resolved to manage the contest, not by pitched battles or regular warfare, but in another method. He accordingly marched into the richest parts of Numidia, captured and burned many fortresses and towns, which were insufficiently or wholly undefended, put the youth to the sword, and gave up every thing else as plunder to his soldiers. From the terror caused by these proceedings, many persons were given up as hostages to the Romans; corn, and other necessaries, were supplied in abundance; and garrisons were admitted wherever Metellus thought fit.

These measures alarmed Jugurtha much more than the loss of the late battle; for he, whose whole security lay in flight, was compelled to pursue; and he who could not defend his own part of the kingdom, was obliged to make war in that which was occupied by others. Under these circumstances, however[174], he adopted what seemed the most eligible plan. He ordered the main body of his army to continue stationary; while he himself, with a select troop of cavalry, went in pursuit of Metellus, and coming upon him unperceived, by means of night marches and by-roads, he fell upon such of the Roman as were straggling about, of whom the greater number, being unarmed, were slain, and several others made prisoners; not one of them, indeed, escaped unharmed; and the Numidians, before assistance could arrive from the camp, fled, as they had been ordered, to the nearest hills.

LV. In the mean time great joy appeared at Rome when the proceedings of Metellus were reported, and when it was known how he was conducting himself and his army conformably to the ancient discipline; how, on adverse ground, he had gained a victory by his valor; how he was securing possession of the enemy's territory; and how he had driven Jugurtha, when elated by the weakness of Aulus, to depend for safety on the desert or on flight. For these successes, accordingly, the senate decreed a thanksgiving[175] to the immortal gods; the city, which had been full of anxiety, and apprehensive as to the event of the war, was now filled with joy; and the fame of Metellus was raised to the utmost height.

The consul's eagerness to gain a complete victory was thus increased; he exerted himself in every possible way, taking care, at the same time, to give the enemy no opportunity of attacking him to advantage. He remembered that envy is the concomitant of glory, and thus, the more renowned he became, the greater was his caution and circumspection. He never went out to plunder, after the sudden attack of Jugurtha, with his troops in scattered parties; when corn or forage was sought, a body of cohorts, with the whole of the cavalry, were stationed as a guard. He himself conducted part of the army, and Marius the rest. The country was wasted, however, more by fire than by spoliation. They had separate camps, not far from each other; whenever there was occasion for force, they formed a union; but, that desolation and terror might spread the further, they acted separately. Jugurtha, meanwhile, continued to follow them along the hills, watching for a favorable opportunity or situation for an attack. He destroyed the forage, and spoiled the water, which was scarce, wherever he found that the enemy were coming. He presented himself sometimes to Metellus, and sometimes to Marius; he would attack their rear upon a march, and instantly retreat to the hills; he would threaten sometimes one point, and sometimes another, neither giving battle nor allowing rest, but making it his great object to retard the progress of the enemy.

LVI. The Roman commander, finding himself thus harassed by artifices, and allowed no opportunity of coming to a general engagement, resolved on laying siege to a large city, named Zama, which was the bulwark of that part of the kingdom in which it was situate; expecting that Jugurtha, as a necessary consequence, would come to the relief of his subjects in distress, and that a battle would then follow. But the king, being apprised by some deserters of the consul's design, reached the place, by rapid marches, before him, and exhorted the inhabitants to defend their walls, giving them, as a reinforcement, a body of deserters; a class of men, who, of all the royal forces, were the most to be trusted, inasmuch as they dared not be guilty of treachery[176]. He also promised to support them, whenever it should be necessary, with his whole army.

Having taken these precautions, he retired into the deserts of the interior; where he soon after learned that Marius, with a few cohorts, had been dispatched from the line of march to bring provisions from Sicca[177], a town which had been the first to revolt from him after his defeat. To this place he hastened by night, accompanied by a select body of cavalry, and attacked the Romans at the gate, just as they were leaving the city; calling to the inhabitants, at the same time, with a loud voice, to surround the cohorts in the rear; adding, that Fortune had given them an opportunity for a glorious exploit; and that, if they took advantage of it, he would henceforth enjoy his kingdom, and they their liberty, without fear. And had not Marius hastened to advance the standards, and to escape from the town, it is certain that all, or the greater part of the inhabitants, would have changed their allegiance; so great is the fickleness which the Numidians exhibit in their conduct. The soldiers of Jugurtha, animated for a time by their king, but finding the enemy pressing them with superior force, betook themselves, after losing a few of their number, to flight.

LVII. Marius arrived at Zama. This town, built on a plain, was better fortified by art than by nature. It was well supplied with necessaries, and contained plenty of arms and men. Metellus, having made arrangements suitable for the time and the place, encompassed the whole city with his army, assigning to each of his officers his post of command. At a given signal, a loud shout was raised on every side, but without exciting the least alarm in the Numidians, who awaited the attack full of spirit and resolution. The assault was consequently commenced; the Romans were allowed to act each according to his inclination; some annoyed the enemy with slings and stones from a distance; others came close up to the walls, and attempted to undermine or scale them, desiring to engage in close combat with the besieged. The Zamians, on the other hand, rolled down stones, and hurled burning stakes, javelins[178], and wood smeared with pitch and sulphur, on the nearest assailants.

Nor was caution a sufficient protection to those who kept aloof; for darts, discharged from engines or by the hand, inflicted wounds on most of them; and thus the brave and the timid, though of unequal merit, were exposed to equal danger.

LVIII. While the struggle was thus continued at Zama, Jugurtha, at the head of a large force, suddenly attacked the camp of the Romans, and, through the remissness of those left to guard it, who expected any thing rather than an attack, effected an entrance at one of the gates. Our men, struck with sudden consternation, acted each on his own impulse; some fled, others seized their arms; and many of them were wounded or slain. About forty, however, out of the whole number mindful of the honor of Rome, formed themselves into a body, and took possession of a slight eminence, from which they could not be dislodged by the utmost efforts of the enemy, but hurled back the darts discharged at them, and, as they were few against many, not without execution. If the Numidians came near them, they displayed their courage, and slaughtered, repulsed, and dispersed them, with the greatest fury. Metellus, meanwhile, who was vigorously pursuing the siege, heard a noise, as of enemies, in his rear, and, turning round his horse, perceived a party of soldiers in flight toward him; a certain proof that they were his own men. He instantly, therefore, dispatched the whole of the cavalry to the camp, and immediately afterward Caius Marius, with the cohorts of the allies, entreating him with tears, by their mutual friendship, and by his regard for the public welfare, to allow no stain to rest on a victorious army, and not to let the enemy escape with impunity. Marius soon executed his orders. Jugurtha, in consequence, after being embarrassed in the intrenchments of the camp, while some of his men threw themselves over the ramparts, and others, in their haste, obstructed each other at the gates, fled, with considerable loss, to his strongholds, Metellus, not succeeding in his attempt on the town, retired with his forces, at the approach of night, into his camp.

LIX. On the following day, before he marched out to resume the siege, he ordered the whole of his cavalry to take their station before the camp, on the side where the approach of Jugurtha was to be apprehended; assigning the gates, and adjoining posts, to the charge of the tribunes. He then marched toward the town, and commenced an assault upon the walls as on the day before. Jugurtha, meanwhile, issuing from his concealment, suddenly attacked our men in the camp, of whom those stationed in advance were for the moment alarmed and thrown into confusion; but the rest soon came to their support; nor would the Numidians have longer maintained their ground, had not their foot, which were mingled with the cavalry, done great execution in the struggle; for the horse, relying on the infantry, did not, as is common in actions of cavalry, charge and then retreat, but pressed impetuously forward, disordering and breaking the ranks, and thus, with the aid of the light-armed foot, almost succeeded in giving the army a defeat[179].

LX. The conflict at Zama, at the same time, was continued with great fury. Wherever any lieutenant or tribune commanded, there the men exerted themselves with the utmost vigor. No one seemed to depend for support on others, but every one on his own exertions. The townsmen, on the other side, showed equal spirit. Attacks, or preparations for defense, were made in all quarters[180]. All appeared more eager to wound their enemies than to protect themselves. Shouts, mingled with exhortations, cries of joy, and the clashing of arms, resounded through the heavens. Darts flew thick on every side. If the besiegers, however, in the least relaxed their efforts, the defenders of the walls immediately turned their attention to the distant engagement of the cavalry; they were to be seen sometimes exhibiting joy, and sometimes apprehension, according to the varying fortune of Jugurtha, and, as if they could be heard or seen by their friends, uttering warnings or exhortations, making signs with their hands, and moving their bodies to and fro, like men avoiding or hurling darts. This being noticed by Marius, who commanded on that side of the town, he artfully relaxed his efforts, as if despairing of success, and allowed the besieged to view the battle at the camp unmolested. Then, while their attention was closely fixed on their countrymen, he made a vigorous assault on the wall, and the soldiers mounting their scaling ladders, had almost gained the top, when the townsmen rushed to the spot in a body, and hurled down upon them stones, firebrands, and every description of missiles. Our men made head against these annoyances for a while, but at length, when some of the ladders were broken, and those who had mounted them dashed to the ground, the rest of the assailants retreated as they could, a few indeed unhurt, but the greater number miserably wounded. Night put an end to the efforts of both parties.

LXI. When Metellus saw that all his attempts were vain; that the town was not to be taken; that Jugurtha was resolved to abstain from fighting, except from an ambush, or on his own ground, and that the summer was now far advanced, he withdrew his army from Zama, and placed garrisons in such of the cities that had revolted to him as were sufficiently strong in situation or fortifications. The rest of his forces he settled in winter quarters, in that part of our province nearest to Numidia[181].

This season of repose, however, he did not, like other commanders, abandon to idleness and luxury; but as the war had been but slowly advanced by fighting, he resolved to try the effect of treachery on the king through his friends, and to employ their perfidy instead of arms. He accordingly addressed himself with large promises, to Bomilcar, the same nobleman who had been with Jugurtha at Rome, and who had fled from thence, notwithstanding he had given bail, to escape being tried for the murder of Massiva; selecting this person for his instrument, because, from his great intimacy with Jugurtha, he had the best opportunities of betraying him. He prevailed on him, in the first place, to come to a conference with him privately, when, having given him his word, "that, if he should deliver up Jugurtha, alive or dead, the senate would grant him a pardon, and the full possession of his property," he easily brought him over to his purpose, especially as he was naturally faithless, and also apprehensive that, if peace were made with the Romans, he himself would be surrendered to justice by the terms of it.

LXII. Bomilcar took the earliest opportunity of addressing Jugurtha, at a time when he was full of anxiety, and lamenting his ill success. He exhorted and implored him, with tears in his eyes, to take at length some thought for himself and his children, as well as for the people of Numidia, who had so much claim upon him. He reminded him that they had been, defeated in every battle; that the country was laid waste; that numbers of his subjects had been captured or slain; that the resources of the kingdom were greatly reduced; that the valor of his soldiers, and his own fortune, had been already sufficiently tried; and that he should beware, lest, if he delayed to consult for his people, his people should consult for themselves. By these and similar appeals, he prevailed with Jugurtha to think of a surrender. Embassadors were accordingly sent to the Roman general, announcing that Jugurtha was ready to submit to whatever he should desire, and to trust himself and his kingdom unconditionally to his honor. Metellus, on receiving this statement, summoned such of his officers as were of senatorial rank, from their winter quarters; of whom, with, others whom he thought eligible, he formed a council. By a resolution of this assembly, in conformity with ancient usage, he demanded of Jugurtha, through his embassadors, two hundred thousand pounds' weight of silver, all his elephants, and a portion of his horses and arms. These requisitions being immediately complied with, he next desired that all the deserters should be brought to him in chains. A large number of them were accordingly brought; but a few, when the surrender first began to be mentioned, had fled into Mauretania to king Bocchus.

When Jugurtha, however, after being thus despoiled of arms, men and money, was summoned to appear in person at Tisidium[182], to await the consul's commands, he began again to change his mind, dreading, from a consciousness of guilt, the punishment due to his crimes. Having spent several days in hesitation, sometimes, from disgust at his ill success, believing any thing better than war, and sometimes considering with himself how grievous would be the fall from sovereignty to slavery, he at last determined, notwithstanding that he had lost so many and so valuable means of resistance, to commence hostilities anew.

At Rome, meanwhile, the senate, having been consulted about the provinces, had decreed Numidia to Metellus.

LXIII. About the same time, as Caius Marius, who happened to be at Utica, was sacrificing to the gods[183], an augur told him that great and wonderful things were presaged to him; that he might therefore pursue whatever designs he had formed, trusting to the gods for success; and that he might try fortune as often as he pleased, for that all his undertakings would prosper. Previously to this period an ardent longing for the consulship had possessed him; and he had, indeed, every qualification for obtaining it, except antiquity of family; he had industry, integrity, great knowledge of war, and a spirit undaunted in the field; he was temperate in private life, superior to pleasure and riches, and ambitious only of glory. Having been born at Arpinum, and brought up there during his boyhood, he employed himself, as soon as he was of age to bear arms, not in the study of Greek eloquence, nor in learning the refinements of the city, but in military service; and thus, amid the strictest discipline, his excellent genius soon attained full vigor. When he solicited the people, therefore, for the military tribuneship, he was well known by name, though most were strangers to his face, and unanimously elected by the tribes. After this office he attained others in succession, and conducted himself so well in his public duties, that he was always deemed worthy of a higher station than he had reached. Yet, though such had been his character hitherto (for he was afterward carried away by ambition), he had not ventured to stand for the consulship. The people, at that time, still disposed of[184] other civil offices, but the nobility transmitted the consulship from hand to hand among themselves. Nor had any commoner appeared, however famous or distinguished by his achievements, who would not have been thought unworthy of that honor, and, as it were, a disgrace to it[185].

LXIV. But when Marius found that the words of the augur pointed in the same direction as his own inclinations prompted him, he requested of Metellus leave of absence, that he might offer himself a candidate for the consulship. Metellus, though eminently distinguished by virtue, honor, and other qualities valued by the good, had yet a haughty and disdainful spirit, the common failing of the nobility. He was at first, therefore, astonished at so extraordinary an application, expressed surprise at Marius's views, and advised him, as if in friendship, "not to indulge such unreasonable expectations, or elevate his thoughts above his station; that all things were not to be coveted by all men; that his present condition ought to satisfy him; and, finally, that he should be cautious of asking from the Roman people what they might justly refuse him." Having made these and similar remarks, and finding that the resolution of Marius was not at all affected by them, he told him "that he would grant what he desired as soon as the public business would allow him".[186] On Marius repeating his request several times afterward, he is reported to have said, "that he need not be in a hurry to go, as he would be soon enough if he became a candidate with his own son."[187] Metellus's son was then on service in the camp with his father[188], and was about twenty years old.

This taunt served only to rouse the feelings of Marius, as well for the honor at which he aimed, as against Metellus. He suffered himself to be actuated, therefore, by ambition and resentment, the worst of counselors. He omitted nothing henceforward, either in deeds or words, that could increase his own popularity. He allowed the soldiers, of whom he had the command in the winter quarters, more relaxation of discipline than he had ever granted them before. He talked of the war among the merchants, of whom there was a great number at Utica, censoriously with respect to Metellus, and vauntingly with regard to himself; saying "that if but half of the army were granted him, he would in a few days have Jugurtha in chains; but that the war was purposely protracted by the consul, because, being a man of vanity and regal pride, he was too fond of the delights of power." All these assertions appeared the more credible to the merchants, as, by the long continuance of the war, they had suffered in their fortunes; and to impatient minds no haste is sufficient.

LXV. There was then in our army a Numidian named Gauda, the son of Mastanabal, and grandson of Masinissa, whom Micipsa, in his will, had appointed next heir to his immediate successors. This man had been debilitated by ill-health, and, from the effect of it, was somewhat impaired in his understanding. He had petitioned Metellus to allow him a seat, like a prince, next to himself, and a troop of horse for a bodyguard; but Metellus had refused him both; the seat, because it was granted only to those whom the Roman people had addressed as kings, and the guard, because it would be an indignity to Roman cavalry to act as guards to a Numidian. While Gauda was discontented at these refusals, Marius paid him a visit, and prompted him, with his assistance, to seek revenge for the affronts put upon him by the general; inflating his mind, which was as weak as his body,[189] with flattering speeches, telling him that he was a prince, a great man, and the grandson of Masinissa; that if Jugurtha were taken or killed, he would immediately become king of Numidia; and that this event might soon happen, if he himself were sent as consul to the war.

Thus partly the influence of Marius himself, and partly the hope of obtaining peace, induced Gauda, as well as most of the Roman knights, both soldiers and merchants,[190] to write to their friends at Rome, in a style of censure, respecting Metellus's management of the war, and to intimate that Marius should be appointed general. The consulship, accordingly, was solicited for him by numbers of people, with the most honorable demonstrations in his favor.[191] It happened that the people too, at this juncture, having just triumphed over the nobility by the Mamilian law,[192] were eager to raise commoners to office. Hence every thing was favorable to Marius's views.

LXVI. Jugurtha, meantime, who, after relinquishing his intention to surrender, had renewed the war, was now hastening the preparations for it with the utmost diligence. He assembled an army; he endeavored, by threats or promises, to recover the towns that had revolted from him; he fortified advantageous positions;[193] he repaired or purchased arms, weapons, and other necessaries, which he had given up on the prospect of peace; he tried to seduce the slaves of the Romans, and even tempted with bribes the Romans themselves who occupied the garrisons; he, indeed, left nothing untried or neglected, but put every engine in motion.

Induced by the entreaties of their king, from whom, indeed, they had never been alienated in affection, the leading inhabitants of Vacca, a city in which Metellus, when Jugurtha began to treat for peace, had placed a garrison, entered into a conspiracy against the Romans. As for the common people of the town, they were, as is generally the case, and especially among the Numidians, of a fickle disposition, factious and turbulent, and therefore already desirous of a change, and adverse to peace and quiet. Having arranged their plans, they fixed upon the third day following for the execution of them, because that day, being a festival, celebrated throughout Africa, would promise merriment and dissipation rather than alarm. When the time came, they invited the centurions and military tribunes, with Titus Turpilius Silanus, the governor of the town, to their several houses, and butchered them all, except Turpilius, at their banquets; and then fell upon the common soldiers, who, as was to be expected on such a day, when discipline was relaxed, were wandering about without their arms. The populace followed the example of their chiefs, some of them having been previously instructed to do so, and others induced by a liking for such disorders, and, though ignorant of what had been done or intended, finding sufficient gratification in tumult and variety.

LXVII. The Roman soldiers, perplexed with sudden alarm, and not knowing what was best for them to do, were in trepidation. At the citadel,[194] where their standards and shields were, was posted a guard of the enemy; and the city-gates, previously closed, prevented escape. Women and children, too, on the roofs of the houses,[195] hurled down upon them, with great eagerness, stones and whatever else their position furnished. Thus neither could such twofold danger be guarded against, nor could the bravest resist the feeblest; the worthy and the worthless, the valiant and the cowardly, were alike put to death unavenged. In the midst of this slaughter, while the Numidians were exercising every cruelty, and the town was closed on all sides, Turpilius was the only one, of all the Italians, that escaped unhurt. Whether his flight was the consequence of compassion in his entertainer, of compact, or of chance, I have never discovered; but since, in such a general massacre, he preferred inglorious safety to an honorable name, he seems to have been a worthless and infamous character.[196]

LXVIII. When Metellus heard of what had happened at Vacca, he retired for a time, overpowered with sorrow, from the public gaze; but at length, as indignation mingled with his grief, he hastened, with the utmost spirit, to take vengeance for the outrage. He led forth, at sunset, the legion that was in winter quarters with him, and as many Numidian horse as he could, and arrived, about the third hour on the following day, at a certain plain surrounded by rising grounds. Here he acquainted the soldiers, who were now exhausted with the length of their march, and averse to further exertion,[197] that the town of Vacca was not above a mile distant, and that it became them to bear patiently the toil that remained, with the hope of exacting revenge for their countrymen, the bravest and most unfortunate of men. He likewise generously promised them the whole of the plunder. Their courage being thus revived, he ordered them to resume their march, the cavalry maintaining an extended line in front, and the infantry, with their standards concealed, keeping the closest order behind.

LXIX. The people of Vacca, perceiving an army coming toward them, judged rightly at first that it was Metellus, and shut their gates; but, after a while, when they saw that their fields were not laid waste, and that the front consisted of Numidian cavalry, they imagined that it was Jugurtha, and went out with great joy to meet him. A signal being immediately given, both cavalry and infantry commenced an attack; some cut down the multitude pouring from the town, others hurried to the gates, others secured the towers, revenge and the hope of plunder prevailing over their weariness. Thus Vacca triumphed only two days in its treachery; the whole city, which was great and opulent, was given up to vengeance and spoliation. Turpilius, the governor, whom we mentioned as the only person that escaped, was summoned by Metellus to answer for his conduct, and not being able to clear himself, was condemned, as a native of Latium,[198] to be scourged and put to death.

LXX. About this time, Bomilcar, at whose persuasion Jugurtha had entered upon the capitulation which he had discontinued through fear, being distrusted by the king, and distrusting him in return, grew desirous of a change of government. He accordingly meditated schemes for Jugurtha's destruction, racking his invention night and day. At last, to leave nothing untried, he sought an accomplice in Nabdalsa, a man of noble birth and great wealth, who was in high regard and favor with his countrymen, and who, on most occasions, used to command a body of troops distinct from those of the king, and to transact all business to which Jugurtha, from fatigue, or from being occupied with more important matters, was unable to attend;[199] employments by which he had gained both honors and wealth. By these two men in concert, a day was fixed for the execution of their treachery; succeeding matters they agreed to settle as the exigences of the moment might require. Nabdalsa then proceeded to join his troops, which he kept in readiness, according to orders, among the winter quarters of the Romans,[200] to prevent the country from being ravaged by the enemy with impunity.

But as Nabdalsa, growing alarmed at the magnitude of the undertaking, failed to appear at the appointed time, and allowed his fears to hinder their plans, Bomilcar, eager for their execution, and disquieted at the timidity of his associate, lest he should relinquish his original intentions and adopt some new course, sent him a letter by some confidential person, in which he "reproached him with pusillanimity and irresolution, and conjured him by the gods, by whom he had sworn, not to turn the offers of Metellus to his own destruction;" assuring him "that the fall of Jugurtha was approaching; that the only thing to be considered was whether he should perish by their hand or by that of Metellus; and that, in consequence, he might consider whether to choose rewards, or death by torture."

LXXI. It happened that when this letter was brought, Nabdalsa, overcome with fatigue, was reposing on his couch, where, after reading Bomilcar's letter, anxiety at first, and afterward, as is usual with a troubled mind, sleep overpowered him. In his service there was a certain Numidian, the manager of his affairs, a person who possessed his confidence and esteem, and who was acquainted with all his designs except the last. He, hearing that a letter had arrived, and supposing that there would be occasion, as usual, for his assistance or suggestions, went into the tent, and, while his master was asleep, took up the letter thrown carelessly upon the cushion behind his head,[201] and read it; and, having thus discovered the plot, set off in haste to Jugurtha. Nabdalsa, who awoke soon after, missing the letter, and hearing of the whole affair, and how it had happened, at first attempted to pursue the informer, but finding that pursuit was vain, he went himself to Jugurtha to try to appease him; saying that the disclosure which he intended to make, had been anticipated by the perfidy of his servant; and beseeching him with tears, by his friendship, and by his own former proofs of fidelity, not to think that he could be guilty of such treachery.

LXXII. To these entreaties the king replied with a mildness far different from his real feelings. After putting to death Bomilcar, and many others whom he knew to be privy to the plot, he refrained from any further manifestation of resentment, lest an insurrection should be the consequence of it. But after this occurrence he had no peace either by day or by night; he thought himself safe neither in any place, nor with any person, nor at any time; he feared his subjects and his enemies alike; he was always on the watch, and was startled at every sound; he passed the night sometimes in one place, and sometimes in another, and often in places little suited to royal dignity; and sometimes, starting from his sleep, he would seize his arms and raise an alarm. He was indeed so agitated by extreme terror, that he appeared under the influence of madness.

LXXIII. Metellus, hearing from some deserters of the fate of Bomilcar, and the discovery of the conspiracy, made fresh preparations for action, and with the utmost dispatch, as if entering upon an entirely new war. Marius, who was still importuning him for leave of absence, he allowed to go home; thinking that as he served with reluctance, and bore him personal enmity, he was not likely to prove a very useful officer.

The common people at Rome, having learned the contents of the letters written from Africa concerning Metellus and Marius, had listened to the accounts given of both with eagerness. But the noble birth of Metellus, which had previously been a motive for paying him honor, had now become a cause of unpopularity; while the obscurity of Marius's origin had procured him favor. In regard to both, however, party feeling had more influence than the good or bad qualities of either. The factious tribunes,[202] too, inflamed the populace, charging Metellus, in their harangues, with offenses worthy of death, and exaggerating the excellent qualities of Marius. At length the people were so excited that all the artisans and rustics, whose whole subsistence and credit depended on their labor, quitting their several employments, attended Marius in crowds, and thought less of their own wants than of his exaltation. Thus the nobility being borne down, the consulship, after the lapse of many years,[203] was once more given to a man of humble birth. And afterward, when the people were asked by Manilius Mancinus, one of their tribunes, whom they would appoint to carry on the war against Jugurtha, they, in a full assembly, voted it to Marius. The senate had previously decreed it to Metellus; but that decree was thus rendered abortive.[204]

LXXIV. During this period, Jugurtha, as he was bereft of his friends (of whom he had put to death the greater number, while the rest, under the influence of terror, had fled partly to the Romans, and partly to Bocchus), as the war, too, could not be carried on without officers, and as he thought it dangerous to try the faith of new ones after such perfidy among the old, was involved in doubt and perplexity; no scheme, no counsel, no person could satisfy him; he changed his route and his captains daily; he hurried sometimes against the enemy, and sometimes toward the deserts; depended at one time on flight, and at another on resistance; and was unable to decide whether he could less trust the courage or the fidelity of his subjects. Thus, to whatever direction he turned his thoughts, the prospect was equally disheartening.

In the midst of his irresolution, Metellus suddenly made his appearance with his army. The Numidians were assembled and drawn up by Jugurtha, as well as time permitted; and a battle was at once commenced. Where the king commanded in person, the struggle was maintained for some time; but the rest of his force was routed and put to flight at the first onset. The Romans took a considerable number of standards and arms, but not many prisoners; for, in almost every battle, their feet afforded more security to the Numidians than their swords.

LXXV. In consequence of this defeat, Jugurtha, feeling less confidence in the state of his affairs than ever, retreated with the deserters, and part of his cavalry, first into the deserts, and afterward to Thala,[205] a large and opulent city, where lay the greater portion of his treasures, and where there was magnificent provision for the education of his children. When Metellus was informed of this, although he knew that there was, between Thala and the nearest river, a dry and desert region fifty miles broad, yet, in the hope of finishing the war if he should gain possession of the town, he resolved to surmount all difficulties, and to conquer even Nature herself. He gave orders that the beasts of burden, therefore, should be lightened of all the baggage excepting ten days' provision; and that they should be laden with skins and other utensils for holding water. He also collected from the fields as many laboring cattle as he could find, and loaded them with vessels of all sorts, but chiefly wooden, taken from the cottages of the Numidians. He directed such of the neighboring people, too, as had submitted to him after the retreat of Jugurtha, to bring him as much water as they could carry, appointing a time and a place for them to be in attendance. He then loaded his beasts from the river, which, as I have intimated, was the nearest water to the town, and, thus provided, set out for Thala.

When he came to the place at which he had desired the Numidians to meet him, and had pitched and fortified his camp, so copious a fall of rain is said to have happened, as would have furnished more than sufficient water for his whole army. Provisions, too, were brought him far beyond his expectations; for the Numidians, like most people after a recent surrender, had done more than was required of them. [206] The men, however, from a religious feeling, preferred using the rain-water; the fall of which greatly increased their courage, for they thought of themselves the peculiar care of the gods. On the next day, to the surprise of Jugurtha, they arrived at Thala. The inhabitants, who thought themselves secured by difficulties of the approach to them, were astonished at so strange and unexpected a sight, but, nevertheless, prepared for their defense. Our men showed equal alacrity on their side.

LXXVI. But Jugurtha himself, believing that Metellus, who, by his exertions, had triumphed over every obstacle, over arms, deserts, seasons, and finally over Nature herself that controls all, nothing was impossible, fled with his children, and a great portion of his treasure, from the city during the night. Nor did he ever, after this time, continue[207] more than one day or night in any place; pretending to be hurried away by business, but in reality dreading treachery, which he thought he might escape by change of residence, as schemes of such a kind are the result of leisure and opportunity.

Metellus, seeing that the people of Thala were determined on resistance, and that the town was defended both by art and situation, surrounded the walls with a rampart and a trench. He then directed his machines against the most eligible points, threw up a mound, and erected towers upon it to protect[208] the works and the workmen. The townsmen, on the other hand, were exceedingly active and diligent; and nothing was neglected on either side. At last the Romans, though exhausted with much previous fatigue and fighting, got possession, forty days after their arrival, of the town, and the town only; for all the spoil had been destroyed by the deserters; who, when they saw the walls shaken by the battering-ram, and their own situation desperate, had conveyed the gold and silver, and whatever else is esteemed valuable, to the royal palace, where, after being sated with wine and luxuries, they destroyed the treasures, the building, and themselves, by fire, and thus voluntarily submitted to the sufferings which, in case of being conquered, they dreaded at the hands of the enemy.

LXXVII. At the very time that Thala was taken, there came to Metellus embassadors from the city of Leptis,[209] requesting him to send them a garrison and a governor; saying "that a certain Hamilcar, a man of rank, and of a factious disposition, against whom the magistrates and the laws were alike powerless, was trying to induce them to change sides; and that unless he attended to the matter promptly, their own safety,[210] and the allies of Rome, would be in the utmost danger." For the people at Leptis, at the very commencement of the war with Jugurtha, had sent to the consul Bestia, and afterward to Rome, desiring to be admitted into friendship and alliance with us. Having been granted their request, they continued true and faithful adherents to us, and promptly executed all orders from Bestia, Albinus, and Metellus. They therefore readily obtained from the general the aid which they solicited; and four cohorts of Ligurians were dispatched to Leptis, with Caius Annius to be governor of the place.

LXXVIII. This city was built by a party of Sidonians, who, as I have understood, being driven from their country through civil dissensions, came by sea into those parts of Africa. It is situated between the two Syrtes, which take their name from their nature[211] These are two gulfs almost at the extremity of Africa[212] of unequal size, but of similar character. Those parts of them next to the land are very deep; the other parts sometimes deep and sometimes shallow, as chance may direct; for when the sea swells, and is agitated by the winds, the waves roll along with them mud, sand, and huge stones; and thus the appearance of the gulfs changes with the direction of the wind.

Of this people, the language alone[213] has been altered by their intermarriages with the Numidians; their laws and customs continue for the most part Sidonian; which they have preserved with the greater ease, through living at so great a distance from the king's dominions.[214] Between them and the populous parts of Numidia lie vast and uncultivated deserts.

LXXIX. Since the affairs of Leptis have led me into these regions, it will not be foreign to my subject to relate the noble and singular act of two Carthaginians, which the place has brought to my recollection.

At the time when the Carthaginians were masters of the greater part of Africa, the Cyrenians were also a great and powerful people. The territory that lay between them was sandy, and of a uniform appearance, without a stream or a hill to determine their respective boundaries; a circumstance which involved them in a severe and protracted war. After armies and fleets had been routed and put to flight on both sides, and each people had greatly weakened their opponents, fearing lest some third party should attack both victors and vanquished in a state of exhaustion, they came to an agreement, during a short cessation of arms, "that on a certain day deputies should leave home on either side, and that the spot where they should meet should be the common boundary between the two states." From Carthage, accordingly, were dispatched two brothers, who were named Philaeni,[215] and who traveled with great expedition. The deputies of the Cyrenians proceeded more slowly; but whether from indolence or accident I have not been informed. However, a storm of wind in these deserts will cause obstruction to passengers not less than at sea; for when a violent blast, sweeping over a level surface devoid of vegetation,[216] raises the sand from the ground, it is driven onward with great force, and fills the mouth and eyes of the traveler, and thus, by hindering his view, retards his progress. The Cyrenian deputies, finding that they had lost ground, and dreading punishment at home for their mismanagement, accused the Carthaginians of having left home before the time; quarreling about the matter, and preferring to do any thing rather than submit. The Philaeni, upon this, asked them to name any other mode of settling the controversy, provided it were equitable; and the Cyrenians gave them their choice, "either that they should be buried alive in the spot which they claimed as the boundary for their people, or that they themselves, on the same conditions, should be allowed to go forward to whatever point they should think proper." The Philaeni, having accepted the conditions, sacrificed themselves[217] to the interest of their country, and were interred alive. The people of Carthage consecrated altars to the brothers on the spot; and other honors were instituted to them at home. I now return to my subject.

LXXX. After the loss of Thala, Jugurtha, thinking no place sufficiently secure against Metellus, fled with a few followers into the country of the Getulians, a people savage and uncivilized, and, at that period, unacquainted with even the name of Rome. Of these barbarians he collected a great multitude, and trained them by degrees to march in ranks, to follow standards, to obey the word of command, and to perform other military exercises. He also gained over to his interest, by large presents and larger promises, the intimate friends of king Bocchus, and working upon the king by their means, induced him to commence war against the Romans. This was the more practicable and easy, because Bocchus, at the commencement of hostilities with Jugurtha, had sent an embassy to Rome to solicit friendship and alliance; but a faction, blinded by avarice, and accustomed to sell their votes on every question honorable or dishonorable,[218] had caused his advances to be rejected, though they were of the highest consequence to the war recently begun. A daughter of Bocchus, too, was married to Jugurtha,[219] but such a connection, among the Numidians and Moors, is but lightly regarded; for every man has as many wives as he pleases, in proportion to his ability to maintain them; some ten, others more, but the kings most of all. Thus the affection of the husband is divided among a multitude; no one of them becomes a companion to him,[220] but all are equally neglected.

LXXXI. The two kings, with their armies,[221] met in a place settled by mutual agreement, where, after pledges of amity were given and received, Jugurtha inflamed the mind of Bocchus by observing "that the Romans were a lawless people, of insatiable covetousness, and the common enemies of mankind; that they had the same motive for making war on Bocchus as on himself and other nations, the lust of dominion; that all independent states were objects of hatred to them; at present, for instance, himself; a little before, the Carthaginians had been so, as well as king Perses; and that, in future, as any sovereign became conspicuous for his power, so would he assuredly be treated as an enemy by the Romans."

Induced by these and similar considerations, they determined to march against Cirta, where Metellus had deposited his plunder, prisoners, and baggage. Jugurtha supposed that, if he took the city, there would be ample recompense for his exertions; or that, if the Roman general came to succor his adherents, he would have the opportunity of engaging him in the field. He also hastened this movement from policy, to lessen Bocchus's chance of peace;[222] lest, if delay should be allowed, he should decide upon something different from war.

LXXXII. Metellus, when he heard of the confederacy of the kings, did not rashly, or in every place, give opportunities of fighting, as he had been used to do since Jugurtha had been so often defeated, but, fortifying his camp, awaited the approach of the kings at no great distance from Cirta; thinking it better, when he should have learned something of the Moors,[223] as they were new enemies in the field, to give battle on an advantage. In the mean time he was informed, by letters from Rome, that the province of Numidia was assigned to Marius, of whose election to the consulship he had already heard.

Being affected at these occurrences beyond what was proper and decorous, he could neither restrain his tears nor govern his tongue; for though he was a man eminent in other respects, he had too little firmness in bearing trouble of mind. His irritation was by some imputed to pride; others said that a noble spirit was wounded by insult; many thought him chagrined because victory, just attained, was snatched from his grasp. But to me it is well known that he was more troubled at the honor bestowed on Marius than at the injustice done to himself; and that he would have shown much less uneasiness if the province of which he was deprived had been given to any other than Marius.

LXXXIII. Discouraged, therefore, by such a mortification, and thinking it folly to promote another man's success at his own hazard, he sent deputies to Bocchus, entreating him "not to become an enemy to the Romans without cause;" and observing "that he had a fine opportunity of entering into friendship and alliance with them, which were far preferable to war; that though he might have confidence in his resources, he ought not to change certainties for uncertainties; that a war was easily begun, but discontinued with difficulty; that its commencement and conclusion were not dependent on the same party; that any one, even a coward, might commence hostilities, but that they could be broken off only when the conqueror thought proper; and that he should therefore consult for his interest and that of his kingdom, and not connect his own prosperous circumstances with the ruined fortunes of Jugurtha."

To these representations the king mildly answered, "that he desired peace, but felt compassion for the condition of Jugurtha, to whom if similar proposals were made, all would easily be arranged." Metellus, in reply to this request of Bocchus, sent deputies with overtures, of which the King approved some, and rejected others. Thus, in sending messengers to and fro, the time passed away, and the war, according to the consul's desire, was protracted without being advanced.

LXXXIV. Marius, who, as I said before, had been made consul with great eagerness on the part of the populace, began, though he had always been hostile to the patricians, to inveigh against them, after the people gave him the province of Numidia, with great frequency and violence; he attacked them sometimes individually and sometimes in a body; he said that he had snatched from them the consulship as spoils from vanquished enemies; and uttered other remarks laudatory to himself and offensive to them. Meanwhile he made the provision for the war his chief object; he asked for reinforcements for the legions; he sent for auxiliaries from foreign states, kings, and allies; he also enlisted all the bravest men from Latium, most of whom were known to him by actual service, some few only by report, and induced, by earnest solicitation, even discharged veterans[224] to accompany him. Nor did the senate, though adverse to him, dare to refuse him any thing; the additions to the legions they had voted even with eagerness, because military service was thought to be unpopular with the multitude, and Marius seemed likely to lose either the means of warfare[225], or the favor of the people. But such expectations were entertained in vain, so ardent was the desire of going with Marius that had seized on almost all. Every one cherished the fancy[226] that he should return home laden with spoil, crowned with victory, or attended with some similar good fortune. Marius himself, too, had excited them in no small degree by a speech; for, when all that he required was granted, and he was anxious to commence a levy, he called an assembly of the people, as well to encourage them to enlist, as to inveigh, according to his practice, against the nobility. He spoke, on the occasion, as follows:

LXXXV. "I am aware, my fellow-citizens, that most men do not appear as candidates before you for an office, and conduct themselves in it when they have obtained it, under the same character; that they are at first industrious, humble, and modest, but afterward lead a life of indolence and arrogance. But to me it appears that the contrary should be the case; for as the whole state is of greater consequence than the single office of consulate or praetorship, so its interests ought to be managed[227] with greater solicitude than these magistracies are sought. Nor am I insensible how great a weight of business I am, through your kindness, called upon to sustain. To make preparations for war, and yet to be sparing of the treasury; to press those into the service whom I am unwilling to offend; to direct every thing at home and abroad; and to discharge these duties when surrounded by the envious, the hostile,[228] and the factious, is more difficult, my fellow-citizens, than is generally imagined. In addition to this, if others fail in their undertakings, their ancient rank, the heroic actions of their ancestors, the power of their relatives and connections, their numerous dependents, are all at hand to support them; but as for me, my whole hopes rest upon myself, which I must sustain by good conduct and integrity; for all other means are unavailing.

I am sensible, too, my fellow-citizens, that the eyes of all men are turned upon me; that the just and good favor me, as my services are beneficial to the state, but that the nobility seek occasion to attack me. I must therefore use the greater exertion, that you may not be deceived in me,[229] and that their views may be rendered abortive. I have led such a life, indeed, from my boyhood to the present hour, that I am familiar with every kind of toil and danger; and that exertion, which, before your kindness to me, I practiced gratuitously, it is not my intention to relax after having received my reward. For those who have pretended to be men of worth only to secure their election,[230] it may be difficult to conduct themselves properly in office: but to me, who have passed my whole life in the most honorable occupations, to act well has from habit become nature.

You have commanded me to carry on the war against Jugurtha; a commission at which the nobility are highly offended. Consider with yourselves, I pray you, whether it would be a change for the better, if you were to send to this, or to any other such appointment, one of yonder crowd of nobles[231], a man of ancient family, of innumerable statues, and of no military experience; in order, forsooth, that in so important an office, and being ignorant of every thing connected with it, he may exhibit hurry and trepidation, and select one of the people to instruct him in his duty. For so it generally happens, that he whom you have chosen to direct, seeks another to direct him. I know some, my fellow-citizens, who, after they have been elected[232] consuls, have begun to read the acts of their ancestors, and the military precepts of the Greeks; persons who invert the order of things;[233] for though to discharge the duties of the office[234] is posterior, in point of time, to election, it is, in reality and practical importance, prior to it.

Compare now, my fellow-citizens, me, who am ***a new man,*** with those haughty nobles.[235] What they have but heard or read, I have witnessed or performed.

What they have learned from books, I have acquired in the field; and whether deeds or words are of greater estimation, it is for you to consider.

They despise my humbleness of birth; I contemn their imbecility. My condition[236] is made an objection to me; their misconduct is a reproach to them. The circumstance of birth,[237] indeed, I consider as one and the same to all; but think that he who best exerts himself is the noblest. And could it be inquired of the fathers,[238] of Albinus and Bestia, whether they would rather be the parents of them or of me, what do you suppose that they would answer, but that they would wish the most deserving to be their offspring! If the patricians justly despise me, let them also despise their own ancestors, whose nobility, like mine, had its origin in merit. They envy me the honor that I have received; let them also envy me the toils, the abstinence,[239] and the perils, by which I obtained that honor.

But they, men eaten up with pride, live as if they disdained all the distinctions that you can bestow, and yet sue for those distinctions as if they had lived so as to merit them. Yet those are assuredly deceived, who expect to enjoy, at the same time, things so incompatible as the pleasures of indolence and the rewards of honorable exertion.[240]

When they speak before you, or in the senate, they occupy the greatest part of their orations in extolling their ancestors;[241] for, they suppose that, by recounting the heroic deeds of their forefathers, they render themselves more illustrious. But the reverse of this is the case; for the more glorious were the lives of their ancestors, the more scandalous is their own inaction. The truth, indeed, is plainly this, that the glory of ancestors sheds a light on their posterity,[242] which suffers neither their virtues nor their vices to be concealed. Of this light, my fellow-citizens, I have no share; but I have, what confers much more distinction, the power of relating my own actions. Consider, then, how unreasonable they are; what they claim to themselves for the merit of others, they will not grant to me for my own; alleging, forsooth, that I have no statues, and that my distinction is newly-acquired; but it is surely better to have acquired such distinction myself than to bring disgrace on that received from others.

I am not ignorant, that, if they were inclined to reply to me, they would make an abundant display of eloquent and artful language. Yet, since they attack both you and myself on occasion of the great favor which you have conferred upon me, I did not think proper to be silent before them, lest any one should construe my forbearance into a consciousness of demerit. As for myself, indeed, nothing that is said of me, I feel assured,[243] can do me injury; for what is true, must of necessity speak in my favor; what is false, my life and character will refute. But since your judgment, in bestowing on me so distinguished an honor and so important a trust, is called in question, consider, I beseech you, again and again, whether you are likely to repent of what you have done. I can not, to raise your confidence in me, boast of the statues, or triumphs, or consulships of my ancestors; but, if it be thought necessary, I can show you spears,[244] a banner,[245] caparisons[246] for horses, and other military rewards; besides the scars of wounds on my breast. These are my statues; this is my nobility; honors, not left, like theirs, by inheritance, but acquired amid innumerable toils and dangers.

My speech, they say, is inelegant; but that I have ever thought of little importance. Worth sufficiently displays itself; it is for my detractors to use studied language, that they may palliate base conduct by plausible words. Nor have I learned Greek; for I had no wish to acquire a tongue that adds nothing to the valor[247] of those who teach it. But I have gained other accomplishments, such as are of the utmost benefit to a state; I have learned to strike down an enemy; to be vigilant at my post;[248] to fear nothing but dishonor; to bear cold and heat with equal endurance; to sleep on the ground; and to sustain at the same time hunger and fatigue. And with such rules of conduct I shall stimulate my soldiers, not treating them with rigor and myself with indulgence, nor making their toils my glory. Such a mode of commanding is at once useful to the state, and becoming to a citizen. For to coerce your troops with severity, while you yourself live at ease, is to be a tyrant, not a general.

It was by conduct such as this, my fellow-citizens, that your ancestors made themselves and the republic renowned. Our nobility, relying on their forefathers' merits, though totally different from them in conduct, disparage us who emulate their virtues; and demand of you every public honor, as due, not to their personal merit, but to their high rank. Arrogant pretenders, and utterly unreasonable! For though their ancestors left them all that was at their disposal, their riches, their statues, and their glorious names, they left them not, nor could leave them, their virtue; which alone, of all their possessions, could neither be communicated nor received.

They reproach me as being mean, and of unpolished manners, because, forsooth, I have but little skill in arranging an entertainment, and keep no actor,[249] nor give my cook[250] higher wages than my steward; all which charges I must, indeed, acknowledge to be just; for I learned from my father, and other venerable characters, that vain indulgences belong to women, and labor to men; that glory, rather than wealth, should be the object of the virtuous; and that arms and armor, not household furniture, are marks of honor. But let the nobility, if they please, pursue what is delightful and dear to them; let them devote themselves to licentiousness and luxury; let them pass their age as they have passed their youth, in revelry and feasting, the slaves of gluttony and debauchery; but let them leave the toil and dust of the field, and other such matters, to us, to whom they are more grateful than banquets. This, however, they will not do; for when these most infamous of men have disgraced themselves by every species of turpitude, they proceed to claim the distinctions due to the most honorable. Thus it most unjustly happens that luxury and indolence, the most disgraceful of vices, are harmless to those who indulge in them, and fatal only to the innocent commonwealth.

As I have now replied to my calumniators, as far as my own character required, though not so fully as their flagitiousness deserved, I shall add a few words on the state of public affairs. In the first place, my fellow-citizens, be of good courage with regard to Numidia; for all that hitherto protected Jugurtha, avarice, inexperience, and arrogance[251], you have entirely removed. There is an army in it, too, which is well acquainted with the country, though, assuredly, more brave than fortunate; for a great part of it has been destroyed by the avarice or rashness of its commanders. Such of you, then, as are of military age, co-operate with me, and support the cause of your country; and let no discouragement, from the ill-fortune of others, or the arrogance of the late commanders, affect any one of you. I myself shall be with you, both on the march and in the battle, both to direct your movements and to share your dangers. I shall treat you and myself on every occasion alike; and, doubtless, with the aid of the gods, all good things, victory, spoil, and glory, are ready to our hands; though, even if they were doubtful or distant, it would still become every able citizen to act in defense of his country. For no man, by slothful timidity, has escaped the lot of mortals[252]; nor has any parent wished for his children[253] that they might live forever, but rather that they might act in life with virtue and honor. I would add more, my fellow-citizens, if words could give courage to the faint-hearted; to the brave I think that I have said enough."

LXXXVI. After having spoken to this effect, Marius, when he found that the minds of the populace were excited, immediately freighted vessels with provisions, pay, arms, and other necessaries, and ordered Aulus Manlius, his lieutenant-general, to set sail with them. He himself, in the mean time, proceeded to enlist soldiers, not after the ancient method, or from the classes[254], but taking all that were willing to join him, and the greater part from the lowest ranks. Some said that this was done from a scarcity of better men, and others from the consul's desire to pay court[255] to the poorer class, because it was by that order of men that he had been honored and promoted; and, indeed, to a man grasping at power, the most needy are the most serviceable, persons to whom their property (as they have none) is not an object of care, and to whom every thing lucrative appears honorable. Setting out, accordingly, for Africa, with a somewhat larger force than had been decreed, he arrived in a few days at Utica. The command of the army was resigned to him by Publius Rutilius, Metullus's lieutenant-general; for Metullus himself avoided the sight of Marius, that he might not see what he could not even endure to hear mentioned.

LXXXVII. Marius, having filled up his legions[256] and auxiliary cohorts, marched into a part of the country which was fertile and abundant in spoil, where, whatever he captured, he gave up to his soldiers. He then attacked such fortresses or towns as were ill defended by nature or with troops, and ventured on several engagements, though only of a light character, in different places. The new recruits, in process of time, began to join in an encounter without fear; they saw that such as fled were taken prisoners or slain; that the bravest were the safest; that liberty, their country, and parents,[257] are defended, and glory and riches acquired, by arms. Thus the new and old troops soon became as one body, and the courage of all was rendered equal.

The two kings, when they heard of the approach of Marius, retreated, by separate routes, into parts that were difficult of access; a plan which had been proposed by Jugurtha, who hoped that, in a short time, the enemy might be attacked when dispersed over the country, supposing that the Roman soldiers, like the generality of troops, would be less careful and observant of discipline when the fear of danger was removed.

LXXXVIII. Metellus, meanwhile, having taken his departure for Rome, was received there, contrary to his expectation, with the greatest feelings of joy, being equally welcomed, since public prejudice had subsided, by both the people and the patricians.

Marius continued to attend, with equal activity and prudence, to his own affairs and those of the enemy. He observed what would be advantageous, or the contrary, to either party; he watched the movements of the kings, counteracted their intentions and stratagems, and allowed no remissness in his own army, and no security in that of the enemy. He accordingly attacked and dispersed, on several occasions, the Getulians and Jugurtha on their march, as they were carrying off spoil from our allies;[258] and he obliged the king himself, near the town of Cirta, to take flight without his arms[259] But finding that such enterprises merely gained him honor, without tending to terminate the war, he resolved on investing, one after another, all the cities, which, by the strength of their garrisons or situation, were best suited either to support the enemy, or to resist himself; so that Jugurtha would either be deprived of his fortresses, if he suffered them to be taken, or be forced to come to an engagement in their defense. As to Bocchus, he had frequently sent messengers to Marius, saying that he desired the friendship of the Roman people, and that the consul need fear no act of hostility from him. But whether he merely dissembled, with a view to attack us unexpectedly with greater effect, or whether, from fickleness of disposition he habitually wavered between war and peace, was never fairly ascertained.

LXXXIX. Marius, as he had determined, proceeded to attack the fortified towns and places of strength, and to detach them, partly by force, and partly by threats or offers of reward, from the enemy. His operations in this way, however, were at first but moderate; for he expected that Jugurtha, to protect his subjects, would soon come to an engagement. But finding that he kept at a distance, and was intent on other affairs, he thought it was time to enter upon something of greater importance and difficulty. Amid the vast deserts there lay a great and strong city, named Capsa, the founder of which is said to have been the Libyan Hercules.[260] Its inhabitants were exempted from taxes by Jugurtha, and under mild government, and were consequently regarded as the most faithful of his subjects. They were defended against enemies, not only by walls, magazines of arms, and bodies of troops, but still more by the difficulty of approaching them; for, except the parts adjoining the walls, all the surrounding country is waste and uncultivated, destitute of water, and infested with serpents, whose fierceness, like that of other wild animals, is aggravated by want of food; while the venom of such reptiles, deadly in itself, is exacerbated by nothing so much as by thirst. Of this place Marius conceived a strong desire[261] to make himself master, not only from its importance for the war, but because its capture seemed an enterprise of difficulty; for Metellus had gained great glory by taking Thala, a town similarly situated and fortified; except that at Thala there were several springs near the walls, while the people of Capsa had only one running stream, and that within the town, all the water which they used beside being rain-water. But this scarcity, both here and in other parts of Africa, where the people live rudely and remote from the sea, was endured with the greater ease, as the inhabitants subsist mostly on milk and wild beasts' flesh,[262] and use no salt, or other provocatives of appetite, their food being merely to satisfy hunger or thirst, and not to encourage luxury or excess.

XC. The consul,[263] having made all necessary investigations, and relying, I suppose, on the gods (for against such difficulties he could not well provide by his own forethought, as he was also straitened for want of corn, because the Numidians apply more to pasturage than agriculture, and had conveyed, by the king's order, whatever corn had been raised into fortified places, while the ground at the time, it being the end of summer, was parched and destitute of vegetation), yet, under the circumstances, conducted his arrangements with great prudence. All the cattle, which had been taken for some days previous, he consigned to the care[264] of the auxiliary cavalry; and directed Aulus Manlius, his lieutenant-general, to proceed with the light-armed cohorts to the town of Lares,[265] where he had deposited provisions and pay for the army, telling him that, after plundering the country, he would join him there in a few days. Having by this means concealed his real design, he proceeded toward the river Tana.

XCI. On his march he distributed daily, to each division of the infantry and cavalry, an equal portion of the cattle, and gave orders that water-bottles should be made of their hides; thus compensating, at once, for the scarcity of corn, and providing, while all remained ignorant of his intention, utensils which would soon be of service. At the end of six days, accordingly, when he arrived at the river, a large number of bottles had been prepared. Having pitched his camp, with a slight fortification, he ordered his men to take refreshment, and to be ready to resume their march at sunset; and, having laid aside all their baggage, to load themselves and their beasts only with water. As soon as it seemed time, he quitted the camp, and, after marching the whole night,[266] encamped again.

The same course he pursued on the following night, and on the third, long before dawn, he reached a hilly spot of ground, not more than two miles distant from Capsa, where he waited, as secretly as possible, with his whole force. But when daylight appeared, and many of the Numidians, having no apprehensions of an enemy, went forth out of the town, he suddenly ordered all the cavalry, and with them the lightest of the infantry, to hasten forward to Capsa, and secure the gates. He himself immediately followed, with the utmost ardor, restraining his men from plunder.

When the inhabitants perceived that the place was surprised, their state of consternation and extreme dread, the suddenness of the calamity, and the consideration that many of their fellow-citizens were without the walls in the power of the enemy, compelled them to surrender. The town, however, was burned; of the Numidians, such as were of adult age, were put to the sword; the rest were sold, and the spoil divided among the soldiers. This severity, in violation of the usages of war, was not adopted from avarice or cruelty in the consul, but was exercised because the place was of great advantage to Jugurtha, and difficult of access to us, while the inhabitants were a fickle and faithless race, to be influenced neither by kindness nor by terror.

XCII. When Marius had achieved so important an enterprise, without any loss to his troops, he who was great and honored before became still greater and still more honored. All his undertakings,[267] however ill-concerted, were regarded as proofs of superior ability; his soldiers, kept under mild discipline, and enriched with spoil, extolled him to the skies; the Numidians dreaded him as some thing more than human; and all, indeed, allies as well as enemies, believed that he was either possessed of supernatural power, or had all things directed for him by the will of the gods.

After his success in this attempt, he proceeded against other towns; a few, where they offered resistance, he took by force; a greater number, deserted in consequence of the wretched fate of Capsa, he destroyed by fire; and the whole country was filled with mourning and slaughter.

Having at length gained possession of many places, and most of them without loss to his army, he turned his thoughts to another enterprise, which, though not of the same desperate character as that at Capsa, was yet not less difficult of execution. [268] Not far from the river Mulucha, which divided the kingdoms of Jugurtha and Bocchus, there stood, in the midst of a plain,[269] a rocky hill, sufficiently broad at the top for a small fort; it rose to a vast height, and had but one narrow ascent left open, the whole of it being as steep by nature as it could have been rendered by labor and art. This place, as there were treasures of the king in it, Marius directed his utmost efforts to take.[270] But his views were furthered more by fortune than by his own contrivance. In the fortress there were plenty of men and arms for its defense, as well as an abundant store of provisions, and a spring of water; while its situation was unfavorable for raising mounds, towers, and other works; and the road to it, used by its inhabitants, was extremely steep, with a precipice on either side. The vineae were brought up with great danger, and without effect; for, before they were advanced any considerable distance, they were destroyed with fire or stones. And from the difficulties of the ground, the soldiers could neither stand in front of the works, nor act among the vineae,[271] without danger; the boldest of them were killed or wounded, and the fear of the rest increased.

XCIII. Marius having thus wasted much time and labor, began seriously to consider whether he should abandon the attempt as impracticable, or wait for the aid of Fortune, whom he had so often found favorable. While he was revolving the matter in his mind, during several days and nights, in a state of much doubt and perplexity, it happened that a certain Ligurian, a private soldier in the auxiliary cohorts,[272] having gone out of the camp to fetch water, observed, near that part of the fort which was furthest from the besiegers, some snails crawling among the rocks, of which, when he had picked up one or two, and afterward more, he gradually proceeded, in his eagerness for collecting them, almost to the top of the hill. When he found this part deserted, a desire, incident to the human mind, of seeing what he had never seen,[273] took violent possession of him. A large oak chanced to grow out among the rocks, at first, for a short distance, horizontally,[274] and then, as nature directs all vegetables,[275] turning and shooting upward. Raising himself sometimes on the boughs of this tree, and sometimes on the projecting rocks, the Ligurian, as all the Numidians were intently watching the besiegers, took a full survey of the platform of the fortress. Having observed whatever he thought it would afterward prove useful to know, he descended the same way, not unobservantly, as he had gone up, but exploring and noticing all the peculiarities of the path. He then hastened to Marius, acquainted him with what he had done, and urged him to attack the fort on that side where he had ascended, offering himself to lead the way and the attempt. Marius sent some of those about him, along with the Ligurian, to examine the practicability of his proposal, who, according to their several dispositions, reported the affair as difficult or easy. The consul's hopes, however, were somewhat encouraged; and he accordingly selected, from his band of trumpeters and bugle-men, five of the most nimble, and with them four centurions for a guard;[276] all of whom he directed to obey the Ligurian, appointing the next day for commencing the experiment.

XCIV. When, according to their instructions, it seemed time to set out, the Ligurian, after preparing and arranging every thing, proceeded to the place of ascent. Those who commanded the centuries,[277] being previously instructed by the guide, had changed their arms and dress, having their heads and feet bare, that their view upward, and their progress among the rocks, might be less impeded;[278] their swords were slung behind them, as well as their shields, which were Numidian, and made of leather, both for the sake of lightness, and in order that, if struck against any object, they might make less noise. The Ligurian went first, and tied to the rocks, and whatever roots of trees projected through age, a number of ropes, by which the soldiers supporting themselves might climb with the greatest ease. Such as were timorous, from the extraordinary nature of the path, he sometimes pulled up by the hand; when the ascent was extremely rugged, he sent them on singly before him without their arms, which he then carried up after them; whatever parts appeared unsafe,[279] he first tried them himself, and, by going up and down repeatedly in the same place, and then standing aside, he inspired the rest with courage to proceed. At length, after uninterrupted and harassing exertion they reached the fortress, which, on that side, was undefended, for all the occupants, as on other days, were intent on the enemy in the opposite quarter.

Though Marius had kept the attention of the Numidians, during the whole day, fixed on his attacks, yet, when he heard from his scouts how the Ligurian had succeeded, he animated his soldiers to fresh exertions, and he himself, advancing beyond the vineae, and causing a testudo to be formed,[280] came up close under the walls, annoying the enemy, at the same time, with his engines, archers, and slingers, from a distance.

But the Numidians, having often before overturned and burned the vineae of the Romans, no longer confined themselves within the fortress, but spent day and night before the walls, railing at the Romans, upbraiding Marius with madness, threatening our soldiers with being made slaves to Jugurtha, and exhibiting the utmost audacity on account of their successful defense. In the mean time, while both the Romans and Numidians were engaged in the struggle, the one side contending for glory and dominion, the other for their very existence, the trumpets suddenly sounded a blast in the rear of the enemy, at which the women and children, who had gone out to view the contest, were the first to flee; next those who were nearest to the wall, and at length the whole of the Numidians, armed and unarmed, retreated within the fort. When this had happened, the Romans pressed upon the enemy with increased boldness, dispersing them, and at first only wounding the greater part, but afterward making their way over the bodies of those who fell, thirsting for glory, and striving who should be first to reach the wall; not a single individual being detained by the plunder. Thus the rashness of Marius, rendered successful by fortune, procured him renown from his very error.

XCV. During the progress of this affair, Lucius Sylla, Marius's quaestor, arrived in the camp with a numerous body of cavalry, which he had been left at Rome to raise among the Latins and allies.

Of so eminent a man, since my subject brings him to my notice, I think it proper to give a brief account of the character and manners; for I shall in no other place allude to his affairs;[281] and Lucius Sisenna,[282] who has treated that subject the most ably and accurately of all writers, seems to me to have spoken with too little freedom. Sylla, then, was of patrician descent, but of a family almost sunk in obscurity by the degeneracy of his forefathers. He was skilled, equally and profoundly, in Greek and Roman literature. He was a man of large mind, fond of pleasure, but fonder of glory. His leisure was spent in luxurious gratifications, but pleasure never kept him from his duties, except that he might have acted more for his honor with regard to his wife[283]. He was eloquent and subtle, and lived on the easiest terms with his friends.[284] His depth of thought in disguising his intentions, was incredible; he was liberal of most things, but especially of money. And though he was the most fortunate [285] of all men before his victory in the civil war, yet his fortune was never beyond his desert;[286] and many have expressed a doubt whether his success or his merit were the greater. As to his subsequent acts, I know not whether more of shame, or of regret must be felt at the recital of them.

XCVI. When Sylla came with his cavalry into Africa, as has just been stated, and arrived at the camp of Marius, though he had hitherto been unskilled and undisciplined in the art of war, he became, in a short time, the most expert of the whole army. He was besides affable to the soldiers; he conferred favors on many at their request, and on others of his own accord, and was reluctant to receive any in return. But he repaid other obligations more readily than those of a pecuniary nature; he himself demanded repayment from no one; but rather made it his object that as many as possible should be indebted to him. He conversed, jocosely as well as seriously, with the humblest of the soldiers; he was their frequent companion at their works, on the march, and on guard. Nor did he ever, as is usual with depraved ambition, attempt to injure the character of the consul, or of any deserving person.

His sole aim, whether in the council or the field, was to suffer none to excel him; to most he was superior. By such conduct he soon became a favorite both with Marius and with the army.

XCVII. Jugurtha, after he had lost the city of Capsa, and other strong and important places, as well as a vast sum of money, dispatched messengers to Bocchus, requesting him to bring his forces into Numidia as soon as possible, and stating that the time for giving battle was at hand. But finding that he hesitated, and was balancing the inducements to peace and war, he again corrupted his confidants, as on a previous occasion, with presents, and promised the Moor himself a third part of Numidia, should either the Romans be driven from Africa, or the war brought to an end without any diminution of his own territories. Being allured by this offer, Bocchus joined Jugurtha with a large force.

The armies of the kings being thus united, they attacked Marius, on his march to his winter quarters, when scarcely a tenth part of the day remained[287], expecting that the night, which was now coming on, would be a shelter to them if they were beaten, and no impediment if they should conquer, as they were well acquainted with the country, while either result would be worse for the Romans in the dark. At the very moment, accordingly, that Marius heard from various quarters[288] of the enemy's approach, the enemy themselves were upon him, and before the troops could either form themselves or collect the baggage, before they could receive even a signal or an order, the Moorish and Getulian horse, not in line, or any regular array of battle, but in separate bodies, as chance had united them, rushed furiously on our men; who, though all struck with a panic, yet, calling to mind what they had done on former occasions, either seized their arms, or protected those who were looking for theirs, while some, springing on their horses, advanced against the enemy. But the whole conflict was more like a rencounter with robbers than a battle; the horse and foot of the enemy, mingled together without standards or order, wounded some of our men, and cut down others, and surprised many in the rear while fighting stoutly with those in front; neither valor nor arms were a sufficient defense, the enemy being superior in numbers, and covering the field on all sides. At last the Roman veterans, who were necessarily well experienced in war,[289] formed themselves, wherever the nature of the ground or chance allowed them to unite, in circular bodies, and thus secured on every side, and regularly drawn up, withstood the attacks of the enemy.

XCVIII. Marius, in this desperate emergency, was not more alarmed or disheartened than on any previous occasion, but rode about with his troop of cavalry, which he had formed of his bravest soldiers rather than his nearest friends, in every quarter of the field, sometimes supporting his own men when giving way, sometimes charging the enemy where they were thickest, and doing service to his troops with his sword, since, in the general confusion, he was unable to command with his voice.

The day had now closed, yet the barbarians abated nothing of their impetuosity, but, expecting that the night would be in their favor, pressed forward, as their kings had directed them, with increased violence. Marius, in consequence, resolved upon a measure suited to his circumstances, and, that his men might have a place of retreat, took possession of two hills contiguous to each other, on one of which, too small for a camp, there was an abundant spring of water, while the other, being mostly elevated and steep, and requiring little fortification, was suited for his purpose as a place of encampment. He then ordered Sylla, with a body of cavalry, to take his station for the night on the eminence containing the spring, while he himself collected his scattered troops by degrees, the enemy being not less disordered[290], and led them all at a quick march[291] up the other hill. Thus the kings, obliged by the strength of the Roman position, were deterred from continuing the combat; yet they did not allow their men to withdraw to a distance, but, surrounding both hills with a large force, encamped without any regular order. Having then lighted numerous fires, the barbarians, after their custom, spent most of the night in merriment, exultation, and tumultuous clamor, the kings, elated at having kept their ground, conducting themselves as conquerors. This scene, plainly visible to the Romans, under cover of the night and on the higher ground, afforded great encouragement to them.

XCIX. Marius, accordingly, deriving much confidence from the imprudence of the enemy, ordered the strictest possible silence to be kept, not allowing even the trumpets, as was usual, to be sounded when the watches were changed;[292] cavalry, and legions, to sound all and then, when day approached, and the enemy were fatigued and just sinking to sleep, he ordered the sentinels, with the trumpeters of the auxiliary cohorts,[293] their instruments at once, and the soldiers, at the same time, to raise a shout, and sally forth from the camp[294] upon the enemy. The Moors and Getulians, suddenly roused by the strange and terrible noise, could neither flee, nor take up arms, could neither act, nor provide for their security, so completely had fear, like a stupor,[295] from the uproar and shouting, the absence of support, the charge of our troops, and the tumult and alarm, seized upon them all. The whole of them were consequently routed and put to flight; most of their arms, and military standards, were taken; and more were killed in this than in all former battles, their escape being impeded by sleep and the sudden alarm.

C. Marius now continued the route, which he had commenced, toward his winter quarters, which, for the convenience of getting provisions, he had determined to fix in the towns on the coast. He was not, however, rendered careless or presumptuous by his victory, but marched with his army in form of a square[296] just as if he were in sight of the enemy. Sylla, with his cavalry, was on the right;

Aulus Manlius, with the slingers and archers, and Ligurian cohorts, had the command on the left; the tribunes, with the light-armed infantry, the consul had placed in the front and rear. The deserters, whose lives were of little value, and who were well acquainted with the country, observed the route of the enemy. Marius himself, too, as if no other were placed in charge, attended to every thing, went through the whole of the troops, and praised or blamed them according to their desert. He was always armed and on the alert, and obliged his men to imitate his example. He fortified his camp with the same caution with which he marched; stationing cohorts of the legions to watch the gates, and the auxiliary cavalry in front, and others upon the rampart and lines. He went round the posts in person, not from suspicion that his orders would not be observed, but that the labor of the soldiers, shared equally by their general, might be endured by them with cheerfulness. [297] Indeed, Marius, as well at this as at other periods of the war, kept his men to their duty rather by the dread of shame[298] than of severity; a course which many said was adopted from desire of popularity, but some thought it was because he took pleasure in toils to which he had been accustomed from his youth, and in exertions which other men call perfect miseries. The public interest, however, was served with as much efficiency and honor as it could have been under the most rigorous command.

CI. At length, on the fourth day of his march, when he was not far from the town of Cirta, his scouts suddenly made their appearance from all quarters at once; a circumstance by which the enemy was known to be at hand. But as they came in from different points, and all gave the same account, the consul, doubting in what form to draw up his army, made no alteration in it, but halted where he was, being already prepared for every contingency. Jugurtha's expectations, in consequence, disappointed him; for he had divided his force into four bodies, trusting that one of them, assuredly,[299] would surprise the Romans in the rear. Sylla, meanwhile, with whom they first came in contact, having cheered on his men, charged the Moors, in person and with his officers,[300] with troop after troop of cavalry, in the closest order possible; while the rest of his force, retaining their position, protected themselves against the darts thrown from a distance, and killed such of the enemy as fell into their hands.

While the cavalry was thus engaged, Bocchus, with his infantry, which his son Volux had brought up, and which, from delay on their march, had not been present in the former battle, assailed the Romans in the rear. Marius was at that moment occupied in front, as Jugurtha was there with his largest force. The Numidian king, hearing of the arrival of Bocchus, wheeled secretly about, with a few of his followers, to the infantry,[301] and exclaimed in Latin, which he had learned to speak at Numantia, "that our men wore struggling in vain; for that he had just slain Marius with his own hand;" showing, at the same time, his sword besmeared with blood, which he had, indeed, sufficiently stained by vigorously cutting down our infantry[302].

When the soldiers heard this, they felt a shock, though rather at the horror of such an event, than from belief in him who asserted it; the barbarians, on the other hand, assumed fresh courage, and advanced with greater fury on the disheartened Romans, who were just on the point of taking to flight, when Sylla, having routed those to whom he had been opposed, fell upon the Moors in the flank. Bocchus instantly fled. Jugurtha, anxious to support his men, and to secure a victory so nearly won, was surrounded by our cavalry, and all his attendants, right and left, being slain, had to force a way alone, with great difficulty, through the weapons of the enemy. Marius, at the same time, having put to flight the cavalry, came up to support such of his men as he had understood to be giving ground. At last the enemy were defeated in every quarter. The spectacle on the open plains was then frightful;[303] some were pursuing, others fleeing; some were being slain, others captured; men and horses were dashed to the earth; many, who were wounded, could neither flee nor remain at rest, attempting to rise, and instantly falling back; and the whole field, as far as the eye could reach, was strewed with arms and dead bodies, and the intermediate spaces saturated with blood.

CII. At length the consul, now indisputably victor, arrived at the town of Cirta, whither he had at first intended to go. To this place, on the fifth day after the second defeat of the barbarians, came messengers from Bocchus, who, in the king's name, requested of Marius to send him two persons in whom he had full confidence, as he wished to confer with them on matters concerning both the interest of the Roman people and his own. Marius immediately dispatched Sylla and Aulus Manlius; who, though they went at the king's invitation, thought proper, notwithstanding, to address him first, in the hope of altering his sentiments, if he were unfavorable to peace, or of strengthening his inclination, if he were disposed to it. Sylla, therefore, to whose superiority, not in years but in eloquence, Manlius yielded precedence, spoke to Bocchus briefly as follows:

"It gives us great pleasure, King Bocchus, that the gods have at length induced a man, so eminent as yourself, to prefer peace to war, and no longer to stain your own excellent character by an alliance with Jugurtha, the most infamous of mankind; and to relieve us, at the same time, from the disagreeable necessity of visiting with the same punishment your errors and his crimes. Besides, the Roman people, even from the very infancy[304] of their state, have thought it better to seek friends than slaves, thinking it safer to rule over willing than forced subjects. But to you no friendship can be more suitable than ours; for, in the first place, we are at a distance from you, on which account there will be the less chance of misunderstanding between us, while our good feeling for you will be as strong as if we were near; and, secondly, because, though we have subjects in abundance, yet neither we, nor any other nation, can ever have a sufficiency of friends. Would that such had been your inclination from the first; for then you would assuredly, before this time, have received from the Roman people more benefits than you have now suffered evils. But since Fortune has the chief control in human affairs, and it has pleased her that you should experience our force as well as our favor, now, when, she gives you this fair opportunity, embrace it without delay, and complete the course which you have begun. You have many and excellent means of atoning, with great ease, for past errors by future services. Impress this, however, deeply on your mind, that the Roman people are never outdone in acts of kindness; of their power in war you have already sufficient knowledge."

To this address Bocchus made a temperate and courteous reply, offering a few observations, at the same time, in extenuation of his error; and saying "that he had taken arms, not with any hostile feeling, but to defend his own dominions, as part of Numidia, out of which he had forcibly driven Jugurtha,[305] was his by right of conquest, and he could not allow it to be laid waste by Marius; that when he formerly sent embassadors to the Romans, he was refused their friendship; but that he would say nothing more of the past, and would, if Marius gave him permission, send another embassy to the senate." But no sooner was this permission granted, than the purpose of the barbarian was altered by some of his friends, whom Jugurtha, hearing of the mission of Sylla and Manlius, and fearful of what was intended by it, had corrupted with bribes.

CIII. Marius, in the mean time, having settled his army in winter quarters, set out, with the light-armed cohorts and part of the cavalry, into a desert part of the country, to besiege a fortress of Jugurtha's, in which he had placed a garrison consisting wholly of Roman deserters. And now again Bocchus, either from reflecting on what he had suffered in the two engagements, or from being admonished by such of his friends as Jugurtha had not corrupted, selected, out of the whole number of his adherents, five persons of approved integrity and eminent abilities, whom he directed to go, in the first place, to Marius, and afterward to proceed, if Marius gave his consent, as embassadors to Rome, granting them full powers to treat concerning his affairs, and to conclude the war upon any terms whatsoever. These five immediately set out for the Roman winter-quarters, but being beset and spoiled by Getulian robbers on the way, fled, in alarm and ill plight,[306] to Sylla, whom the consul, when he went on his expedition, had left as pro-praetor with the army. Sylla received them, not, as they had deserved, like faithless enemies, but with the greatest ceremony and munificence; from which the barbarians concluded that what was said of Roman avarice was false, and that Sylla, from his generosity, must be their friend. For interested bounty,[307] in those days, was still unknown to many; by whom every man who was liberal was also thought benevolent, and all presents were considered to proceed from kindness. They therefore disclosed to the quaestor their commission from Bocchus, and asked him to be their patron and adviser; extolling, at the same time, the power, integrity, and grandeur of their monarch, and adding whatever they thought likely to promote their objects, or to procure the favor of Sylla. Sylla promised them all that they requested; and, being instructed how to address Marius and the senate, they tarried in the camp about forty days.[308]

CIV. When Marius, having failed in the object[309] of his expedition, returned to Cirta, and was informed of the arrival of the embassadors, he desired both them and Sylla to come to him, together with Lucius Bellienus, the praetor from Utica, and all that were of senatorial rank in any part of the country, with whom he discussed the instructions of Bocchus to his embassadors; to whom permission to proceed to Rome was granted by the consul. In the mean time a truce was asked, a request to which assent was readily expressed by Sylla and the majority; the few, who advocated harsher measures, were men inexperienced in human affairs, which, unstable and fluctuating, are always verging to opposite extremes.[310]

The Moors having obtained all that they desired, three of them started for Rome with Oneius Octavius Rufus, who, as quaestor, had brought pay for the army to Africa; the other two returned to Bocchus, who heard from them, with great pleasure, their account both of other particulars, and especially of the courtesy and attention of Sylla.

To his three embassadors that went to Rome, when, after a deprecatory acknowledgment that their king had been in error, and had been led astray by the treachery of Jugurtha, they solicited for him friendship and alliance, the following answer was given: "The senate and people of Rome are wont to be mindful of both services and injuries; they pardon Bocchus, since he repents of his fault, and will grant him their alliance and friendship when he shall have deserved them."

CV. When this reply was communicated to Bocchus, he requested Marius, by letter, to send Sylla to him, that, at his discretion,[311] measures might be adopted for their common interest. Sylla was accordingly dispatched, attended with a guard of cavalry, infantry, and Balearic slingers, besides some archers and a Pelignian cohort, who, for the sake of expedition, were furnished with light arms, which, however, protected them, as efficiently as any others, against the light darts of the enemy. As he was on his march, on the fifth day after he set out, Volux, the son of Bocchus, suddenly appeared on the open plain with a body of cavalry, which amounted in reality to not more than a thousand, but which, as they approached in confusion and disorder, presented to Sylla and the rest the appearance of a greater number, and excited apprehensions of hostility. Every one, therefore, prepared himself for action, trying and presenting[312] his arms and weapons; some fear was felt among them, but greater hope, as they were now conquerors, and were only meeting those whom they had often overcome. After a while, however, a party of horse sent forward to reconnoiter, reported, as was the case, that nothing but peace was intended.

CVI. Volux, coming forward, addressed himself to Sylla, saying that he was sent by Bocchus his father to meet and escort him. The two parties accordingly formed a junction, and prosecuted their journey, on that day and the following, without any alarm. But when they had pitched their camp, and evening had set in,

Volux came running, with looks of perplexity, to Sylla, and said that he had learned from his scouts that Jugurtha was at hand, entreating and urging him, at the same time, to escape with him privately in the night. Sylla boldly replied, "that he had no fear of Jugurtha, an enemy so often defeated; that he had the utmost confidence in the valor of his troops; and that, even if certain destruction were at hand, he would rather keep his ground, than save, by deserting his followers, a life at best uncertain, and perhaps soon to be lost by disease." Being pressed, however, by Volux, to set forward in the night, he approved of the suggestion, and immediately ordered his men to dispatch their supper,[313] to light as many fires as possible in the camp, and to set out in silence at the first watch.

When they were all fatigued with their march during the night, and Sylla was preparing, at sunrise, to pitch his camp, the Moorish cavalry announced that Jugurtha was encamped about two miles in advance. At this report, great dismay fell upon our men; for they believed themselves betrayed by Volux, and led into an ambuscade. Some exclaimed that they ought to take vengeance on him at once, and not suffer such perfidy to remain unpunished.

CVII. But Sylla, though he had similar thoughts, protected the Moor from violence; exhorting his soldiers to keep up their spirits; and saying, "that a handful of brave men had often fought successfully against a multitude; that the less anxious they were to save their lives in battle, the greater would be their security; and that no man, who had arms in his hands, ought to trust for safety to his unarmed heels, or to turn to the enemy, in however great danger, the defenseless and blind parts of his body".[314] Having then called almighty Jupiter to witness the guilt and perfidy of Bocchus, he ordered Volux, as being an instrument of his father's hostility,[315] to quit the camp.

Volux, with tears in his eyes, entreated him to entertain no such suspicions; declaring "that nothing in the affair had been caused by treachery on his part, but all by the subtlety of Jugurtha, to whom his line of march had become known through his scouts. But as Jugurtha had no great force with him, and as his hopes and resource were dependent on his father Bocchus, he assuredly would not attempt any open violence, when the son of Bocchus would himself be a witness of it. He thought it best for Sylla, therefore, to march boldly through the middle of his camp, and that as for himself, he would either send forward his Moors, or leave them where they were, and accompany Sylla alone." This course, under such circumstances, was adopted; they set forward without delay, and, as they came upon Jugurtha unexpectedly, while he was in doubt and hesitation how to act, they passed without molestation. In a few days afterward, they arrived at the place to which their march was directed.

CVIII. There was, at this time, in constant and familiar intercourse with Bocchus, a Numidian named Aspar, who had been sent to him by Jugurtha, when he heard of Sylla's intended interview, in the character of embassador, but secretly to be a spy on the Mauretanian king's proceedings. There was also with him a certain Dabar, son of Massugrada, one of the family of Masinissa,[316] but of inferior birth on the maternal side, as his father was the son of a concubine. Dabar, for his many intellectual endowments, was liked and esteemed by Bocchus, who, having found him faithful[317] on many former occasions, sent him forthwith to Sylla, to say that "he was ready to do whatever the Romans desired; that Sylla himself should appoint the place, day, and hour,[318] for a conference; that he kept all points, which he had settled with him before, inviolate;[319] and that he was not to fear the presence of Jugurtha's embassador as any restraint[320] on the discussion of their common interests, since, without admitting him, he could have no security against Jugurtha's treachery". I find, however, that it was rather from African duplicity[321] than from the motives which he professed, that Bocchus thus allured both the Romans and Jugurtha with the hopes of peace; that he frequently debated with himself whether he should deliver Jugurtha to the Romans, or Sylla to Jugurtha; and that his inclination swayed him against us, but his fears in our favor.

CIX. Sylla replied, "that he should speak on but few particulars before Aspar, and discuss others at a private meeting, or in the presence of only a few;" dictating, at the same time, what answer should be returned by Bocchus.[322] Afterward, when they met, as Bocchus had desired, Sylla stated, "that he had come, by order of the consul, to inquire whether he would resolve on peace or on war." Bocchus, as he had been previously instructed by Sylla, requested him to come again at the end of ten days, since he had as yet formed no determination, but would at that time give a decisive answer. Both then retired to their respective camps.[323] But when the night was far advanced, Sylla was secretly sent for by Bocchus. At their interview, none but confidential interpreters were admitted on either side, together with Dabar, the messenger between them, a man of honor, and held in esteem by both parties. The king at once commenced thus:

CX. "I never expected that I, the greatest monarch in this part of the world, and the richest of all whom I know, should ever owe a favor to a private man. Indeed, Sylla, before I knew you, I gave assistance to many who solicited me, and to others without solicitation, and stood in need of no man's assistance.

But at this loss of independence, at which others are wont to repine, I am rather inclined to rejoice. It will be a pleasure to me[324] to have once needed your friendship, than which I hold nothing dearer to my heart. Of the sincerity of this assertion you may at once make trial, take my arms, my soldiers, my money, or whatever you please, and use it as your own. But do not suppose, as long as you live, that your kindness to me has been fully requited; my sense of it will always remain undiminished, and you shall, with my knowledge, wish for nothing in vain. For, as I am of opinion, it is less dishonorable to a prince to be conquered in battle than to be surpassed in generosity.

With respect to your republic, whose interests you are sent to guard, hear briefly what I have to say. I have neither made war upon the Roman people, nor desired that it should be made; I have merely defended my territories with arms against an armed force. But from hostilities, since such is your pleasure, I now desist. Prosecute the war with Jugurtha as you think proper. The river Malucha, which was the boundary between Miscipsa and me, I shall neither pass myself, nor suffer Jugurtha to come within it. And if you shall ask any thing besides, worthy of me and of yourself, you shall not depart with a refusal."

CXI. To this speech Sylla replied, as far as concerned himself, briefly and modestly; but spoke, with regard to the peace and their common concerns, much more at length. He signified to the king "that the senate and people of Rome, as they had the superiority in the field, would think themselves little obliged by what he promised; that he must do something which would seem more for their interest than his own; and that for this there was now a fair opportunity, since he had Jugurtha in his power, for, if he delivered him to the Romans, they would feel greatly indebted to him, and their friendship and alliance, as well as that part of Numidia which he claimed,[325] would readily be granted him." Bocchus at first refused to listen to the proposal, saying that affinity, the ties of blood,[326] and a solemn league, connected him with Jugurtha; and that he feared, if he acted insincerely, he might alienate the affections of his subjects, by whom Jugurtha was beloved, and the Romans disliked. But at last, after being frequently importuned, his resolution gave way,[327] and he engaged to do every thing in accordance with Sylla's wishes. They then concerted measures for conducting a pretended treaty of peace, of which Jugurtha, weary of war, was extremely desirous. Having settled their plans, they separated.

CXII. On the next day Bocchus sent for Aspar, Jugurtha's envoy, and acquainted him that he had ascertained from Sylla, through Dabar, that the war might be concluded on certain conditions; and that he should therefore make inquiry as to the sentiments of his king. Aspar proceeded with joy to Jugurtha's camp, and having received full instructions from him, returned in haste to Bocchus at the end of eight days, with intelligence "that Jugurtha was eager to do whatever might be required, but that he put little confidence in Marius, as treaties of peace, concluded with Roman generals, had often before proved of no effect; that if Bocchus, however, wished to consult the interests of both,[328] and to have an established peace, he should endeavor to bring all parties together to a conference, as if to settle the conditions, and then deliver Sylla into his hands, for when he had such a man in his power, a treaty would at once be concluded by order of the senate and people of Rome; as a man of high rank, who had fallen into the hands of the enemy, not from want of spirit, but from zeal for the public interest, would not be left in captivity".

CXIII. The Moor, after long meditation on these suggestions, at length expressed his assent to them, but whether in pretense or sincerity I have not been able to discover. But the inclinations of kings, as they are violent, are often fickle, and at variance with themselves. At last, after a time and place were fixed for coming to a conference about the treaty, Bocchus addressed himself at one time to Sylla and at another to the envoy of Jugurtha, treating them with equal affability, and making the same professions to both. Both were in consequence equally delighted, and animated with the fairest expectations. But on the night preceding the day appointed for the conference, the Moor, after first assembling his friends, and then, on a change of mind, dismissing them, is reported to have had many anxious struggles with himself, disturbed alike in his thoughts and his gestures, which, even when he was silent, betrayed the secret agitation of his mind. At last, however, he ordered that Sylla should be sent for, and, according to his desire, laid an ambush for

Jugurtha.

As soon as it was day, and intelligence was brought that Jugurtha was at hand, Bocchus, as if to meet him and do him honor, went forth, attended by a few friends, and our quaestor, as far as a little hill, which was full in the view of the men who were placed in ambush. To the same spot came Jugurtha with most of his adherents, unarmed, according to agreement; when immediately, on a signal being given, he was assailed on all sides by those who were lying in wait. The others were cut to pieces, and Jugurtha himself was delivered bound to Sylla, and by him conducted to Marius.

CXIV. At this period war was carried on unsuccessfully by our generals Quintus Caepio and Marcus Manlius, against the Gauls; with the terror of which all Italy was thrown into consternation. Both the Romans of that day, indeed, and their descendants, down to our own times, maintained the opinion that all other nations must yield to their valor, but that they contended with the Gauls, not for glory, but merely in self-defense. But after the war in Numidia was ended, and it was announced that Jugurtha was coming in chains to Rome, Marius, though absent from the city, was created consul, and Gaul decreed to him as his province. On the first of January he triumphed as consul, with great glory. At that time[329] the hopes and dependence of the state were placed on him.

NOTES FOR THE JUGURTHINE WAR

[1] I. Intellectual power-- ***Virtute***. See the remarks on ***virtus***, at the commencement of the Conspiracy of Catiline. A little below, I have rendered ***via virtutis***, "the path of true merit."

[2] Worthy of honor-- ***Clarus***. "A person may be called ***clarus*** either on account of his great actions and merits; or on account of some honor which he has obtained, as the consuls were called ***clarissimi viri***; or on account of great expectations which are formed from him. But since the worth of him who is ***clarus*** is known by all, it appears that the mind is here called ***clarus*** because its nature is such that pre-eminence is generally attributed to it, and

the attention of all directed toward it." ***Dietsch***.

[3] Abandons itself--***Pessum datus est***. Is altogether sunk and overwhelmed.

[4] Impute their delinquency to circumstances, etc.--Suam quisque culpam ad negotia transferunt. Men excuse their indolence and inactivity, by saying that the weakness of their faculties, or the circumstances in which they are placed, render them unable to accomplish any thing of importance. But, says Seneca, Satis natura, homini dedit roboris, si illo utamur;--nolle in causa, non posse praetenditur. "Nature has given men sufficient powers, if they will but use them; but they pretend that they can not when the truth is that they will not." "***Negotia*** is a common word with Sallust, for which other writers would use ***res, facta***." Gerlach. "Cajus rei nos ipsi sumus auctores, ejus culpam rebus externis attribuimus." ***Muller***. "Auctores" is the same as the [Greek: ***aitioi***].

[5] Useless--***Aliena***. Unsuitable, not to the purpose, not contributing to the improvement of life.

[6] Instead of being mortal--***Pro mortalibus***. There are two senses in which these words may be taken: ***as far as mortals can***, and ***instead of being mortals***. Kritz and Dietsch say that the latter is undoubtedly the true sense. Other commentators are either silent or say little to the purpose. As for the translators, they have studied only how to get over the passage delicately. The latter sense is perhaps favored by what is said in c. 2, that "the illustrious achievements of the mind are, like the mind itself, immortal."

[7] II. They all rise and fall, etc.--Omnia orta occidunt, et aucta senescunt. This is true of things in general, but is here

spoken only of the qualities of the body, as De Brosses clearly perceived.

[8] Has power over all things--*Habet cuncta*. "All things are in its power." Dietsch. "*Sub ditione tenet*. So Jupiter, Ov. Met. i. 197:
  Quum mihi qui fulmen, qui vos habeoque regoque."
Burnouf. So Aristippus said, **Habeo Laidem, non habeor a Laide**, [Greek: **echo ouk echomai**]. Cic. Epist. ad Fam. ix. 26.

[9] III. Civil and military offices--*Magistratus et imperia*. "Illo vocabule civilia, hoc militaria munera, significantur." **Dietsch**.

[10] To rule our country or subjects, etc.--Nam vi quidem regere patriam aut parentes, etc. Cortius, Gerlach, Kritz, Dietsch, and Muller are unanimous in understanding *parentes* as the participle of the verb *pareo*. That this is the sense, says Gerlach, is sufficiently proved by the conjunction *aut*; for if Sallust had meant *parents*, he would have used *ut*; and in this opinion Allen coincides. Doubtless, also, this sense of the word suits extremely well with the rest of the sentence, in which changes in government are mentioned. But Burnouf, with Crispinus, prefers to follow Aldus Manutius, who took the word in the other signification, supposing that Sallust borrowed the sentiment from Plato, who says in his Epistle ad Dionis Propinquos: [Greek: Patera de hae maetera ouch osion haegoumai prosbiazesthai, mae noso paraphrosunaes hechomenous. Bian de patridi politeias metabolaes aeae prospherein, otan aneu phugon, kai sphagaes andron, mae dunaton hae ginesthae taen ariostaen.] And he makes a similar observation in his Crito: [Greek: Pantachou poiaetaen, o an keleuoi hae polis te, kai hae patris.--Biazesthai de ouch osion oute maetera, oute patera poly de touton eti aetton taen

patrida.] On which sentiments Cicero, ad Fam. i. 9, thus comments: Id enim jubet idem ille Plato, quem ego auctorem vehementer sequor; tantum contendere in republica quantum probare tuis civibus possis: vim neque parenti, neque patriae afferre oportere. There is also another passage in Cicero, Cat. i. 3, which seems to favor this sense of the word: Si te parentes timerent atque odissent tui, neque eos ulla ratione placare posses, ut opinor, ab eorum oculis aliquo concederes; nunc te patria, quae communis est omnium nostrum parens odit ac metuit, etc. Of the first passage cited from Plato, indeed, Sallust's words may seem to be almost a translation. Yet, as the majority of commentators have followed Cortius, I have also followed him. Sallust has the word in this sense in Jug., c. 102; Parentes abunde habemus. *So Vell. Pat. ii. 108:* Principatis constans ex voluntate parentium.

[11] Lead to--*Portendant*. "*Portendere* in a *pregnant sense*, meaning not merely to indicate, but *quasi secum ferre*, to carry along with them." *Kritzius*.

[12] IV, Presumptuously--*Per insolentiam*. The same as *insolenter*, though some refer it, not to Sallust, but to quis existumet, *in the sense of* strangely, *i. e.* foolishly or ignorantly. I follow Cortius's interpretation.

[13] At what periods I obtained office, what sort of men, etc. --*Quibus ego temporibus maqistratus adeptus sum, et quales viri*, etc. --"Sallust obtained the quaestorship a few years after the conspiracy of Catiline, about the time when the state was agitated by the disorders of Clodius and his party. He was tribune of the people, A.U.C. 701, the year in which Clodius was killed by Milo. He was praetor in 708, when Caesar had made himself ruler. In the expression *quales viri,* etc., he alludes chiefly to Cato, who, when he stood

for the praetorship, was unsuccessful." ***Burnouf.*** Kritzius defends ***adeptus sum.***

[14] What description of persons have subsequently entered the senate--"Caesar chose the worthy and unworthy, as suited his own purposes, to be members of the senate." ***Burnouf.***

[15] Quintus Maximus--Quintus Fabius Maximus, of whom Ennius says,
Unus qui nobis cunctando restituit rem;
Non ponebat enim rumores ante salutem.

[16] Publius Scipio--Scipio Africanus the Elder, the conqueror of Hannibal. See c. 5.

[17] To the pursuit of honor--***Ad vertutem. Virtus*** in the same sense as in ***virtutis via,*** c. 1.

[18] The wax--***Ceram illam.*** The images or busts of their ancestors, which the nobility kept in the halls of their houses, were made of wax. See Plin. H. N. xxxv., 2.

[19] Men of humble birth--***Homines novi.*** See Cat., c. 23.

[20] V. Threw every thing, religious and civil, into confusion--Divina et humana cuncta permiscuit. "All things, both divine and human, were so changed, that their previous condition was entirely subverted." ***Dietsch***.

[21] Civil dissensions--***Studiis civilibus***. This is the sense in which most commentators take ***studia***; and if this be right, the whole phrase must be understood as I have rendered it. So Cortius; "Ut non prius finirentur [***studia civilia***] nisi bello et vastitate Italiae."

Sallust has ***studia partium*** Jug. c. 42; and Gerlach quotes from Cic. pro Marcell. c. 10: "Non enim consiliis solis et studiis, sed armis etiam et castris dissidebamus".

[22] More than any other enemy--***Maxime***.

[23] Since the Roman name became great--Post magnitudinem nominis Romani. "I know not why interpreters should find any difficulty in this passage. I understand it to signify simply ***since*** the Romans became so great as they were in the time of Hannibal; for, ***before*** that period they had suffered even heavier calamities, especially from the Gauls." ***Cortius***.

[24] Syphax--"He was King of the Masaesyli in Numidia; was at first an enemy to the Carthaginians (Liv. xxiv. 48), and afterward their friend (Liv. xxviii. 17). He then changed sides again, and made a treaty with Scipio; but having at length been offered the hand of Sophonisba, the daughter of Asdrubal, in marriage, he accepted it, and returned into alliance with the Carthaginians. Being subsequently taken prisoner by Masinissa and Laelius, the lieutenant of Scipio, (Liv. xxx. 2) he was carried into Italy, and died at Tibur (Liv. xxx. 45)." ***Burnouf***.

[25] His reign--***Imperii***. Cortius thinks that the grant of the Romans ceased with the life of Masinissa, and that his son, Micipsa, reigned only over that part of Numidia which originally belonged to his father. But in this opinion succeeding commentators have generally supposed him to be mistaken.

[26] VII. During the Numantine war--***Bella Numantino***. Numantia, which stood near the source of the Durius or ***Douro*** in Spain, was so strong in its situation and fortifications, that it with stood the

Romans for fourteen years. See Florus, ii. 17,18; Vell. Pat. ii. 4.

[27] VIII. Rather by attention to them as a body, than by practicing on individuals--***Publice quam privatim.*** "Universae potius civitatis, quam privatorum gratiam quaerendo." ***Burnouf.*** The words can only be rendered periphrastically.

[28] IX. In a short time--***Statim***. If what is said in c. 11 be correct, that Jugurtha was adopted within three years of Micipsa's death, his adoption did not take place till twelve years after the taking of Numantia, which surrendered in 619, and Micipsa died in 634. ***Statim*** is therefore used with great latitude, unless we suppose Sallust to mean that Micipsa signified to Jugurtha his intention to adopt him immediately on his return from Numantia, and that the formal ceremony of the adoption was delayed for some years.

[29] X. I received you--into my kingdom--***In meuum regnum accepi***. By these words it is only signified that Micipsa received Jugurtha into his palace so as to bring him up with his own children. The critics who suppose that there is any allusion to the adoption, or a pretended intention of it on the part of Micipsa, are evidently in the wrong.

[30] Pre-eminent merit--***Gloria***. Our English word ***glory*** is too strong.

[31] By the fidelity which you owe to my kingdom--Per regni fidem. This seems to be the best of all the explanations that have been offered of these words. "Per fidem quam tu rex (futurus) mihi regi praestare debes." ***Bournouf.*** "Per fidem quae decet in regno, i. e. ***regem.***" Dietsch. "Per eam fidem, qua esse decet eum qui regnum obtinet. ***Kritzius***.

[32] It is not armies, or treasures, etc.--[Greek: Ou tode to chrusoun skaeptron to taen basileian diasozon estin, alla oi polloi philoi skaeptron basileioin ulaethestaton kai asphalestaton.] "It is not this golden scepter that can preserve a kingdom; but numerous friends are to princes their trust and safest scepter." Xen. Cyrop., viii. 7,14.

[33] And who can be a greater friend than one brother to another? --***Quis autem amicior, quam frater fratri?*** "[Greek: Nomiz adelphous tous alaethinous philous] Menander." ***Wasse***.

[34] That I have not adopted a better son, &c--Ne ego meliores liberos sumsissevidear quam genuisse. As there is no allusion to Micipsa's adoption of any other son than Jugurtha, Sallust's expression ***liberos sumsisse*** can hardly be defended. It is necessary to give ***son*** in the singular, in the translation.

[35] XI. Had spoken insincerely--***Ficta locutum***. Jugurtha saw that Micipsa pretended more love for him than he really felt. Compare c. 6,7.

[36] Which is regarded by the Numidians as the seat of honor--Quad apud Numidas honori ducitur. "I incline," says Sir Henry Steuart, "to consider those manuscripts as the most correct, in which the word ***et*** is placed immediately before apud, Quod et apud Numidas honori ducitur." Sir Henry might have learned, had he consulted the commentators, that " ***the word*** et ***is placed immediately before*** apud" in no manuscript; that Lipsius was the first who proposed its insertion; and that Crispinus, the only editor who has received it into his text, is ridiculed by Wasse for his folly. "Lipsius," says Cortius, "cum sciret apud Romanos etiam medium locum honoratiorem

fuisse, corrigit: ***quod et apud Numidas honori ducitur***. Sed quis talia ab historico exegerit? Si de Numidis narrat, non facile aliquis intulerit, aliter propterea fuisse apud Romanos."

[37] To the other seat--***In alteram partem***. We must suppose that the three seats were placed ready for the three princes; that Adherbal sat down first, in one of the outside seats; the one, namely, that would be on the right hand of a spectator facing them; and that Hiempsal immediately took the middle seat, on Adherbal's right hand, so as to force Jugurtha to take the other outside one. Adherbal had then to remove Hiempsal *in alteram partem*, that is, to induce him to take the seat corresponding to his own, on the other side of the middle one.

[38] Chief lictor--***Proximus lictor***. "The ***proximus lictor*** was he who, when the lictors walked before the prince or magistrate in a regular line, one behind the other, was last, or next to the person on whom they attended." ***Cortius***. He would thus be ready to receive the great man's commands, and be in immediate communication with him. We must suppose either that Sallust merely speaks in conformity with the practice of the Romans, or, what is more probable, that the Roman custom of being preceded by lictors had been adopted in Numidia.

[39] Hut of a maid-servant--***Tugurio muliers ancillae*** Rose renders *tugurio* "a mean apartment," and other translators have given something similar, as if they thought that the servant must have had a room in the house. But she, and other Numidian servants, may have had huts apart from the dwelling-house. ***Tugurium*** undoubtedly signifies *a hut* in general.

[40] XIII. Into our province--***In Provinciam***. "The word ***province***, in this place, signifies that part of Africa which, after the destruction of Carthage, fell to the Romans by the right of conquest,

in opposition to the kingdom of Micipsa." ***Wasse***.

[41] Having thus accomplished his purposes--***Patratis consiliis***. After ***consiliis***, in all the manuscripts, occur the words postquam omnis Numidia potiebatur, which were struck out by Cortius, as being ***turpissima glossa***. The recent editors, Gerlach, Kritz, Dietsch, and Burnouf, have restored them.

[42] His intimate friends--***Hospitibus***. Persons probably with whom he had been intimate at Numantia, or who had since visited him in Numidia.

[43] The senate--gave audience to both parties--senatus utrisque datur. "The embassadors of Jugurtha, and Adberbal in person, are admitted into the senate-house to plead their cause." ***Burnouf***.

[44] By deputation--***Procuratione***. He was to consider himself only the ***procurator***, manager, or deputed governor, of the kingdom.

[45] Kindred--and relatives--***Cognatorum--affinium***. ***Cognatus*** is a blood relation; ***affinis*** is properly a relative by marriage.

[46] Hereditary--***Ab stirpe***.

[47] Next to this--***Secundum ea***. "Priscianus, lib. xiii., de praepositione agens, ***Secundum***, inquit, quando pro [Greek: kata ei meta] loco praepositionis est. ***Sallustius in Jugurthino:*** secundum ea, uti deditis uterer.--***Videlicet hoc dicit***, Secundum in Sallustii exemple, ***post*** vel ***proxime*** significare." ***Rivius***.

[48] As I had no power to form the character of Jugurtha--Neque mihi in manu fuit, qualis Jugurtha foret. "In manu fuit is simply

in potestate fuit--Ter. Hec., iv. 4, 44: Uxor quid faciat in manu non est mea." Cortius.

[49] Dishonored, afflicted--Deformatus aerumnis.

[50] Above all others--***Potissimum***.

[51] One of us has been murdered, and I, the other, have scarcely escaped the hand of lawlessness--Alter eorum necatus, alterius ipse ego manus impias vix effugi. This is the general reading, but it cannot be right. Adherbal speaks of himself and his brother as two persons, and of Jugurtha as a third, and says that **of those two** the one (*alter*) has been killed; he would then naturally proceed to speak of himself as the other; *i. e.* he would use the word *alter* concerning himself, not apply it to Jugurtha. Allen, therefore, proposes to read **alter necatus, alter manus impias vix effugi**. This mode of correction strikes out too much; but there is no doubt that the second *alter* should be in the nominative case.

[52] From being friendly, has become hostile to me--Ex necessariis adversa facta sunt. "Si omnia mihi incolumia manerent, neque quidquam rerum mearum (s. praesidiorum) amisissem, neque Jugurtha aliique mihi ex necessariis inimici facti essent."***Kritzius***.

[53] But would that I could see him, etc.--***Quod utinam illum--videam***. The *quod*, in *quod utinam*, is the same as that in *quod si*, which we commonly translate, **but if**. *Quod*, in such expressions, serves as a particle of connection, between what precedes and what follows it; the Latins being fond of connection by means of relatives. See Zumpt's Lat. Grammar on this point, Sect. 63, 82, Kenrick's translation. Kritzius writes ***quodutinam***, ***quodsi***, ***quodnisi***, etc., as one word. Cortius injudiciously interprets ***quod*** in this passage as having

facientem understood with it.

[54] My life or death depends on the aid of others--Cujus vitae necisque ex opibus alienis pendet. On the aid of the Romans. Unless they protected him, he expected to meet with the same fate as Hiempsal at the hands of Jugurtha.

[55] Without disgrace--**Sine dedecore**. That is, if he did not succeed in getting revenge on Jugurtha.

[56] By your regard for yourselves, etc.--I have here departed from the text of Cortius, who reads **per, vos, liberos atque parentes**, i. e. vos (obsecro) per liberos, etc., as most critics would explain it, though Cortius himself prefers taking **vos** as the nominative case, and joining it with **subvenite**, which follows. Most other editions have **per vos, per liberos, atque parentes vestros**, to which I have adhered. **Per vos**, though an adjuration not used in modern times, is found in other passages of the Roman writers. Thus Liv. xxix. 18: **Per vos, fidemque vestram**. Cic. pro Planc., c. 42; Per vos, per fortunas vestras.

[57] To sink into ruin--**Tabescere**. "Paullatim interire." **Cortius**. Lucret. ii. 1172: Omnia paullatim tabescere el ire Ad capulum. "This speech," says Gerlach, "though of less weighty argument than the other speeches of Sallust, is composed with great art. Neither the speaker nor his cause was adapted for the highest flights of eloquence; but Sallust has shrouded Adherbal's weakness in excellent language. That there is a constant recurrence to the same topics, is no ground for blame; indeed, such recurrence could hardly be avoided, for it is natural to all speeches in which the orator earnestly labors to make his hearers adopt his own feelings and views. The Romans were again and again to be supplicated, and again and again

to be reminded of the character and services of Masinissa, that they might be induced, if not by the love of justice, yet by the dread of censure, to relieve the distresses of his grandson.... He omits no argument or representation that could move the pity of the Romans; and if his abject prostration of mind appears more suitable to a woman than a man, it is to be remembered that it is purposely introduced by Sallust to exhibit the weakness of his character."

[58] XV. Aemilius Scaurus--He was ***princeps senatus***(see c. 25), and seems to be pretty faithfully characterized by Sallust as a man of eminent abilities, but too avaricious to be strictly honest. Cicero, who alludes to him in many passages with commendation (Off., i. 20, 30; Brut. 29; Pro Muraen., 7; Pro Fonteio, 7), mentions an anecdote respecting him (De Orat. ii. 70), which shows that he had a general character for covetousness. See Pliny, H. N, xxxvi. 14. Valerius Maximus (iii. 7, 8) tells another anecdote of him, which shows that he must have been held in much esteem, for whatever qualities, by the public. Being accused before the people of having taken a bribe from Mithridates, he made a few remarks on his own general conduct; and added, "Varius of Sucro says that Marcus Scaurus, being bribed with the king's money, has betrayed the interests of the Roman people. Marcus Scaurus denies that he is guilty of what is laid to his charge. Which of the two do you believe?" The people dismissed the accusation; but the words of Scaurus may be regarded as those of a man rather seeking to convey a notion of his innocence, than capable of proving it. The circumstance which Cicero relates is this: Scaurus had incurred some obloquy for having, as it was said, taken possession of the property of a certain rich man, named Phyrgio Pompeius, without being entitled to it by any will; and being engaged as an advocate in some cause, Mommius, who was pleading on the opposite side, seeing a funeral pass by at the time, said, "Scaurus, yonder is a dead man, on his way to the grave; if you can but get possession of his property!" I mention these matters, because it has been thought that Sallust,

from some ill-feeling, represents Scaurus as more avaricious than he really was.

[59] His ruling passion--**Consueta libidine**. Namely, avarice.

[60] XVI. Lucius Opimius--His contention with the party of C. Gracchus may be seen in any history of Rome. For receiving bribes from Jugurtha he was publicly accused, and being condemned, ended his life, which was protracted to old age, in exile and neglect. Cic. Brut. 33; Planc. 28.

[61] XVII. Only two divisions, Asia and Europe--Thus Varro, de L. L. iv.13, ed. Bip. "As all nature is divided into heaven and earth, so the heaven is divided into regions, and the earth into Asia and Europe." See Bronkh. ad Tibull., iv. 1, 176.

[62] The strait connecting our sea with the ocean--Fretum nostri maris et oceani. *That is, the* Fretum Gaditanum, or Strait of Gibraltar. By *our see*, he means the Mediterranean. See Pomp. Mela, i. 1.

[63] A vast sloping tract--Catabathmos--Declivem latitudinem, quem locum Catabathmon incolae appellant. Catabathmus--vallis repente convexa**, Plin. H. N. v 5.** Catabathmus, vallis devexa in Aegyptum, Pomp. Mela, i. 8. I have translated **declivem latitudinem** in conformity with these passages. **Catabathmus**, a Greek word, means a descent. *There were two, the* major *and* minor; Sallust speaks of the **major**.

[64] Most of them die by the gradual decay of age--Plerosque senectus dissolvit "A happy expression; since the effect of old age on the bodily frame is not to break it in pieces suddenly, but to

dissolve it, as it were, gradually and imperceptibly." ***Burnouf***.

[65] King Hiempsal--"This is not the prince that was murdered by Jugurtha, but the king who succeeded him; he was grandson of Masinissa, son of Gulussa, and father of Juba. After Juba was killed at Thapsus, Caesar reduced Numidia to the condition of a province, and appointed Sallust over it, who had thus opportunities of gaining a knowledge of the country, and of consulting the books written in the language of it." ***Burnouf***.

[66] XVIII. Getulians and Lybians--***Gaetuli et Libyes***, "See Pompon. Mel. i. 4; Plin. H. N. v. 4, 6, 8, v. 2, xxi. 13; Herod, iv. 159, 168." ***Gerlach***. The name ***Gaetuli***, is, however, unknown to Herodotus. They lay to the south of Numidia and Mauretania. See Strabo, xvii. 3. ***Libyes*** is a term applied by the Greek writers properly to the Africans of the North coast, but frequently to the inhabitants of Africa in general.

[67] His army, which was composed of various nations--This seems to have been an amplification of the adventure of Hercules with Geryon, who was a king in Spain. But all stories that make Hercule a leader of armies appear to be equally fabulous.

[68] Medes, Persians and Armenians--De Brosses thinks that these were not real Medes, etc., but that the names were derived from certain companions of Hercules. The point is not worth discussion.

[69] Our sea--The Mediterranean. See above, c. 17.

[70] More toward the Ocean--***Intra oceanum magis***. "***Intra oceanum*** is differently explained by different commentators. Cortius, Muller and Gerlach, understand the parts bounded by the ocean, lying close upon it, and stretching toward the west; while Langius thinks that

the regions more remote from the Atlantic Ocean, and extending toward the east, are meant. But Langius did not consider that those who had inverted keels of vessels for cottages, could not have strayed far from the ocean, but must have settled in parts bordering upon it. *And this is what is signified by* intra oceanum. For *intra aliquam rem* is not always used to denote what is actually *in a thing,* and circumscribed by its boundaries, but what approaches toward it, and reaches close to it." Kritzius. He then instances *intra modum, intra legem; Hortensii scripta intra famam sunt*, Quintil. xi. 8, 8. But the best example which he produces is Liv. xxv. 11: *Fossa ingens ducta, et vallum*, intra eam *erigitur*. Cicero, in Verr. iii. 89, has also, he notices, the same, expression, **Locus** intra oceanum jam nullus est--quo non nostrorum hominum libido iniquitasque pervaserit, *i. e..* locus oceano conterminus. Burnouf absurdly follows Langius.

[71] Numidians--***Numidas***. The same as ***Nomades***, or wanderers; a term applied to pastoral nations, and which, as Kritzius observes, the Africans must have had from the Greeks, perhaps those of Sicily.

[72] More to the sun--***sub sole magis***. I have borrowed this expression from Rose. The Getulians were more southward.

[73] These soon built themselves towns--That is, the united Medes, Armenians, and Libyans.

[74] Medes--into Moors--***Mauris pro Medis***. A most improbable, not to say impossible corruption.

[75] Of the Persians--***Persarum***. That is, of the Persians and Getulians united.

[76] The two parties--*Utrique*. The older Numidians, and the younger, who had emigrated toward Carthage.

[77] Those who had spread toward our sea--for the Libyans are less warlike than the Getulians--Magis hi, qui ad nostrum mare processerant; quia Libyes quam Gaetuli minus bellicosi. The Persians and Getulians (under the name of Numidians), and their colonists, who were more toward the Mediterranean, and were more warlike than the Libyans (who were united with the Medes and Armenians) took from them portions of their territories by conquest. This is clearly the sense, as deducible from the preceding portion of the text.

[78] Lower Africa--*Africa pars inferior*. The part nearest to the sea. The ancients called the maritime parts of a country the lower parts**, and the inland parts** the higher, taking the notion, probably, from the course of the rivers. Lower Egypt was the part at the mouth of the Nile.

[79] XIX. Hippo--"It is not Hippo Regius" (now called *Bona*) "that is meant, but another Hippo, otherwise called *Diarrhytum* or *Zarytum*, situate in Zengitana, not far from Utica. This is shown by the order in which the places are named, as has already been observed by Cortius." *Kritzius*.

[80] Leptis--There were two cities of this name. Leptis Major, now *Lebida*, lay between the two Syrtes; Leptis Minor, now *Lempta*, between the smaller Sytis and Carthage. It is the latter that is meant here, and in c. 77, 78.

[81] Next to the Catabathmos--*Ad Catabathmon*. *Ad* means, on the side of the country toward the Catabathmos. "Catabathmon *initium* ponens Sallustius ab eo *discedit*." Kritzius.

[82] Along the sea-coast--***Secundo mari***. "Si quis secundum mare pergat" ***Wasse.***

[83] Of Therseans--***Theraeon***. From the island of Thera, one of the Sporades, in the Aegean Sea, now called ***Santorin***. Battus was the leader of the colony. See Herod., iv. 145; Strab., xvii. 8; Pind. Pyth., iv.

[84] Two Syrtes--See c. 78.

[85] Leptis--That is, ***Leptis Major***. See above on this c.

[86] Altars of the Philaeni--see c. 79.

[87] To the south of Numidia--***Super Numidiam***. "Ultra Numidiam, meridiem versus." ***Burnouf***.

[88] Had lately possessed--***Novissime habuerant***. In the interval between the second and third Punic wars.

[89] XXI. Both armies took up, etc.--I have omitted the word ***interim*** at the beginning of this sentence, as it would be worse than useless in the translation. It signifies, during the interval before the armies came to an engagement; but this is sufficiently expressed at the termination of the sentence.

[90] Cirta--Afterward named ***Sittianorum Colonia***, from P. Sittius Nucerinus (mentioned in Cat., c. 21), who assisted Caesar in the African war, and was rewarded by him with the possession of this city and its lands. It is now called ***Constantina***, from Constantine the Great, who enlarged and restored it when it had fallen into decay.

Strabo describes it, xvii. 3.

[91] Twilight was beginning to appear--*Obscuro etiam tum lumine*. Before day had fairly dawned.

[92] Romans--*Togatorum*. Romans, with, perhaps, some of the allies, engaged in merchandise, or other peaceful occupations, and therefore wearing the *toga*. They are called *Italici* in c. 26.

[93] Three young men--*Tres adolescentes*. Cortius includes these words in brackets, regarding them as the insertion of some sciolist. But a sciolist, as Burnouf observes, would hardly have thought of inserting *tres adolescentes*. The words occur in all the MSS., and are pretty well confirmed by what is said below, c. 25, that when the senate next sent a deputation, they took care to make it consist of majores natu, nobiles. *See on* adolescens, Cat., c. 38.

[94] XXII. Told much less than the truth--*Sed is rumor clemens erat*. "It fell below the truth, not telling the whole of the atrocity that had been committed." **Gruter.** "Priscian (xviii. 26) interprets *clemens* 'non nimius,' alluding to this passage of Sallust."
Kritzius. All the later commentators have adopted this interpretation, except Burnouf, who adopts the supposition of Ciacconius, that a vague and uncertain rumor is meant.

[95] Right of nations--*Jure gentium.* "That is, the right of avenging himself." **Rupertus.**

[96] XXIV. Pays no regard--*Neque--in animo habeat.* This letter of Adherbal's, both in matter and tone, is very similar to his speech in c. 14.

[97] I have experienced, even before--*Jam antea expertus sum.* He means, in the result of his speech to the senate.

[98] XXV. Chief of the senate--*Princeps senatus.* "He whose name was first entered in the censors' books was called *Princeps Senatus*, which title used to be given to the person who of those alive had been censor first (***qui primus censor, ex iis qui viverent, fuisset***), but after the year 544, to him whom the censors thought most worthy, Liv., xxvii. 13. This dignity, although it conferred no command or emolument, was esteemed the very highest, and was usually retained for life, Liv., xxxiv. 44; xxxix. 52. It is called ***Principatus***; and hence afterward the Emperor was named ***Princeps***, which word properly denotes rank, and not power." Adam's Rom. Antiq., p. 3.

[99] At length the evil incitements of ambition prevailed--Vicit tamen in avido ingenio pravum consilium. "Evil propensities gained the ascendency in his ambitious disposition."

[100] XXVI. The Italians--***Italici.*** See c. 21.

[101] XXVII. By the Sempronian law--***Lege Sempronia.*** This was the ***Lex Sempronia de Provinciis.*** In the early ages of the republic, the provinces were decreed by the senate to the consuls after they were elected; but by this law, passed A.U.C. 631, the senate fixed on two provinces for the future consuls before their election (Cic. Pro Dom., 9; De Prov. Cons., 2), which they, after entering on their office, divided between themselves by lot or agreement. The law was passed by Caius Gracchus. See Adam's Rom. Antiq., p. 105.

[102] Publius Scipio Nasica--"The great-grandson of him who was pronounced by the senate to be ***vir optimus***; and son of him who, though holding no office at the time, took part in putting to death

Tiberius Gracchus. He was consul with Bestia, A.U.C. 643, and died in his consulship. Cic. Brut., 34." ***Burnouf.***

[103] Lucius Bestia Calpurnius--"He had been on the side of the nobility against the Gracchi, and was therefore in favor with the senate. After his consulship he was accused and condemned by the Mamilian law (c. 40), for having received money from Jugurtha, Cic. Brut. c. 34. De Brosses thinks that he was the grandfather of that Bestia who was engaged in the conspiracy of Catilina." Burnouf.

[104] XXIX. For the sake of giving confidence--***Fidei causa.*** "In order that Jugurtha might have confidence in Bestia, Sextius the quaestor was sent as a sort of hostage into one of Jugurtha's towns." ***Cortius.***

[105] As if by an evident majority of voices--Quasi per saturam exquisitis sententiis. "The opinions being taken in a confused manner," or, as we say, *in the lump*. The sense manifestly is, that there was (or was said to be) such a preponderating majority in Jugurtha's favor, that it was not necessary to ask the opinion of each individual in order. ***Satura***, which some think to be always an adjective, with ***lanx*** understood, though ***lanx***, according to Scheller, is never found joined with it in ancient authors, was a plate filled with various kinds of fruit, such as was annually offered to the gods. "Lanx plena diversis frugibus in templum Cereris infertur, quae satura nomine appellatur," Acron. ad Hor. Sat., i. 1, *init*. "Lanx. referta variis multisque primitiis, sacris Cereris inferebatur," Diomed., iii. p. 483."Satura, cibi genus ex variis rebus conditum," Festus ***sub voce***. See Casaubon. de Rom. Satira, ii. 4; Kritzius ad h. l., and Scheller's Lex. v., ***Satur.*** In the Pref. to Justinian's Pandects, that work is called opus sparsim et quasi per saturam collectum, utile cum inutilibus mixtim.

[106] To preside at the election of magistrates--Ad magistratus rogandos. *The presiding magistrate had* to ask the consent of the people, saying *Velitis, jubeatis--rogo Quirites.*

[107] XXX. To give in full--*Perscribere.* "To write at length." The reader might suppose, at first, that Sallust transcribed this speech from some publication; but in that case, as Burnouf observes, he would rather have said *ascribere.* Besides, the following *hujuscemodi* shows that Sallust did not profess to give the exact words of Memmius. And the speech is throughout marked with Sallustian phraseology. "The commencement of it, there is little doubt, is imitated from Cato, of whose speech *De Lusitanis* the following fragment is extant in Aul. Gell. xiii. 24: Multa me dehortata sunt huc prodere, anni, aetas, vox vires, senectus." Kritzius.

[108] XXXI. During the last fifteen years--*His annis quindecim.* "It was at this time, A.U.C. 641, twenty-two years since the death of Tiberius Gracchus, and ten since that of Caius; Sallust, or Memmius, not to appear to make too nice a computation, takes a mean." *Burnouf.* The manuscripts, however, vary; some read *fifteen*, and others *twelve*. Cortius conjectured *twenty*, as a rounder number, which Kritzius and Dietsch have inserted in their texts. *Twenty* is also found in the Editio Victoriana, Florence, 1576.

[109] Your defenders have perished--*Perierint vestri defensores.* Tiberius and Caius Gracchus, and their adherents.

[110] Liberty of speech--*Libertatem.* Liberty of speech is evidently intended.

[111] Every civil and religions obligation--*Divina et humana omnia.*

"They offended against the laws, when they took bribes from an enemy; against the honor of Rome when they did what was unworthy of it, and greatly to its injury; and against gods and men, against all divine and human obligations, when they granted to a wicked prince not only impunity, but even rewards, for his crimes." ***Dietsch.***

[112] Slaves purchased with money, etc.--***Servi, aere parati,*** etc. This is taken from another speech of Cato, of which a portion is preserved in Aul. Gell. x. 3: Servi injurias nimis aegre ferunt; quid illos bono genere natos, magna virtute praeditos, animi habuisse atque habituros, dum vivent? "Slaves are apt to be too impatient of injuries; and what feelings do you think that men of good family, and of great merit, must have had, and will have as long as they live?"

[113] Public spirit--***Pietas.*** Under this word are included all duties that we ought to perform to those with whom we are intimately connected, or on whom we are dependent, as our parents, our country, and the gods. I have borrowed my translation of the word from Rose.

[114] The marks of favor which proceed from you--***Beneficia vestra.*** Offices of state, civil and military.

[115] A greater disgrace to lose, etc.--Quod majus dedecus est parta amitere quam omnino non paravisse. [Greek: Aischion de echontas aphairethaenai ae ktomenous atychaesai] Thucyd. ii. 62.

[116] These times please you less than those, etc.--Illa quam haec tempora magis placent, ***etc.*** "Those times, which immediately succeeded the deaths of the Gracchi, and which were distinguished for the tyranny of the nobles, and the humiliation of the people; these times, in which the people have begun to rouse their spirit and exert their liberty." ***Burnouf.***

[117] Embezzlement of the public money--*Peculatus aerarii.* "Peculator, qui furtum facit pecuniae publicae." Ascon. Pedian. in Cic. Verr i.

[118] Kings--I have substituted the plural for the singular. "No name was more hated at Rome than that of a king; and no sentiment, accordingly, could have been better adapted to inflame the minds of Memmius's hearers, than that which he here utters." **Dietsch.**

[119] If the crimes of the wicked are suppressed, etc.--Si injuriae non sint, haud saepe auxilii egeas. "Some foolishly interpret *auxilium* as signifying *auxilium tribunicium*, the aid of the tribunes; but it is evident to me that Sallust means aid against the injuries of bad men, *i.e. revenge or punishment."* Kritzius. "If injuries are repressed, or prevented, there will be less need for the help of good men and it will be of less consequence if they become inactive." **Dietsch.**

[120] XXXII. Lucius Cassius--This is the man from whom came the common saying *cui bono?* "Lucius Cassius, whom the Roman people thought the most accurate and wisest of judges, was accustomed constantly to inquire, in the progress of a cause, *cui bono fuisset*, of what advantage any thing had been." Cic. pro Rosc. Am. 80. "His tribunal," says Valerius Maximus (iii. 7), "was called, from his excessive severity, the rock of the accused." It was probably on account of this quality in his character that he was now sent into Numidia.

[121] Under guarantee of the public faith--*Interposita fide publica.* See Cat.47, 48. So a little below, *fidem suam interponit. Interpono* is "to pledge."

[121] Under guarantee of the public faith--*Interposita fide publica.* See Cat. 47, 48. So a little below, *fidem suam interponit. Interpono* is "to pledge."

[122] XXXIII. In the garb, as much as possible, of a suppliant--Cultu quam maxime miserabili. "In such a garb as accused persons, or suppliants, were accustomed to adopt, when they wished to excite compassion, putting on a mean dress, and allowing their hair and beard to grow." ***Burnouf.***

[123] XXXIV. Enjoined the prince to hold his peace--A single tribune might, by such intervention, offer an effectual opposition to almost any proceeding. On the great power of the tribunes, see Adam's Rom. Ant., under the head "Tribunes of the People."

[124] Every other act to which anger prompts--Aliis omnibus, qua ira fieri amat. "These words have given rise to wonderful hallucinations; for Quintilian, ix. 3. 17, having observed that many expressions of Sallust are borrowed from the Greek, as Vulgus amat fieri, all interpreters, from Cortius downward, have thought that the structure of Sallust's words must be Greek, and have taken *ira,* in this passage, for an ablative, and *quae* for a nominative plural. Gerlach has even gone so far as to take liberties with the words cited By Quintilian, and to correct them, please the gods, into quae in Vulgus amat fieri. But how could there have been such want of penetration in learned critics, such deficiency in the knowledge of the two languages, that, when the imitation of the Greek, noticed by Quintilian, has reference merely to the word [Greek: philei], ***amat***, they should think of extending it to the dependence of a singular verb on a neuter plural? With truth, indeed, though with much simplicity, does Gerlach observe, that you will in vain seek for instances of this mode of expression in other writers." ***Kritzius.*** Dietsch agrees with

Kritzius; and there will, I hope, be no further doubt that *quae* is the accusative and *ira* the nominative; the sense being, "which anger loves or desires to be done." Another mode of explanation has been suggested, namely, to understand *multitudo* as the nominative case to *amat*, making *ira* the ablative; but this method is far more cumbersome, and less in accordance with the style of Sallust. The words quoted by Quintilian do not refer, as Cortius erroneously supposes, to this passage, but to some part of Sallust's works that is now lost.

[125] XXXV. Should be disturbed--*Movere* is the reading of Cortius; *moveri* that of most other editors, in conformity with most of the MSS. and early editions.

[126] The times at which he resorted to particular places--Loca atque tempora cuncta. "All his places and times." There can be no doubt that the sense is what I have given in the text.

[127] In accordance with the law of nations, etc.--As the public faith had been pledged to Jugurtha for his security, his retinue was on the same footing as that of embassadors, the persons of whose attendants are considered as inviolable as their own, as long as they commit no offense against the laws of the country in which they are resident. If any such offense is committed by an attendant of an embassador, an application is usually made by the government to the embassador to deliver him up for trial. Bomilcar seems to have been apprehended without any application having been made to Jugurtha; as, in our own country, the Portuguese embassador's brother, who was one of his retinue, was apprehended and executed for a murder, by Oliver Cromwell. See, on this point, Grotius De Jure Bell, et Pac., xviii, 8; Vattel, iv. 9; Burlamaqui on Politic Law, part iv. ch. 15. Jugurtha, says Vattel, should have given up Bomilcar; but such was not Jugurtha's object.

[128] At the commencement of the proceedings--*In priori actione.* That is, when Bomilcar was apprehended and charged with the murder.

[129] His other subjects would be deterred from obeying him--Reliquos popularis metus invaderet parendi sibi. "Fear of obeying him should take possession of his other subjects."

[130] That it was a venal city, etc.--***Urbem venalem,*** etc. I consider, with Cortias, that this is the proper way of taking these words. Some would render them ***O venal city,*** etc., because Livy, Epit. lxiv., has ***O urbem venalem,*** but this seems to require that the verb should be in the second person; and it is probable that in Livy we should either eject the O or read ***inveneris.*** Florus, iii. 1, gives the words in the same way as Sallust.

[131] XXXVI. As propraetor--***Pro praetore.*** With the power of lieutenant-general.

[132] XXXVII. Throughout the year--***Totius anni.*** That is, all that remained of the year.

[133] On the edge of a steep hill--In praerupti montis extremo. "In extremo ***a scholiast rightly interprets*** in margine," Gerlach. Cortius, whom Langius follows, considers that ***in extremo*** means at the bottom; a notion which Kritzius justly condemns; for, as Gerlach asks, what would that have to do with the strength of the place? Muller would have us believe that ***in extremo*** means ***at the top***; but if Sallust had meant to say that the city was at the top, he would hardly have chosen the word ***extremus*** for the purpose. Doubtless, as Gerlach observes, the city was on the top of the hill, which was broad enough to hold it; but the words ***in extremo*** signify that the walls were

even with the side of the hill. Of the site of the town of Suthul no traces are now to be found.

[134] Vineae--Defenses made of hurdles or other wood, and often covered with raw hides, to defend the soldiers who worked the battering-ram. The word that comes nearest to *vineae* in our language is *mantelets*. Before this word, in many editions, occurs the phrase *ob thesauros oppidi potiundi*, which Cortius, whom I follow, omits.

[135] XXXIII. That their defection might thus be less observed--Ita delicta occultiora fore. Cortius transferred these words to this place from the end of the preceding sentence; Kritzius and Dietsch have restored them to their former place. Gerlach thinks them an intruded gloss.

[136] The chief centurion--*Centurio primi pili.* There were sixty centurions in a Roman legion; the one here meant was the first, or oldest, centurion of the Triarii, or Pilani.

[137] As death was the alternative--Quia mortis metu mutabant. Neither manuscripts nor critics are agreed about this passage. Cortius, from a suggestion of Palmerius, adopted *mutabant*; most other editors have *mutabantur*; but both are to be taken in the same sense; for *mutabant* is equivalent to *mutabant se*. Cortius's interpretation appears the most eligible: "Permutabantur cum metuenda morte," i.e. there were those conditions on one side, and death on the other, and if they did not accept the conditions, they must die. Kritzius fancifully and strangely interprets, propter mortis metum se mutabant, i.e., alia videbantur atque erant, or the acceptance of the terms appeared excusable to the soldiers, because they were threatened with death if they did not accept them. It is worth while to notice the variety of readings exhibited in the manuscripts collated by Cortius:

ten exhibit *mutabantur*; three, *minitabantur*; three, *multabantur*; three, *tenebantur*; one, *tenebatur*; one, *cogebantur*; one, *cogebatur*; one, *angustiabantur*; one, *urgebantur*; and one mortis metuebant pericula. **There is also, he adds, in some copies,** mutabant, which the Bipont editors and Mueller absurdly adopted.

[138] XXXIX. Under all the circumstances of the case--***Ex copia rerum.*** From the number of things which he had to consider.

[139] XL. The Latins and Italian allies--Per homines nominis Latini, et socios Italicos. "The right of voting was not extended to all the Latin people till A.U.C. 664, and the Italian allies did not obtain it till some years afterward." ***Kritzius.*** So that at this period, which was twenty years earlier, their influence could only be employed in an underhand way. Compare c.42.

[140] Marcus Scaurus--See c. 15. That he was appointed on this occasion, is an evident proof of his commanding influence.

[141] But the investigation, notwithstanding, was conducted, etc.--Sed quaes tuo exercita, etc. Scaurus, it is probable, did what he could to mitigate the violence of the proceedings. Cicero, however, says that Caius Gallus ***sacerdos***, with four ***consulares***, Bestia, Caius Cato, Albinus, and Opimius, were condemned and exiled by this law of Mamilius. See Brut., c. 34.

[142] XLI. Took, snatched, and seized--Ducere, ***trahere, rapere***. "***Ducere*** conveys the notion of cunning and fraud; ***trahere*** of some degree of force; ***rapere*** of open violence." ***Muller***. The words chiefly refer to offices in the state, as is apparent from what follows.

[141] The parents and children of the soldiers, etc.--

Quid quod usque proximos
  Revellis agri terminos, et ultra
Limites clientium
  Salis avarus? Pellitur paternos
In sinu ferens deos
  Et uxor et vir, sordidosque natos.

Hor. Od., ii. 18.

What can this impious av'rice stay?
Their sacred landmarks torn away.
You plunge into your neighbor's grounds,
And overleap your client's bounds,
Helpless the wife and husband flee,
And in their arms, expell'd by thee,
Their household gods, adored in vain,
Their infants, too, a sordid train.

[144] Among the nobility--**Ex nobilitate.** Cortius injudiciously omits those words. The reference is to the Gracchi.

[145] By means of the allies and Latins--See on, c. 40.

[146] But to a reasonable man it is more agreeable to submit, etc.--Sed bono vinci satius est, quam malo more injuriam vincere. Bono, *sc.* viro. "That is, if the nobility had been truly worthy characters, they would rather have yielded to the Gracchi, than have revenged any wrong that they had received from them in an unprincipled manner." **Dietsch.** Thus this is a reflection on the nobles; in which notion of the passage Allen concurs with Dietsch. Others, as Cortius, think it a reflection on the too great violence of the Gracchi. The brevity with which Sallust had expressed himself makes it difficult to

decide. Kritzius, who thinks that the remark is in praise of the Gracchi, supplies the ellipse thus: "Sane concedi debet Gracchis non satis moderatum animum fuiase; quae res ipsis adeo interitum attulit*; sed* sic quoque egregii viri putandi sunt; nam bono vinci," etc. Langius and Burnouf join **bono** with **more**, but do not differ much in their interpretations of the passage from that given by Dietsch.

[147] XLIII. Of a character uniformly irreproachable--Fama tamen aequabili et inviolata. Aequabilis is uniform, always the same, keeping an even tenor.

[148] Regarded all things as common to himself and his colleague--Ali omnia sibi cum collega ratus. "Other matters, unconnected with the war against Jugurtha, he thought that he would have to manage in conjunction with his colleague, and that, consequently, he might give but partial attention to them; but that the war in Numidia was committed to his sole care." **Cortius.** Other interpretations of these words have been suggested; but they are fanciful and unworthy of notice.

[149] Princes--**Reges.** Who these were, the commentators have not attempted to conjecture.

[150] XLIV. By Spurius Albinus, the proconsul.--A Spurio Albino proconsule. *This is the general reading. Cortius has,* Spurii Albini pro consule*, with which we may understand* agentis *or* imperantis, but can hardly believe it to be what Sallust wrote. Kritzius reads, **Spurii Albini proconsulis**.

[151] In a stationary camp--***Stativis castris***. In contradistinction to that which the soldiers formed at the end of a day's march.

[152] But neither had the camp been fortified, etc.--Sed neque muniebantur ea (se. castra), neque more militari vigiliae deducebantur. "*The words* sed neque muniebantur ea are wanting in almost all the manuscripts, as well as in all the editions, except that of Cyprianus Popma." *Kritzius*. Gerlach, however, had, previously to Kritz, inserted them in his text though in brackets; for he supposed them to be a mere conjecture of some scribe, who was not satisfied with a single *neque*. But they have been found in a codex of Fronto, by Angelo Mai, and have accordingly been received as genuine by Kritz and Dietsch. Potter and Burnouf have omitted the *ea*, thinking, I suppose, that in such a position it could hardly be Sallust's; but the verb requires a nominative case to prevent it from being referred to the following *vigiliae*.

[153] Foreign wine--*Vino advectitio* Imported. Africa does not abound in wine.

[154] XLV. With regard to other things--Caeteris. Cortius, whom Gerlach follows, considers this word as referring to the men or officers; but Kritzius and Dietsch, with better judgment, understand *rebus*.

[155] Numerous sentinels--*Vigilias crebras*. At short intervals, says Kritzius, from each other.

[156] XLVI. Villages--*Mapalibus*. See c. xviii. The word is here used for a collection of huts, a village.

[157] Here the consul, to try the disposition of the inhabitants, and, should they allow him, to take advantage of the situation of the place, etc.--Huc consul, simul tentandi gratia, et si paterentur, opportuniatis loci, praesidium imponit. *This is a* locus

veratissimus, about which no editor has satisfied himself. I have deserted Cortius and followed Dietsch, who seems to have settled the passage, on the basis of Havercamp's text, with more judgment than any other commentator. Cortius read, Huc consul simul tentandi gratia, si paterent opportunitates loci, *etc., taking* opportuniatates in the sense of *munitiones*, "defenses;" but would Sallust have said that Metellus put a garrison in the place, to try if its defenses would be open to him? *Havercamp's reading is,* simul tentan si gratia, et si paterentur opportunitates loci, *etc. Palmerius conjectured* simul tentandi gratia, si paterentur; et opportunitate loci, which Gerlach and Kritsius adopt, except that they change the place of the *et*, and put it before *si*. Allen thinks that he has amended the passage by reading Huc consul, simul si paterentur tentandi, et opportunitatis loci, gratia; but this conjecture is liable to similar objection with that of Cortius. Other varieties of reading it is needless to notice. But it is observable that four manuscripts, as Kritzius remarks, have *propter opportunitates,* which led me long ago to suppose that the true reading must be simul tentandi gratia, simul propter opportunitates loci. Simul propter might easily have been corrupted into *si paterentur*.

[158] Frequent arrival of supplies--*Commeatum.* "Frumenti et omnium rerum quarum in bello usus est, largam copiam." *Kritzius*. I follow the text of Cortius (retaining the words *juvaturum ecercitum*) which Kritzius sufficiently justifies. There is a variety of readings, but all much the same in sense.

[159] Extraordinary earnestness--*Impensius modo.* Cortius and Kritzius interpret this *modo* as the ablative case of modus; i. e. quam modus erat, *or* supra modum; but Dietsch and Burnouf question the propriety of this interpretation, and consider the *modo* to be

the same as that in **tantummodo, dummodo,** etc. The same expression occurs again in c. 75.

[160] XLVIII. Running parallel with the stream--***Tractu pari.*** It may be well to illustrate this and the following chapter by a copy of the lines which Cortius has drawn, "to excite," as he says, "the imagination of his readers:"

```
        River Muthul, flowing from the south
    ------------------------------------------------
                            I  Hill on
        North               I  which
        <-----------    I       I  Jugurtha
                        I       I  posted
                        I       I  himself
    ------------------------------------------------
        Range of hills, parallel I with the Muthul
                        I
                        I  Route of Metellus
                        I
```

[161] XLIX. In a transverse direction--***Transverso itinere***. It lay on the flank of the Romans as they marched toward the river, in dextero latere, c.49, fin.

[162] Well acquainted with the country--***Prudentes.*** "Periti loci et regionis." ***Cortius.*** Or it may mean knowing what they were to do, while the enemy would be ***imperiti,*** surprised and perplexed.

[163] Would crown--***Confirmaturum***. Would establish, settle, put the last hand to them.

[164] Was seen--***Conspicitur.*** This is the reading adopted by Cortius,

Mueller, and Allen, as being that of all the manuscripts. Havercamp, Kritzius, and Dietsch admitted into their texts, on the sole authority of Donatus ad Ter. Eun. ii. 3, ***conspicatur***, i.e. (Metellus) catches sight of the enemy. The latter reading, perhaps, makes a better connection.

[165] Rendering it uncertain--***Incerti.*** Presenting such an appearance that a spectator could not be certain what they were.

[166] He drew up these in the right wing--in three lines--In dextero latere triplicibus subsidiis aciem instruxit. In the other passages in which Sallust has the word ***subsidia*** (Cat. c. 59), he uses it for ***the lines behind the front.*** Thus he says of Catiline, Octo cohortes in fronte constituit; reliqua signa in subsidiis arctius collocat; ***and of Petreius,*** Cohortes veteranas--in fronte; post eas reliquum exercitum in subsidiis locat. But whether he uses the word in the same sense here; whether we might, as Cortius thinks (whom Gerlach and Dietsch follow), call the division of Metellus's troops ***quadruple*** instead of ***triple,*** or whether he arranged them as De Brosses and others suppose, in the usual disposition of Hastati, Principes, and Triarii, who shall place beyond dispute? The probability, however, if Sallust is consistent with himself in his use of the word, lies with Cortius. Gerlach refers to Caesar, De Bell, Civ., iii. 89: "Celeriter ex tertia acie singulas cohortes detraxit, atque ex his quartam instituit; but this does not illustrate Sallust's use of the word ***subsidia***: Caesar forms a fourth ***acies***; Metellus draws up one ***acies*** triplicibus subsidia".

[167] With the front changed into a flank--***Transversis principiis.*** He made the whole army wheel to the left, so that what was their front line, or ***principia,*** as they faced the enemy on the hill, became their flank as they marched from the mountain toward the river.

[168] L. Behind the front line--*Post principia.* The *principia* are the same as those mentioned in the preceding note, that is, the front line when the army faced that of Jugurtha on the hill, but which presented its flank to the enemy when the army was on its march. So that Marius commanded in the center ("in medio agmine," says Dietsch), while Metellus took the lead with the cavalry of the left wing. See the following note.

[169] Cavalry on the left wing--which, on the march, had become the van--Sinistrae ulae equitibus--qui in agmine principes facti erant. When Metellus halted (c. 49, fin.), and drew up his troops fronting the hill on which Jugurtha was posted, he placed all his cavalry in the wings; consequently, when the army wheeled to the left, and marched forward, the cavalry of the left wing became the van.

[170] LI. Of the whole struggle--*Totius negotii.* That is, on the side of the Romans.

[171] LII. The enemy's ignorance of the country--Regio hostibus ignara. Ignara *for* ignota; a country unknown to the enemy.

[172] LIII. Fatigued and exhausted--*Fessi lassique.* I am once more obliged to desert Cortius, who reads *laetique*. The sense, as Kritzius and Dietsch observe, shows that *laeti* can not be the reading, for there must evidently be a complete antithesis between the two parts of the sentence; an antithesis which would be destroyed by the introduction of *laeti*. Gerlach, though he retains *laeti* in his text, condemns it in his notes.

[173] LIV. Which could only be conducted, etc.--Quod, nisi ex illius lubidine, geri non posset. **Cortius omits the** non **before** posset,

but almost every other editor, except Allen, has retained it, from a conviction of necessity.

[174] Under these circumstances, however--*Ex copia tamen.* With *copia* we must understand *consiliorum* or *rerum,* as at the end of c. 39. All the manuscripts, except two, have *inopia*, which editors have justly rejected as inconsistent with the sense.

[175] LV. A thanksgiving--*Supplicia.* The same as *supplicatio,* on which the reader may consult Adam's Rom. Ant., or Dr. Smith's Dictionary.

[176] LVI. Dared not be guilty of treachery--*Fallere nequibant.* "Through dread of the severest punishments if they should fall into the hands of the Romans. Valerius Maximus, ii. 7, speaks of deserters having been deprived of their hands by Quintus Fabius Maximus; of others who were crucified or beheaded by the elder Africanus; of others who were thrown to wild beasts by Africanus the younger; and of others who were sentenced by Paulus Aemilius to be trampled to death by elephants. Hence it appears that the punishment of deserters was left to the pleasure of the general." *Burnouf.*

[177] Sicca--It stood on the banks of the Bagradas, at some distance from the coast, and contained a celebrated Temple of Venus. Val. Max., ii. 6. D'Anville thinks it the same as the modern *Kef.*

[178] LVII. Javelins--*Pila.* This *pilum* may have been, as Mueller suggests, similar to the *falarica* which Livy (xxi. 8) says that the Saguntines used against their besiegers. Falarica erat Saguntinis, missile telum hastili abiegno--id, sicut in pilo, quadratum stuppa circumligabant, linebantque pice:--quod cum medium accensum mitteretur, etc. Of Sallust's other words, in the latter part of this sentence,

the sense is clear, but the readings of different editors are extremely various. Cortius and Gerlach have sudes, pila praeterea picem sulphure et taeda mixtam ardentia mittere: but it can scarcely be believed that Sallust wrote ***picem--taeda mixtam.*** Havercamp gives pice et sulphure taedam mixtam ardentia mittere, which has been adopted by Kritzius and Dietsch, except that they have changed ***ardentia,*** on the authority of some of the manuscripts, into ***ardenti***.

[179] LIX. And thus, with the aid of the light-armed foot, almost succeeded in giving the enemy a defeat--Ita expeditis peditibus suis hostes paene victos dare. Cortius, Kritzius, and Allen, concur in regarding ***expeditis peditibus*** as an ablative of the instrument, i.e. as equivalent to ***per expeditos pedites*** and ***victos dare*** as nothing more than ***vincere.*** This appears to be the right mode of explanation; but most of the translators, French as well as English, have taken ***expeditis peditibus*** as a dative, and given to the passage the sense that "the cavalry delivered up the enemy, when nearly conquered, to be dispatched by the light-armed foot."

[180] LX. Attacks, or preparations for defense, were made in all quarters--***Oppugnare aut parare omnibus locis.*** There is much discussion among the critics whether these verbs are to be referred to the besiegers or the besieged. Cortius and Gerlach attribute ***oppugnare*** to the Romans, and ***parare*** to the men of Zama; a distinction which Kritzius justly condemns. There can be little doubt that they are spoken of both parties equally.

[181] LXI. The rest of his forces--in that part of our province nearest to Numidia--Caeterum exercitum in provinciam, quae proxima est Numidiae, hiemandi gratia collocat. ***"The words*** quae proxima est Numidiae Cortius would eject as superfluous and spurious. But it is to be understood that Metellus did not distribute his troops through

the whole of the province, but in that part which is nearest to Numidia, in order that they might be easily assembled in case of an attack of the enemy or any other emergency. There is, therefore, no need to read with the Bipont edition and Mueller, *qua proxima,* etc. though this is in itself not a bad conjecture." **Kritzius**.

[182] LXII. Was summoned to appear in person at Tisidium, etc.--***Cum ipse ad imperandum Tisidium vocaretur.*** The gerund is used, as grammarians say, in a passive sense. "The town of Tisidium is nowhere else mentioned. Strabo (xvii. 3, p. 488, Ed. Tauch.) speaks of a place named [Greek: ***Tisiaioi***], which was utterly destroyed, and not a vestige of it left." **Gerlach**.

[183] LXIII. Sacrificing to the gods--***Per hostias dis supplicante.*** Supplicating or worshiping the gods with sacrifices, and trying to learn their intentions as to the future by inspection of the entrails. "Marius was either a sincere believer in the absurd superstitions and dreams of the soothsayers, or pretended to be so, from a knowledge of the nature of mankind, who are eager to listen to wonders, and are ore willing to be deceived than to be taught." **Burnouf.** See Plutarch, Life of Marius. He could interpret omens for himself, according to Valerius Maximus, i. 5.

[184] The people--disposed of, etc.--Etiam tum alios magistratus plebes, consulatum nobilitas, inter se per manus tradebat. The commentators have seen the necessity of understanding a verb with ***plebes.*** Kritzius suggests ***habebat;*** Gerlach ***grebat*** or ***accipiebat***.

[185] A disgrace to it--***Pollutus.*** He was considered, as it were, unclean. See Cat., c. 23, *fin*.

[186] LXIV. As soon as the public business would allow him--Ubi

primum potuisset per negotia publica. As soon as he could through (regard to) the public business.

[187] With his own son--***Cum filio suo.*** With the son of Metellus. He tells Marius that it would be soon enough for him to stand for the consulship in twenty-three years' time, the legitimate age for the consulship being forty-three.

[188] In the camp with his father--***Contubernio patris.*** He was among the young noblemen in the consul's retinue, who were sent out to see military service under him. This was customary. See Cic. Pro Cael. Pro Planc. 11.

[189] LXV. Which was as weak as his body--***Ob morbos--parum valido.*** Sallust had already expressed this a few lines above.

[190] Merchants--***Negotiatores.*** "Every one knows that Romans of equestrian dignity were accustomed to trade in the provinces." ***Burnouf.***

[191] With the most honorable demonstrations in his favor --***Honestissima suffragatione.*** "***Suffragatio*** was the zealous recommendation of those who solicited the votes of their fellow-citizens in favor of some candidate. See Festus, s.v. ***Suffragatores,*** p. 266, Lindem." ***Dietsch.*** It was honorable, in the case of Marius, as it was without bribery, and seemed to have the good of the republic in view.

[192] The Mamilian law--See c. 40.

[193] LXVI. Advantageous positions--***Suos locos.*** Places favorable for his views. See Kritzius on c. 54.

[194] LXVII. Were in trepidation. At the citadel, etc.--I have translated this passage in conformity with the texts of Gerlach, Kritzius, Dietsch, Mueller, and Allen, who put a point between *trepidare* and *ad arcem*. Cortina, Havercamp, and Burnouf have *trepidare ad arcem*, without any point. Which method gives the better sense, any reader can judge.

[195] On the roofs of the houses--***Pro tectis aedificiorum***. In front of the roofs of the houses; that is, at the parapets. "In prima tectorum parte." ***Kritzius***. The roofs were flat.

[196] Worthless and infamous character--***Improbus intestabilisque***. These words are taken from the twelve tables of the Roman law: See Aul. Gell. vi. 7, xv. 3. Horace, in allusion to them, has intestabilis et sacer***, Sat. ii. 3.181,*** Intestabilis signified a person to be of so infamous a character that he was not allowed to give evidence in a court of justice.

[197] LXVIII. Averse to further exertion--***Tum abnuentes omnia***. Most of the translators have understood by these words that the troops refused to obey orders; but Sallust's meaning is only that they expressed, by looks and gestures, their unwillingness to proceed.

[198] LXIX As a native of Latium--***Nam is civis ex Latio erat***. "As he was a Latin, he was not protected by the Porcian law (see Cat., c. 51), though how far this law had power in the camp, is not agreed." ***Allen***. Gerlach thinks that it had the same power in the camp as elsewhere, with reference to Roman citizens. But Roman citizenship was not extended to the Latins till the end of the Social War, A.U.C. 662. Plutarch, however, in his Life of Caius Gracchus (c. 9), speaks of Livius Drusus having been abetted by the patricians in proposing a law for exempting the Latin soldiers from being flogged, about thirty

years earlier; and it seems to have been passed, but, from this passage of Sallust, appears not to have remained in force. Lipsius touches on this obscure point in his *Militia Romana*, v. 18, but settles nothing. Plutarch, in his Life of Marius, c. 8, says that Turpilius was an old retainer of the family of Metellus, whom he attended, in this war, as *præfectus fabrum*, or master of the artificers; that, being afterward appointed governor of Vacca, he exercised his office with great justice and humanity, that his life was spared by Jugurtha at the solicitation of the inhabitants; that, when he was brought to trial, Metellus thought him innocent, and that he would not have been condemned but for the malice of Marius, who exasperated the other members of the council against him. He adds, that after his death, his innocence became apparent, and that Marius boasted of having planted in the breast of Metellus an avenging fury, that would not fail to torment him for having put to death the innocent friend of his family. Hence Sir Henry Steuart has accused Sallust of wilfully misrepresenting the character of Turpilius, as well as the whole transaction. But as much credit is surely due to Sallust as to Plutarch.

[199] LXX. To which Jugurtha--was unable to attend--Quae Jugartha, fesso, aut majoribus astricto, superaverant. "Which had remained to (or been too much for) Jugurtha, when weary, or engaged in more important affairs."

[200] Among the winter-quarters of the Romans--Inter hiberna Romanorum. It is stated in c. 61, as Kritzius observes, that Metellus, when he put his army into winter-quarters, had, at the same time, placed garrisons in such of Jugurtha's towns as had revolted to him. The forces of the Romans being thus dispersed, Nabdalsa might justly be said to have his army *inter hiberna*, "*among* their winter-quarters."

[201] LXXI. Behind his head--*Super caput*. On the back of the bolster that supported his head; part of which might be higher than the head itself.

[202] LXXIIL The factious tribunes--*Seditiosi magistratus*.

[203] After the lapse of many years--*Post multas tempestates*. Apparently the period since A.U.C. 611, when Quintus Pompeius, who, as Cicero says (in Verr. ii. 5), was *humile atque obscuro loco natus*, obtained the consulship; that is, a term of forty-three or forty-four years.

[204] That decree was thus rendered abortive--*Ea res frustra fuit*. By a *lex Sempronia*, a law of Caius Gracchus, it was enacted that the senate should fix the provinces for the future consuls before the *comitia* for electing them were held. But from Jug. c. 26, it appears that the consuls might settle by lot, or by agreement between themselves, which of those two provinces each of them should take. How far the senate were allowed or accustomed in general, to interfere in the arrangement, it is not easy to discover: but on this occasion they had taken on themselves to pass a resolution in favor of the patrician. Lest similar scenes, however, to those of the Sempronian times should be enacted, they yielded the point to the people.

[205] LXXV. Thala--The river on which this town stood is not named by Sallust, but it appears to have been the Bagrada. It seems to have been nearly destroyed by the Romans, after the defeat of Juba, in the time of Julius Caesar; though Tacitus, Ann. iii. 21, mentions it as having afforded a refuge to the Romans in the insurrection of the Numidian chief, Tacfarinas. D'Anville and Dr. Shaw, *Travels in Bombay*, vol. i. pt. 2, ch. 5, think it the same with Telepte, now *Ferre-anah*; but this is very doubtful. See Cellar. iv. 5. It was in ruins in the time of Strabo.

[206] Had done more than was required of them--*Officia intenderant*. "Auxit *intenditque* saevitiam exacerbatus indicio filii sui Drusi" Suet. Tib. 62.

[207] LXXVI. Nor did he ever--continue, etc.--Neque postea--moratus, simulabat*, etc.--Most editors take* moratus *for* morans; Allen places a colon after it, as if it were for *moratus est*.

[208] And erected towns upon it to protect, etc.--Et super aggerem impositis turribus epus et administros tutari. "And protected the work and the workmen with towers placed on the mound." Impositis turribus is not the ablative absolute, but the ablative of the instrument.

[209] LXXVII. Leptis--Leptis Major, now *Lebida*. In c. 19, Leptis Minor is meant.

[210] Their own safety--*Suam salutem*: i.e. the safety of the people of Leptis.

[211] LXXVIII. Which take their name from their nature--Quibus nomen ex re inditum. From [Greek: *surein*], *to draw,* because the stones and sand were drawn to and fro by the force of the wind and tide. But it has been suggested that this etymology is probably false; it is less likely that their name should be from the Greek than from the Arabic, in which *sert* signifies a desert tract or region, a term still applied to the desert country bordering on the Syrtea. See Ritter, Allgem. vergleich, Geog. vol. i. p. 929. The words which, in Havercamp, close this description of the Syrtes, "Syrtes ab tractu nominatae", and which Gruter and Putschius suspected not to be Sallust's, Cortius omitted; and his example has been followed by

Muller and Burnouf; Gerlach, Kritzius, and Dietsch, have retained them. Gerlach, however, thinks them a gloss, though they are found in every manuscript but one.

[212] Almost at the extremity of Africa--*Prope in extrema Africa.* "By *extrema Africa* Gerlach rightly understands the eastern part of Africa, bordering on Egypt, and at a great distance from Numidia." *Kritzius*.

[213] The language alone--*Lingua modo*.

[214] From the king's dominions--*Ab imperio regis.* "Understand Masinissa's, Micipsa's, or Jugurtha's." *Burnouf*.

[215] LXXIX. Philaeni--The account of these Carthaginian brothers with a Greek name, *philainoi, praise-loving*, is probably a fable. Cortius thinks that the inhabitants, observing two mounds rising above the surrounding level, fancied they must have been raised, not by nature, but by human labor, and invented a story to account for their existence. "The altars," according to Mr. Rennell (Geog. of Herod., p. 640), "were situated about seven ninths of the way from Carthage to Cyrene; and the deception," he adds, "would have been too gross, had it been pretended that the Carthaginian party had traveled seven parts in nine, while the Cyrenians had traveled no more than two such parts of the way." Pliny (II. N. v. 4) says that the altars were of sand; Strabo (lib. iii.) says that in his time they had vanished. Pomponius Mela and Valerius Maximus repeat the story, but without adding any thing to render it more probable.

[216] Devoid of vegetation--*Nuda gignentium*. So c. 93, cunota gignentium natura. *Kritzius justly observes that* gignentia is not to be taken in the sense of *genita*, as Cortius and others interpret,

but in its own active sense; the ground was bare of all that was productive, *or* of whatever generates any thing. This interpretation is suggested by Perizonius ad Sanctu Minerv. i. 15.

[217] Sacrificed themselves--***Seque vitamque--condonavere***. "Nihil aliud est quam ***vitam suam***, sc.[Greek: ***eu dia dyoin***]." ***Allen***.

[218] LXXX. Sell--honorable or dishonorable--Omnia honesta atque inhonesta vendere. See Cat. c. 30. They had been bribed by Jugurtha to use their influence against Bocchus.

[219] A daughter of Bocchus, too, was married to Jugurtha--Jugurthae filia Bocchi nupserat. Several manuscripts and old editions have ***Boccho***, making Bocchus the son-in-law of Jugurtha. But Plutarch (Vit. Mar. c. 10, Sull. c. 8) and Florus (iii. 1) agree in speaking of him as Jugurtha's father-in-law. Bocchus was doubtless an older man than Jugurtha, having a grown up son, Volux, c. 105. Castilioneus and Cortius, therefore, saw the necessity of reading ***Bocchi***, and, other editors have followed them, except Gerlach, "who," says Kritzius, "has given ***Bocchi*** in his larger, and ***Boccho*** in his smaller and more recent edition, in order that readers using both may have an opportunity of making a choice."

[220] No one of them becomes a companion to him--Nulla pro socia obtinet The use of ***obtinet*** absolutely, or with the word dependent on it understood, prevails chiefly among the later Latin writers. Livy, however, has ***fama obtinuit***, xxi. 46. "The ***tyro*** is to be reminded," says Dietsch, "that ***obtinet*** is not the same as ***habetar***, but is always for ***locum obtinet***."

[221] LXXXI. The two kings, with their armies--The text has only

exercitus.

[222] To lessen Bocchus's chance of peace--Bocchi pacem imminuere. He wished to engage Bocchus in some act of hostility against the Romans, so as to render any coalition between them impossible.

[223] LXXXII. Should have learned something of the Moors --***Cognitis Mauris, i.e.*** after knowing something of the Moors, ***and not before***. ***Cognitis militibus*** is used in the same way in c. 39; and Dietsch says that ***amicitia Jugurthae parum cognita*** is for ***nondum cognita***, c. 14.

[224] LXXXIV. Discharged veterans--***Homines emeritis stipendiis.*** Soldiers who had completed their term of service.

[225] Means of warfare--***Usum belli.*** That is ea quae belli usus posceret, troops and supplies.

[226] Cherished the fancy--***Animis trahebant.*** "***Trahere animo*** is always to revolve in the mind, not to let the thought of a thing escape from the mind." ***Kritzius***.

[227] LXXXV. Its interests ought to be managed, etc.--Majore cura illam administrari quam haec peti debere. Cortius injudiciously omits the word ***illam***. No one has followed him but Allen.

[228] Hostile--***Occursantis.*** Thwarting, opposing.

[229] That you may not be deceived in me--***Ut neque vos capiamini.*** "This verb is undoubtedly used in this passage for ***decipere***. Compare Tibull. Eleg. iii. 6, 45: Nec vos aut capiant pendentia

brachia collo, Aut fallat blanda sordida tingua prece. Cic. Acad. iv. 20: *Sapientis vim maximam esse cavere, ne capiatur.*" Gerlach.

[230] To secure their election--*Per ambitionem. Ambire* is to canvass for votes; to court the favor of the people.

[231] Of yonder crowd of nobles--*ex illo globo nobilitatis. Illo,* [Greek: *deiktikos*].

[232] I know some--who after they have been elected, etc.--"At whom Marina directs this observation, it is impossible to tell. Gerlach referring to Cic. Quest. Acad. ii. 1, 2, thinks that Lucullus is meant. But if he supposes that Lucullus was present to the mind of Marius when he spoke, he is egregiously deceived, for Marius was forty years antecedent to Lucullus. It is possible, however, that *Sallust*, thinking of Lucullus when he wrote Marius's speech, may have fallen into an anachronism, and have attributed to Marius, whose character he had assumed, an observation which might justly have been made in his own day." *Kritzius*.

[233] Persons who invert the order of things--*Homines Praeposteri.* Men who do that last which should be done first.

[234] For though to discharge the duties of the office, etc.--Nam gerere, quam fieri, tempore posterius, re atque usu prius est. With *gerere* is to be understood *consulatum*; with *fieri, consulem.* This is imitated from Demosthenes, Olynth. iii.: [Greek: To gar prattein ton legein kai cheirotonein, usteron on tae taxei, proteron tae dynamei kai kreitton esti.] "Acting is posterior in order to speaking and voting, but prior and superior in effect."

[235] With those haughty nobles--Cum illorum superbui. Virtus

Scipiades et mitis sapientia Laeli.

[236] My condition *Mihi fortuna*. "That is, my lot, or condition, in which I was born, in which I had no hand in producing." **Dietsch**.

[237] The circumstance of birth, etc. Naturam unam et communem omnium existumo. "Nascendi sortem" is the explanation which Dietsch gives to **naturam**. One man is **born** as well as another, but the difference between men is made by their different modes of action; a difference which the nobles falsely suppose to proceed from fortune. "Voltaire, Mohammed, Act.I., sce. iv., has expressed the sentiment of Sallust exactly:

Les mortels sont egaux, ce n'est point la naissance,
C'est la seule vertu qui fait leur difference." **Burnouf.**

[238] And could it be inquired of the fathers, etc.--Ac, si jam ex patribus Alibini aut Bestiae quaeri posset**, etc.** Patres, in this passage, is not, as Anthon imagines, the same as **majores**; as is apparent from the word **gigni**. The fathers of Albinus and Bestia were probably dead at the time that Marius spoke. The passage which Anthon quotes from Plutarch to illustrate **patres**, is not applicable, for the word there is [Greek: pragonoi: Epunthaneto ton paronton, ei mae kai tous ekeinon oiontai progonous auto mallon an emxasthai paraplaesious ekgonous apolitein, ate dae maed autous di eugeneian, all ap aretaes kai kalon ergon endoxous genomenous.] Vit. Mar. c. 9. "He would then ask the people whether they did not think that the ancestors of those men would have wished rather to leave a posterity like him, since they themselves had not risen to glory by their high birth, but by their virtue and heroic achievements?" **Langhorne**.

[239] Abstinence--**Innocentiae**. Abstinence from all vicious indulgence.

[240] Honorable exertion--*Virtutis*. See notes on Cat. c. 1, and Jug. c. 1.

[241] They occupy the greatest part of their orations in extolling their ancestors--***Pleraque oratione majores suos extollunt.*** "They extol their ancestors in the greatest part of their speech."

[242] The glory of ancestors sheds a light on their posterity, Juvenal, viii.138:

>Incipit ipsorum contra te stare parentum
>Nobilitas, claramque facem praeferre pudendis.

>Thy fathers' virtues, clear and bright, display
>Thy shameful deeds, as with the light of day.

[243] I feel assured--***Ex animi sententia***. "It was a common form of strong asseveration." ***Gerlach.***

[244] Spears--***Hastas***. "A ***hasta pura***, that is a spear without iron, was anciently the reward of a soldier the first time that he conquered in battle, Serv. ad Virg. Aen. vi. 760; it was afterward given to one who had struck down an enemy in a sally or skirmish, Lips. ad Polyb. de Milit. Rom. v.17." ***Burnouf.***

[245] A banner--***Vexillum***. "Standards were also military rewards. Vopiscus relates that ten ***hastae purae***, and four standards of two colors, were presented to Aurelian. Suetonius (Aug. 25) says that Agrippa was presented by Augustus, after his naval victory, with a standard of the color of the sea. These standards therefore, were not, as Badius Ascensius thinks, always taken from the enemy; though this was sometimes the case, as appears from Sil. Ital. x.v. 261:

Tunc hasta viris, tunc martia cuique
Vexilla, ut meritum, et praedae libamina, dantur." *Burnouf.*

[246] Caparisons--*Phaleras*. "Sil. Ital. xv. 255:

Phaleris hic pectora fulget:
Hic *torque* aurato circumdat bellica collae.

Juvenal, xv. 60:

Ut laeti *phaleris* omnes et *torquibus* omnes.

These passages show that *phalerae*, a name for the ornaments of horses, were also decorations of men; but they differed from the *torques*, or collars, in this respect, that the *phalerae* hung down over the breast, and the *torques* only encircled the neck. See Lips. ad Polyb. de Milit. Rom. v. 17." *Burnouf.*

[247] Valor--*Virtutem.* "The Greeks, those illustrious instructors of the world, had not been able to preserve their liberty; their learning therefore had not added to their valor. *Virtus*, in this passage, is evidently *fortitudo bellica*, which, in the opinion of Marius, was *the only virtue.*" Burnouf. See Plutarch, Vit. Mar. c. 2.

[248] To be vigilant at my post--*Praesidia agitare*. Or "to keep guard at my post." "*Praesidia agitare* signifies nothing more than to protect a party of foragers or the baggage, or to keep guard round a besieged city." *Vortius.*

[249] Keep no actor--*Histrionem nullum--habeo*. "Luxuriae peregrinae origo ab exercitu Asiatico (Manlii sc. Vulsonis, A.U.C. 563) invecta

in urbem est.----Tum psaltriae sambucistriaeque et convivalia *ludionum* obiectamenta, addita epulis." Liv. xxxix. 6. "By this army returning from Asia was the origin of foreign luxury imported into the city.----At entertainments--were introduced players on the harp and timbrel, with **buffoons** for the diversion of the guests." **Baker**. Professor Anthon, who quotes this passage, says that **histrio** "here denotes a buffoon kept for the amusement of the company." But such is not the meaning of the word **histrio**. It signifies one who in some way *acted*, either by dancing and gesticulation, or by reciting, perhaps to the music of the sambucistriae or other minstrels. See Smith's Dict. of Gr. and Rom. Ant. Art. **Histrio**, sect. 2. Scheller's Lex. sub. vv. **Histrio, Ludio**, and **Salto**. The emperors had whole companies of actors, **histriones aulici**, for their private amusement. Suetonius says of Augustus (c. 74) that at feasts he introduced acroamata et histriones. ***See also Spartian.*** Had***. c. 19; Jul. Capitol.*** Verus, c.8.

[250] My cook--***Coquum***. Livy, in the passage just cited from him, adds tum coquus villisimum antiquis mancipium, et estimatione et usu in pretio esse; ut quod ministerium fuerat, ars haberi coepta. "The cook, whom the ancients considered as the meanest of their slaves both in estimation and use, became highly valuable." **Baker**.

[251] Avarice, inexperience, and arrogance--Avaritiam, imperitiam, superbiam. "The President De Brosses and Dotteville have observed, that Marius, in these words, makes an allusion to the characters of all the generals that had preceded him, noticing at once the avarice of Calpurnius, the inexperience of Albinus, and the pride of Metellus." ***Le Brun***.

[252] For no man, by slothful timidity, has escaped the lot of mortals--Etenim ignavia nemo immortalis factus. The English translators have rendered this phrase as if they supposed the sense to

be, "No man has gained immortal renown by inaction." But this is not the signification. What Marius means, is, that no man, however cautiously and timidly he may avoid danger, has prolonged his life to immortality. Taken in this sense, the words have their proper connection with what immediately follows: neque quisquam parens liberis, uti aeterni forent, optavit. The sentiment is the same as in the verse of Horace: ***Mors et fugacem persequitur virum***; or in these lines of Tyrtaeus:

[Greek: Ou gar kos thanaton ge psygein eimarmenon estin
    Andr', oud' haen progonon hae genos athanaton
    Pollaki daeiotaeta phygon kai doupon akonton
    Erchetai, en d' oiko moira kichen thanaton.]

    To none, 'mong men, escape from death is giv'n,
    Though sprung from deathless habitants of heav'n:
    Him that has fled the battle's threatening sound,
    The silent foot of fate at home has found.

The French translator, Le Brun, has given the right sense: "Jamais la lachete n'a preserve de la mort;" and Dureau Delamalle: "Pour etre un lache, on n'en serait pas plus immortel." ***Ignavia*** is properly ***inaction***; but here signifies ***a timid shrinking from danger***.

[253] Nor has any parent wished for his children, etc.--[Greek: Ou gar athanatous sphisi paidas euchontai genesthai, all' agathous kai eukleeis.] "Men do not pray that they may have children that will never die, but such as will be good and honorable." Plato, Menex. 20. "This speech, differing from the other speeches in Sallust both in words and thoughts, conveys a clear notion of that fierce and objurgatory eloquence which was natural to the rude manners and bold character of Marius. It is a speech which can not be called polished

and modulated, but must rather be termed rough and ungraceful. The phraseology is of an antique cast, and some of the wordscoarse.----But it is animated and fervid, rushing on like a torrent; and by language of such a character and structure, the nature and manners of Marius are excellently represented." **Gerlach**.

[254] LXXXVI. Not after the ancient method, or from the classes--Non more majorum, neque ex classibus. By the regulation of Servius Tullius, who divided the Roman people into six classes, the highest class consisting of the wealthiest, and the others decreasing downward in regular gradation, none of the sixth class, who were not considered as having any fortune, but were *capite censi*, "rated by the head," were allowed to enlist in the army. The enlistment of the lower order, commenced, it is said, by Marius, tended to debase the army, and to render it a fitter tool for the purposes of unprincipled commanders. See Aul. Gell., xvi. 10.

[255] Desire to pay court--*Per ambitionem*.

[256] LXXXVII. Having filled up his legions, etc. Their numbers had been thinned in actions with the enemy, and Metellus perhaps took home some part of the army which did not return to it.

[257] Their country and parents, etc--*Patriam parentesque*, etc. Sallust means to say that the soldiers would see such to be the general effect and result of vigorous warfare; not that they had any country or parents to protect in Numidia. But the observation has very much of the rhetorician in it.

[258] LXXXVIII. From our allies--*Ex sociis nostris*. The people of the province.

[259] Obliged the king himself--to take flight without his arms

Ipsumque regem--armis exuerat. He attacked Jugurtha so suddenly and vigorously that he was compelled to flee, leaving his arms behind him.

[260]: LXXXIX. The Libyan Hercules--**Hercules Libys**. "He is one of the forty and more whom Varro mentions, and who, it is probable, were leaders of trading expeditions or colonies. See *supra*, c. 18. A Libyan Hercules is mentioned by Solinus xxvii." **Bernouf**.

[261] Marius conceived a strong desire--Marium maxima cupido invaserat. "A strong desire had seized Marius."

[262] Wild beasts' flesh--**Ferina carne**. Almost all our translators have rendered this "venison." But the Africans lived on the flesh of whatever beasts they took in the chase.

[263] XC. The consul, etc.--Here is a long and awkward parenthesis. I have adhered to the construction of the original. The "yet," *tamen*, that follows the parenthesis, refers to the matter included in it.

[264] He consigned to the care, etc.--Equitibus auxiliariis agendum attribuit. "He gave to be driven by the auxiliary cavalry."

[265] The town of Lares--**Oppidum Laris**. Cortius seems to have been right in pronouncing **Laris** to be an accusative plural. Gerlach observes that Lares occurs in the Itinerary of Antonius and in St. Augustine, Adv. Donatist., vi. 28.

[266] XCI. After marching the whole night.--He seems to have marched in the night for the sake of coolness.

[267] XCII. All his undertakings, etc.--Omnia non bene consulta in virtutem trahebantur. "All that he did rashly was attributed to

his ***consciousness of*** extraordinary power." If they could not praise his prudence, they praised his resolution and energy.

[268] Difficult of execution--***Difficilem***. There seemed to be as many impediments to success as in the affair at Capsa, though the undertaking was not of so perilous a nature.

[269] In the midst of a plain--***Inter caeteram planitiem***. By ***caeteram*** he signifies that ***the rest*** of the ground, except the part on which the fort stood, was plain and level.

[270] Directed his utmost efforts to take--Summa vi capere intendit***. It is to be observed that*** summa vi ***refers to*** intendit, not to ***capere. Summa ope*** animum ***intendit ut caperet***.

[271] Among the vineae--***Inter vineas***. "***Inter***, for which Mueller, from a conjecture of Glareanus, substituted ***intra*** is supported by all the manuscripts, and ought not to be altered, although ***intra*** would have been more exact, as the signification of ***inter*** is of greater extent, and includes that of ***intra***. ***Inter*** is used when a thing is inclosed on each side; ***intra***, when it is inclosed on all sides. If the soldiers, therefore, are considered as surrounded with the ***vineae***, they should be described as ***intra vineas***; but as there is no reason why they may not also be contemplated as being inclosed only laterally by the ***vineae***, the phrase ***inter vineas*** may surely in that case be applied to them. Gronovius and Drakenborch ad Liv., i. 10, have observed how often these propositions are interchanged when referred to ***time***." Kritzius. On ***vineae***, see c. 76.

[272] XCIII. A certain Ligurian--in the auxiliary cohorts--The Ligurians were not numbered among the Italians or ***socii*** in the Roman

army, but attached to it only as auxiliaries.

[273] A desire--of seeing what he had never seen--More humani ingenii, cupido ignara visundi invadit. This is the reading of Cortius, to which Muller and Allen adhere. Gerlach inserted in his text, **More humani ingeni, cupido difficilia faciundi animum vortit**; which Kritzius, Orelli, and Dietsch, have adopted, and which Cortius acknowledged to be the reading of the generality of the manuscripts, except that they vary as to the last two words, some having **animad vortit**. The sense of this reading will be, "the desire of doing something difficult, which is natural to the human mind, drew off his thoughts from gathering snails, and led him to contemplate something of a more arduous character." But the reading of Cortius gives so much better a sense to the passage, that I have thought proper to follow it. Burnouf, with Havercamp and the editions antecedent to Cortius, reads more humanae cupidinis ignara visundi animum vortit, of which the first five words are taken from a quotation of Aulus Gellius, ix. 12, who, however, may have transcribed them from some other part of Sallust's works, now lost.

[274] Horizontally--**Prona**. This word here signifies **forward**, not **downward**, as Anthon and others interpret, for trees growing out of a rock or bank will not take a **descending** direction.

[275] As nature directs all vegetables--Quo cuncta gignentium natura fert. ***It is to be observed that the construction is*** natura fert cuncta gignentium, ***for*** cuncta gignentia. ***On*** gignentia, i.e. vegetable, or ***whatever produces any thing***, see c. 79, and Cat., c. 53.

[276] Four centurions for a guard--Praesidio qui forent, quatuor centuriones. It is a question among the commentators whether the

centurions were attended by their centuries or not; Cortius thinks that they were not, as ten men were sufficient to cause an alarm in the fortress, which was all that Marius desired. But that Cortius is in the wrong, and that there were common soldiers with the centurions, appears from the following considerations: 1. Marius would hardly have sent, or Sallust have spoken of, *four* men as a guard to *six*. 2. Why should centurions only have been selected, and not common soldiers as well as their officers? 3. An expression in the following chapter, *laqueis--quibus allevati milites facilius escenderent*, seems to prove that there were others present besides the centurions and the trumpeters. The word *milites* is indeed wanting in the text of Cortius, but appears to have been omitted by him merely to favor his own notion as to the absence of soldiers, for he left it out, as Kritzius says, *summa libidine, ne uno quidem codice assentiente*, "purely of his own will, and without the authority of a single manuscript." Taking a fair view of the passage, we seem necessarily led to believe that the centurions were attended by a portion, if not the whole, of their companies. See the following note.

[277] XCIV. Those who commanded the centuries--Illi qui centuriis praeerant. This is the reading of several manuscripts, and of almost all the editions before that of Kritzius, and may be tolerated if we suppose that the centurions were attended by their men, and that Sallust, in speaking of the change of dress, meant to include the men, although he specifies only the officers. Yet it is difficult to conceive why Sallust should have used such a periphrase for *centuriones*. Seven of the manuscripts, however, have qui adsensuri erant, *which Kritzius and Dietsch have adopted. Two have* qui ex centuriis praeerant. *Allen, not unhappily, conjectures,* qui praesidio erant. *Cortius suspected the phrase,* qui centuriis praeerant, *and thought it a transformation of the words* qui adscensuris praeerat, which somebody had written in the margin as an

explanation of the following word *duce*, and which were afterward altered and thrust into the text.

[278] Progress--might be less impeded--***Nisus--facilius foret***. The adverb for the adjective. So in the speech of Adherbal, c. 14, ut tutius essem.

[279] Unsafe--***Dubia nisu***. "Not to be depended upon for support." *Nisu* is the old dative for *nisui*.

[280] Causing a testudo to be formed--***Testudine acta***. The soldiers placed their shields over their heads, and joined them close together, forming a defense like the shell of a tortoise.

[281] XCV. For I shall in no other place allude to his affairs--Neque enim allo loco de Sullae rebus dicturi sumus. "These words show that Sallust, at this time, had not thought of writing ***Histories***, but that he turned his attention to that pursuit after he had finished the Jugurthine war. For that he spoke of Sylla in his large history is apparent from several extant fragments of it, and from Plutarch, who quotes Sallust, Vit. Syll., c. 3." **Kritzius.**

[282] Lucius Sisenna--He wrote a history of the civil wars between Sylla and Marius, Vell. Paterc. ii. 9. Cicero alludes to his style as being jejune and puerile, Brut., c. 64, De Legg. i. 2. About a undred and fifty fragments of his history remain.

[283] Except that he might have acted more for his honor with regard to his wife--***Nisi quod de uxore potuit honestius consuli.*** As these words are vague and indeterminate, it is not agreed among the critics and translators to what part of Sylla's life Sallust refers. I suppose, with Rupertus, Aldus, Manutius, Crispinus, and De Brosses,

that the allusion is to his connection with Valeria, of which the history is given by Plutarch in his life of Sylla, which the English reader may take in Langhorne's translation: "A few months after Metella's death, he presented the people with a show of gladiators; and as, at that time, men and women had no separate places, but sat promiscuously in the theater, a woman of great beauty, and of one of the best families, happened to sit near Sylla. She was the daughter of Messala, and sister to the orator Hortensius; her name was Valeria; and she had lately been divorced from her husband. This woman, coming behind Sylla, touched him, and took off a little of the nap of his robe, and then returned to her place. Sylla looked at her, quite amazed at her familiarity, when she said, 'Wonder not, my lord, at what I have done; I had only a mind to share a little in your good fortune.' Sylla was far from being displeased; on the contrary, it appeared that he was flattered very agreeably, for he sent to ask her name, and to inquire into her family and character. Then followed an interchange of amorous regards and smiles, which ended in a contract and marriage. The lady, perhaps, was not to blame. But Sylla, though he got a woman of reputation, and great accomplishments, yet came into the match upon wrong principles. Like a youth, he was caught with soft looks and languishing airs, things that are wont to excite the lowest of the passions." Others have thought that Sallust refers to Sylla's conduct on the death of his wife Metella, above mentioned, to whom, as she happened to fall sick when he was giving an entertainment to the people, and as the priest forbade him to have his house defiled with death on the occasion, he unfeelingly sent a bill of divorce, ordering her to be carried out of the house while the breath was in her. Cortius, Kritz, and Langius. think that the allusion is to Sylla'a general faithlessness to his wives, for he had several; as if Sallust had used the singular for the plural, **uxore** for **uxoribus**, or **reuxoria**; but if Sallust meant to allude to more than one wife, why should he have restricted himself to the singular?

[284] Lived on the easiest terms with his friends--*Facilis amicitia* The critics are in doubt about the sense of this phrase. I have given that which Dietsch prefers, who says that a man facilis amicitia is "one who easily grants his friends all that they desire, exacts little from them, and is no severe censor of their morals." Cortius explains it ***facilis ad amicitiam***, and Facciolati, in his Lexicon, ***facile sibi amicos parans***, but these interpretations, as Kritzius observes, are hardly suitable to the ablative case.

[285] Most fortunate--***Felicissumo***. Alluding, perhaps, to the title of Felix, which he assumed after his great victory over Marius.

[286] His desert--***Industriam***. That is, the efforts which he made to attain distinction.

[287] XCVII. When scarcely a tenth part of the day remained--Vix decima parte die reliqua. A remarkably exact specification of the time.

[288] From various quarters--***Ex multis.*** From his scouts, who came in from all sides.

[289] The Roman veterans, who were necessarily well experienced in war,--The reading of Cortius is, Romani veteres, novique, et ob ea scientes belli; which he explains by supposing that the new recruits ***were joined with*** the veterans, and that both united were consequently well skilled in war, citing, in support of his supposition, a passage in c. 87: ***Sic brevi spatio*** novi veteresqua ***coaluere, et virtus omnium aequalis facta.*** And Ascensius had previously given a similar explanation, quod etiam veterani adessent. But many later critics have not been induced to believe that Cortius's reading will bear any such interpretation; and accordingly Kritzius, Dietsch, and Orelli, have ejected ***novique***; as

indeed Ciaeconius and Ursinus had long before recommended. Muller, Burnouf, and Allen, retain it, adopting Cortius's interpretation. Gerlach also retains it, but not without hesitation. But it is very remarkable that it occurs in all the manuscripts but one, which has ***Romani veteres boni scientes erant ut quos locus,*** etc.

[290] ***Neque minus hostibus conturbatis***. If the enemy had not been in as much disorder as himself, Marius would hardly have been able to effect his retreat.

[291] ***Pleno gradu.***--"By the ***militaris gradus*** twenty miles were completed in five hours of a summer day; by the ***plenusus***, which is quicker, twenty-four miles were traversed in the same time." Veget. i.9.

[292] XCIX. When the watches were changed--Per vigilias: i. e. at the end of each watch, when the guards were relieved. "The nights, by the aid of a clepsydra, were divided into four watches, the termination of each being marked by the blast of a trumpet or horn. See Viget. in. 8: A tubicine omnes vigiliae committuntur; et finitis horis a cornicine revocantur." Kritzius He also refers to Liv. vii. 35; Lucan. viii. 24; Tacit. Hist. v. 22.

[293] Auxiliary cohorts--***Cohortium***. I have added the word ***auxiliary***. That they were the cohorts of the auxiliaries or allies is apparent, as the word ***legionum*** follows. Kritzius indeed thinks otherwise, supposing that the cohorts had particular trumpeters, distinct from those of the whole legion. But for this notion there seems to be no sufficient ground. Sallust speaks of the ***cohortes sociorum***, c. 58, and ***cohortes Ligurum***, c. 100.

[294] Sally forth from the camp--***Portis erumpere***. Sallust uses the common phrase for issuing from the camp. It can hardly be

supposed, that the Romans had formed a regular camp with gates during the short time that they had been upon the hill, especially as they had fled to it in great disorder.

[295] Stupor--*Vecordia*. A feeling that deprived them of all sense.

[296] C. in form of a square--*Quadrato agmine*. "A hollow square, with the baggage in the center; see Serv. ad Verg. Aen. xii.121. ... Such an *agmen* Sallust, in c. 46, calls *munitum*, as it was prepared to defend itself against the enemy, from whatever quarter they might approach." *Kritzius*.

[297] Might be endured by them with cheerfulness Volentibus esset. *A Greek phrase,* Boulomenois eiae.

[298] Dread of shame--*Pudore.* Inducing each to have a regard to his character.

[299] CI. Trusting that one of them, assuredly, etc.--Ratua es omnibus aque aliquos ab tergo hostibus ventures. By aequo Sallust signifies that each of the four bodies would have an equal chance of coming on the rear of the Romans.

[300] In person and with his officers--*Ipse aliique.* "The *alii*, are the *praefecti equitum,* officers of the cavalry." *Kritzius.*

[301] Wheeled secretly about, with a few of his followers, to the infantry--*Clam--ad pedites convertit*. What infantry are meant, the commentators can not agree, nor is there any thing in the narrative on which a satisfactory decision can be founded. As the arrival of Bocchus is mentioned immediately before, Cortius supposes that the

infantry of Bocchus are signified; and it may be so; but to whatever party the words wore addressed, they were intended to be heard by the Romans, or for what purpose were they spoken in Latin? Jugurtha may have spoken the words in both languages, and this, from what follows, would appear to have been the case, for both sides understood him. ***Quod ubi milites*** (evidently the Roman soldiers) accepere--simul barbari animos tollere**, *etc*. *The*** clam signifies that Jugurtha turned about, or wheeled off, so as to escape the notice of Marius, with whom he had been contending.

[302] By vigorously cutting down our infantry--Satis impigre occiso pedite nostro. "A ces mots il leur montra son epee teinte du sang des notres, dont il venait, en effet, de faire une assez cruelle boucherie." ***De Brosses***. Of the other French translators, Beauzee and Le Brun render the passage in a similar way; Dotteville and Durean Delamalle, as well as all our English translators, take ***pedite*** as signifying ***only one soldier***. Sir Henry Steuart even specifies that it was "a legionary soldier." The commentators, I should suppose, have all regarded the word as having a plural signification; none of them, except Burnouf, who expresses a needless doubt, say any thing on the point.

[303] The spectacle on the open plains was then frightful--Tum spectaculum horribile campis patentibus, etc. The idea of this passage was probably taken, as Ciacconius intimates, from a description in Xenophon, Agesil. ii. 12, 14, part of which is quoted by Longinus, Sect. 19, as an example of the effect produced by the omission of conjunctions: [Greek: Kai symbalontes tas aspidas eothounto, emachonto, apekteinon, apethnaeskon Epei ge maen elaexen hae machae, paraen dae theasasthai entha synepeson allaelois, taen men gaen aimati pe, ormenaen, nekrous de peimenous philious kai polemious met allaelon, aspidas de diatethrummenas, dorata syntethrausmena,

egchoipidia gumna kouleon ta men chamai, ta d'en somasi, ta d'eti meta cheiras.] "Closing their shields together, they pushed, they fought, ... But when the battle was over, you might have seen, where they had fought, the ground clotted with blood, the corpses of friends and enemies mingled together, and pierced shields, broken lances, and swords without their sheaths, strewed on the ground, sticking in the dead bodies, or still remaining in the hands that had wielded them when alive." Tacitus, Agric. c. 37. has copied this description of Sallust, as all the commentators have remarked: Tum vero patentibus locis grande et atrox spectaculum. Sequi, vulnerare, capere, atque eosdem, oblatis aliis, trucidare.... Passim, arma et corpora, et laceri artus, et cruenta humus. "The sight on the open field was then striking and horrible; they pursued, they inflicted wounds, they took ... Every where were seen arms and corpses, mangled limbs, and the ground stained with blood."

[304] Besides, the Roman people, even from the very infancy--The reading of this passage, before the edition of Cortius, was this: Ad hoc, populo Romano jam a principio inopi melius visum amicos, quam servos, quaerere. *Gruter proposed to read* Ad hoc populo Romano inopi melius est visum*, etc., whence Cortius made* Ad hoc, populo Romano jam inopi visum*, etc. But the Bipont editors, observing that* inopi was not quite consistent with *quaerere servos*, altered the passage to *Ad hoc, populo Romano jam a principio reipublicae melius visum*, etc., which seems to be the best emendation that has been proposed, and which I have accordingly followed. Kritzius and Dietsch adopt it, except that they omit *reipublicae*, and put nothing in the place of *inopi*. Gerlach retains *inopi*, on the principle of "quo insolentius, eo verius," and it may, after all, be genuine. Cortius omitted *melius* on no authority but his own.

[305] Out of which he had forcibly driven Jugurtha--Unde ut

Jugurtham expulerit [expulerat] There is here some obscurity. The manuscripts vary between *expulerit* and *expulerat*. Cortius, and Gerlaen in his second edition, adopt *expulerat*, which they of necessity refer to Marius; but to make Bocchus speak thus, is, as Kritzius says, to make him speak very foolishly and arrogantly. Kritzius himself, accordingly, adopts *expulerit*, and supposes that Bocchus invents a falsehood, in the belief that the Romans wouldhave no means of detecting it. But Bocchus may have spoken truth, referring, as Mueller suggests, to some previous transactions between him and Jugurtha, to which Sallust does not elsewhere allude.

[306] In ill plight--*Sine decore*.

[307] For interested bounty--*Largitio*. "The word signifies liberal treatment of others with a view to our own interest; without any real goodwill." **Mueller**. "He intends a severe stricture on his own age, and the manners of the Romans." **Dietsch**.

[308] About forty days. Waiting, apparently, for the return of Marius.

[309] CIV. Having failed in the object, etc.--Infecto, quo intenderat, negotio. Though this is the reading of most of the manuscripts, Kritzius, Mueller, and Dietach, read *confecto*, as if Marius could not have failed in his attempt.

[310] Are always verging to opposite extremes.--Semper in adversa mutant. Rose renders this "are always changing, and constantly for the worse;" and most other translators have given something similar. But this is absurd; for every one sees that all changes in human affairs are not for the worse. *Adversa* is evidently to be taken in the sense which I have given.

[311] CV. At his discretion--*Arbitratu*. Kritzius observes that this word comprehends the notion of plenary powers to treat and decide: *der mit unbeschraenkter Vollmacht unterhandeln koennte*.

[312] Presenting--*Intendere*. The critics are in doubt to what to refer this word; some have thought of understanding *animum*; Cortius, Wasse, and Mueller, think it is meant only of the bows of the archers; Kritzius, Burnouf, and Allen, refer it, apparently with better judgment, to the *arma* and *tela* in general.

[313] CVI. To dispatch their supper--*Coenatos esse*. "The perfect is not without its force; it signifies that Sylla wished his orders to be performed with the greatest expedition." *Kritzius*. He orders them *to have done* supper.

[314] CVII. And blind parts of his body--*Caecum corpus*. Imitated from Xenephon, Cyrop. iii. 3, 45: [Greek: Moron gar to kratein boulomenous, ta tuphla, tou somatos, kai aopla, tauta enantia tattein tois polemiois pheugontas.] "It is folly for those that desire to conquer to turn the blind, unarmed, and handless parts of the body, to the enemy in flight."

[315] At being an instrument of his father's hostility--Quoniam hostilia faceret. "Since he wished to deceive the Romans by pretended friendship." *Mueller*.

[316] CVIII. Of the family of Masinissa--*Ex gente Masinissae*. Massugrada was the son of Masinissa by a concubine.

[317] Faithful--*Fidum*. After this word, in the editions of Cortius, Kritzius, Gerlach, Allen, and Dietsch, follows *Romanis* or esse Romanis. *These critics defend* Romanis on the plea that a dative

is necessary after *fidum*, and that it was of importance, as Castilioneus observes that Dabar should be well disposed toward the Romans, and not have been corrupted, like many other courtiers of Bocchus, by the bribes of Jugurtha. Glarcanus, Badius Ascensius, the Bipont editors, and Burnouf, with, most of the translators, omit ***Romanis***, and I have thought proper to imitate their example.

[318] Place, day, and hour--***Diem, locum, tempus.*** Not only the day, but the time of the day.

[319] That he kept all points, which he had settled with him before, inviolate--***Consulta sese omnia cum illo integra habere***. Kritzius justly observes that most editors, in interpreting this passage, have erroneously given to ***consulta*** the sense of ***consulenda***; and that the sense is, "that all that he had arranged with Sylla before, remained unaltered, and that he was not drawn from his resolutions by the influence of Jugurtha."

[320] And that he was not to fear the presence of Jugurtha's embassador, as any restraint, etc.--Neu Jugurthae legatum pertimesceret, quo res communis licentius gereretur. There is some difficulty in this passage. Burnouf makes the nearest approach to a satisfactory explanation of it. "Sylla," says he, "was not to fear the envoy of Jugurtha, *quo*, on which account (equivalent to ***eoque***, and on that account, ***i. e.*** on account of his freedom from apprehension) their common interests would be more freely arranged." Yet it appears from what follows that fear of Jugurtha's envoy could not be dismissed, and that there could be no freedom of discussion in his presence, as Sylla was to say but little before him, and to speak more at large at a private meeting. These considerations have induced Kritzius to suppose that the word ***remoto***, or something similar, has been lost after ***quo***. The Bipont editors inserted ***cautum esse***

before *quo*, which is without authority, and does not at all assist the sense.

[321] African duplicity--***Punica fide***. "***Punica fides*** was a well-known proverbial expression for treachery and deceit. The origin of it is perhaps attributable not so much to fact, as to the implacable hatred of the Romans toward the Carthaginians." ***Burnouf***.

[322] CIX. What answer should be returned by Bocchus--That is, in the presence of Aspar.

[323] Both then retired to their respective camps--Deinde ambo in sua castra digressi. **Both,** i. e. Bocchus and Sylla, not Aspar and Sylla, as Cortius imagines.

[324] CX. It will be a pleasure to me--***Fuerit mihi***. Some editions, as that of Langius, the Bipont, and Burnouf's, have fuerit mihi pretium. Something of the kind seems to be wanting. "Res in bonis numeranda fuerit mihi." ***Burnouf***. Allen, who omits ***pretium***, interprets, "Grata mihi egestas sit, quae ad tuam, amicitiam coufugiat;" but who can deduce this sense from the passage, unless he have ***pretium***, or something similar, in his mind?

[325] CXI. That part of Numidia which he claimed--Numidiae partem quam nunc peteret. See the second note on c. 102. Bocchus continues, in his speech in the preceding chapter, to signify that a part of Numidia belonged to him.

[326] The ties of blood--***Cognationem***. To this blood-relationship between him and Jugurtha no allusion is elsewhere made.

[327] His resolution gave way--***Lenitur***. Cortius whom Gerlach and

Mueller follow, reads *leniter*, but, with Kritzius and Gerlach, I prefer the verb to the adverb; which, however, is found in the greater number of the manuscripts.

[328] CXII. Interests of both--***Ambobus***. Both himself and Jugurtha.

[329] CXIV. At that time-- ***Ea tempestate***. "In many manuscripts is found ***ex ea tempestate***, by which the sense is wholly perverted. Sallust signifies that Marius did not continue always deserving of such honor; for, as is said in c. 63, 'he was afterward carried headlong by ambition.'" ***Kritzius***.

www.bookjungle.com email: sales@bookjungle.com fax: 630-214-0564 mail: Book Jungle PO Box 2226 Champaign, IL 61825

The Codes Of Hammurabi And Moses
W. W. Davies

The discovery of the Hammurabi Code is one of the greatest achievements of archaeology, and is of paramount interest, not only to the student of the Bible, but also to all those interested in ancient history...

Religion   **ISBN:** *1-59462-338-4*   Pages: 132
MSRP *$12.95*   QTY

The Theory of Moral Sentiments
Adam Smith

This work from 1749. contains original theories of conscience amd moral judgment and it is the foundation for systemof morals.

Philosophy   **ISBN:** *1-59462-777-0*   Pages: 536
MSRP *$19.95*   QTY

Jessica's First Prayer
Hesba Stretton

In a screened and secluded corner of one of the many railway-bridges which span the streets of London there could be seen a few years ago, from five o'clock every morning until half past eight, a tidily set-out coffee-stall, consisting of a trestle and board, upon which stood two large tin cans, with a small fire of charcoal burning under each so as to keep the coffee boiling during the early hours of the morning when the work-people were thronging into the city on their way to their daily toil...

Childrens   **ISBN:** *1-59462-373-2*   Pages: 84
MSRP *$9.95*   QTY

My Life and Work
Henry Ford

Henry Ford revolutionized the world with his implementation of mass production for the Model T automobile. Gain valuable business insight into his life and work with his own auto-biography... "We have only started on our development of our country we have not as yet, with all our talk of wonderful progress, done more than scratch the surface. The progress has been wonderful enough but..."

Biographies/   **ISBN:** *1-59462-198-5*   Pages: 300
MSRP *$21.95*   QTY

The Art of Cross-Examination
Francis Wellman

I presume it is the experience of every author, after his first book is published upon an important subject, to be almost overwhelmed with a wealth of ideas and illustrations which could readily have been included in his book, and which to his own mind, at least, seem to make a second edition inevitable. Such certainly was the case with me; and when the first edition had reached its sixth impression in five months, I rejoiced to learn that it seemed to my publishers that the book had met with a sufficiently favorable reception to justify a second and considerably enlarged edition. ..

Pages: 412

Reference   ISBN: *1-59462-647-2*   MSRP *$19.95*

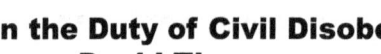

On the Duty of Civil Disobedience
Henry David Thoreau

Thoreau wrote his famous essay, On the Duty of Civil Disobedience, as a protest against an unjust but popular war and the immoral but popular institution of slave-owning. He did more than write—he declined to pay his taxes, and was hauled off to gaol in consequence. Who can say how much this refusal of his hastened the end of the war and of slavery?

Law   ISBN: *1-59462-747-9*   **Pages: 48**   MSRP *$7.45*

Dream Psychology Psychoanalysis for Beginners
Sigmund Freud

Sigmund Freud, born Sigismund Schlomo Freud (May 6, 1856 - September 23, 1939), was a Jewish-Austrian neurologist and psychiatrist who co-founded the psychoanalytic school of psychology. Freud is best known for his theories of the unconscious mind, especially involving the mechanism of repression; his redefinition of sexual desire as mobile and directed towards a wide variety of objects; and his therapeutic techniques, especially his understanding of transference in the therapeutic relationship and the presumed value of dreams as sources of insight into unconscious desires.

Pages: 196

Psychology   ISBN: *1-59462-905-6*   MSRP *$15.45*

The Miracle of Right Thought
Orison Swett Marden

Believe with all of your heart that you will do what you were made to do. When the mind has once formed the habit of holding cheerful, happy, prosperous pictures, it will not be easy to form the opposite habit. It does not matter how improbable or how far away this realization may see, or how dark the prospects may be, if we visualize them as best we can, as vividly as possible, hold tenaciously to them and vigorously struggle to attain them, they will gradually become actualized, realized in the life. But a desire, a longing without endeavor, a yearning abandoned or held indifferently will vanish without realization.

Pages: 360

Self Help   ISBN: *1-59462-644-8*   MSRP *$25.45*

www.bookjungle.com email: sales@bookjungle.com fax: 630-214-0564 mail: Book Jungle PO Box 2226 Champaign, IL 61825

QTY

	Title	ISBN	Price
☐	**The Rosicrucian Cosmo-Conception Mystic Christianity** by *Max Heindel*	ISBN: 1-59462-188-8	$38.95
	The Rosicrucian Cosmo-conception is not dogmatic, neither does it appeal to any other authority than the reason of the student. It is: not controversial, but is: sent forth in the, hope that it may help to clear...	New Age/Religion Pages 646	
☐	**Abandonment To Divine Providence** by *Jean-Pierre de Caussade*	ISBN: 1-59462-228-0	$25.95
	"The Rev. Jean Pierre de Caussade was one of the most remarkable spiritual writers of the Society of Jesus in France in the 18th Century. His death took place at Toulouse in 1751. His works have gone through many editions and have been republished...	Inspirational/Religion Pages 400	
☐	**Mental Chemistry** by *Charles Haanel*	ISBN: 1-59462-192-6	$23.95
	Mental Chemistry allows the change of material conditions by combining and appropriately utilizing the power of the mind. Much like applied chemistry creates something new and unique out of careful combinations of chemicals the mastery of mental chemistry...	New Age Pages 354	
☐	**The Letters of Robert Browning and Elizabeth Barret Barrett 1845-1846 vol II** by **Robert Browning** and **Elizabeth Barrett**	ISBN: 1-59462-193-4	$35.95
		Biographies Pages 596	
☐	**Gleanings In Genesis (volume I)** by *Arthur W. Pink*	ISBN: 1-59462-130-6	$27.45
	Appropriately has Genesis been termed "the seed plot of the Bible" for in it we have, in germ form, almost all of the great doctrines which are afterwards fully developed in the books of Scripture which follow...	Religion/Inspirational Pages 420	
☐	**The Master Key** by *L. W. de Laurence*	ISBN: 1-59462-001-6	$30.95
	In no branch of human knowledge has there been a more lively increase of the spirit of research during the past few years than in the study of Psychology, Concentration and Mental Discipline. The requests for authentic lessons in Thought Control, Mental Discipline and...	New Age/Business Pages 422	
☐	**The Lesser Key Of Solomon Goetia** by *L. W. de Laurence*	ISBN: 1-59462-092-X	$9.95
	This translation of the first book of the "Lernegton" which is now for the first time made accessible to students of Talismanic Magic was done, after careful collation and edition, from numerous Ancient Manuscripts in Hebrew, Latin, and French...	New Age/Occult Pages 92	
☐	**Rubaiyat Of Omar Khayyam** by *Edward Fitzgerald*	ISBN: 1-59462-332-5	$13.95
	Edward Fitzgerald, whom the world has already learned, in spite of his own efforts to remain within the shadow of anonymity, to look upon as one of the rarest poets of the century, was born at Bredfield, in Suffolk, on the 31st of March, 1809. He was the third son of John Purcell...	Music Pages 172	
☐	**Ancient Law** by *Henry Maine*	ISBN: 1-59462-128-4	$29.95
	The chief object of the following pages is to indicate some of the earliest ideas of mankind, as they are reflected in Ancient Law, and to point out the relation of those ideas to modern thought.	Religiom/History Pages 452	
☐	**Far-Away Stories** by *William J. Locke*	ISBN: 1-59462-129-2	$19.45
	"Good wine needs no bush, but a collection of mixed vintages does. And this book is just such a collection. Some of the stories I do not want to remain buried for ever in the museum files of dead magazine-numbers an author's not unpardonable vanity..."	Fiction Pages 272	
☐	**Life of David Crockett** by *David Crockett*	ISBN: 1-59462-250-7	$27.45
	"Colonel David Crockett was one of the most remarkable men of the times in which he lived. Born in humble life, but gifted with a strong will, an indomitable courage, and unremitting perseverance...	Biographies/New Age Pages 424	
☐	**Lip-Reading** by *Edward Nitchie*	ISBN: 1-59462-206-X	$25.95
	Edward B. Nitchie, founder of the New York School for the Hard of Hearing, now the Nitchie School of Lip-Reading, Inc, wrote "LIP-READING Principles and Practice". The development and perfecting of this meritorious work on lip-reading was an undertaking...	How-to Pages 400	
☐	**A Handbook of Suggestive Therapeutics, Applied Hypnotism, Psychic Science** by *Henry Munro*	ISBN: 1-59462-214-0	$24.95
		Health/New Age/Health/Self-help Pages 376	
☐	**A Doll's House: and Two Other Plays** by *Henrik Ibsen*	ISBN: 1-59462-112-8	$19.95
	Henrik Ibsen created this classic when in revolutionary 1848 Rome. Introducing some striking concepts in playwriting for the realist genre, this play has been studied the world over.	Fiction/Classics/Plays 308	
☐	**The Light of Asia** by *sir Edwin Arnold*	ISBN: 1-59462-204-3	$13.95
	In this poetic masterpiece, Edwin Arnold describes the life and teachings of Buddha. The man who was to become known as Buddha to the world was born as Prince Gautama of India but he rejected the worldly riches and abandoned the reigns of power when...	Religion/History/Biographies Pages 170	
☐	**The Complete Works of Guy de Maupassant** by *Guy de Maupassant*	ISBN: 1-59462-157-8	$16.95
	"For days and days, nights and nights, I had dreamed of that first kiss which was to consecrate our engagement, and I knew not on what spot I should put my lips..."	Fiction/Classics Pages 240	
☐	**The Art of Cross-Examination** by *Francis L. Wellman*	ISBN: 1-59462-309-0	$26.95
	Written by a renowned trial lawyer, Wellman imparts his experience and uses case studies to explain how to use psychology to extract desired information through questioning.	How-to/Science/Reference Pages 408	
☐	**Answered or Unanswered?** by *Louisa Vaughan* — Miracles of Faith in China	ISBN: 1-59462-248-5	$10.95
		Religion Pages 112	
☐	**The Edinburgh Lectures on Mental Science (1909)** by *Thomas*	ISBN: 1-59462-008-3	$11.95
	This book contains the substance of a course of lectures recently given by the writer in the Queen Street Hall, Edinburgh. Its purpose is to indicate the Natural Principles governing the relation between Mental Action and Material Conditions...	New Age/Psychology Pages 148	
☐	**Ayesha** by *H. Rider Haggard*	ISBN: 1-59462-301-5	$24.95
	Verily and indeed it is the unexpected that happens! Probably if there was one person upon the earth from whom the Editor of this, and of a certain previous history, did not expect to hear again...	Classics Pages 380	
☐	**Ayala's Angel** by *Anthony Trollope*	ISBN: 1-59462-352-X	$29.95
	The two girls were both pretty, but Lucy who was twenty-one who supposed to be simple and comparatively unattractive, whereas Ayala was credited, as her Bombwhat romantic name might show, with poetic charm and a taste for romance. Ayala when her father died was nineteen...	Fiction Pages 484	
☐	**The American Commonwealth** by *James Bryce*	ISBN: 1-59462-286-8	$34.45
	An interpretation of American democratic political theory. It examines political mechanics and society from the perspective of Scotsman James Bryce	Politics Pages 572	
☐	**Stories of the Pilgrims** by *Margaret P. Pumphrey*	ISBN: 1-59462-116-0	$17.95
	This book explores pilgrims religious oppression in England as well as their escape to Holland and eventual crossing to America on the Mayflower, and their early days in New England...	History Pages 268	

www.bookjungle.com *email: sales@bookjungle.com fax: 630-214-0564 mail: Book Jungle PO Box 2226 Champaign, IL 61825*

QTY

The Fasting Cure *by Sinclair Upton* ISBN: *1-59462-222-1* **$13.95**
In the Cosmopolitan Magazine for May, 1910, and in the Contemporary Review (London) for April, 1910, I published an article dealing with my experiences in fasting. I have written a great many magazine articles, but never one which attracted so much attention... New Age/Self Help/Health Pages 164

Hebrew Astrology *by Sepharial* ISBN: *1-59462-308-2* **$13.45**
In these days of advanced thinking it is a matter of common observation that we have left many of the old landmarks behind and that we are now pressing forward to greater heights and to a wider horizon than that which represented the mind-content of our progenitors... Astrology Pages 144

Thought Vibration or The Law of Attraction in the Thought World ISBN: *1-59462-127-6* **$12.95**
by William Walker Atkinson Psychology/Religion Pages 144

Optimism *by Helen Keller* ISBN: *1-59462-108-X* **$15.95**
Helen Keller was blind, deaf, and mute since 19 months old, yet famously learned how to overcome these handicaps, communicate with the world, and spread her lectures promoting optimism. An inspiring read for everyone... Biographies/Inspirational Pages 84

Sara Crewe *by Frances Burnett* ISBN: *1-59462-360-0* **$9.45**
In the first place, Miss Minchin lived in London. Her home was a large, dull, tall one, in a large, dull square, where all the houses were alike, and all the sparrows were alike, and where all the door-knockers made the same heavy sound... Childrens/Classic Pages 88

The Autobiography of Benjamin Franklin *by Benjamin Franklin* ISBN: *1-59462-135-7* **$24.95**
The Autobiography of Benjamin Franklin has probably been more extensively read than any other American historical work, and no other book of its kind has had such ups and downs of fortune. Franklin lived for many years in England, where he was agent... Biographies/History Pages 332

Name	
Email	
Telephone	
Address	
City, State ZIP	

☐ Credit Card   ☐ Check / Money Order

Credit Card Number	
Expiration Date	
Signature	

Please Mail to: Book Jungle
PO Box 2226
Champaign, IL 61825
or Fax to: 630-214-0564

ORDERING INFORMATION

web: *www.bookjungle.com*
email: *sales@bookjungle.com*
fax: *630-214-0564*
mail: *Book Jungle PO Box 2226 Champaign, IL 61825*
or PayPal *to sales@bookjungle.com*

Please contact us for bulk discounts

DIRECT-ORDER TERMS

**20% Discount if You Order
Two or More Books**
Free Domestic Shipping!
Accepted: Master Card, Visa,
Discover, American Express

www.ingramcontent.com/pod-product-compliance
Lightning Source LLC
Chambersburg PA
CBHW080240170426
43192CB00014BA/2506